CHILDREN OF
THE REVELS

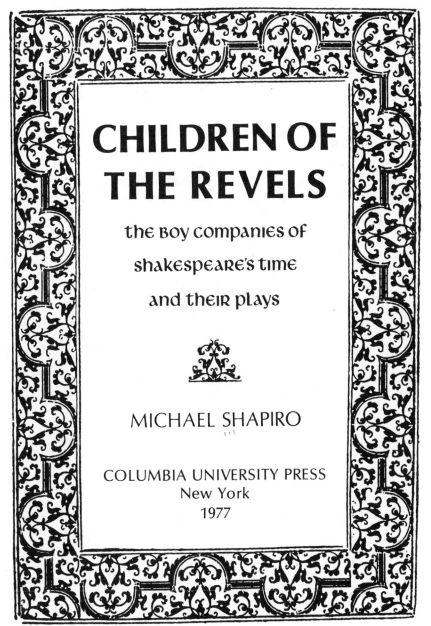

CHILDREN OF THE REVELS

the boy companies of

shakespeare's time

and their plays

MICHAEL SHAPIRO

COLUMBIA UNIVERSITY PRESS
New York
1977

Library of Congress Cataloging in Publication Data

Shapiro, Michael, 1938–
    Children of the revels.

    Includes bibliographical references and index.
    1. Theater—England—London—History.
2. Children as actors.   I. Title.
PN2590.B6S5   792'.09421   76-47585
ISBN 0-231-04112-8

Columbia University Press
New York—Guildford, Surrey

TO ELIZABETH

Acknowledgments

HOW fitting to begin a book on plays in their social context by reviewing the network of personal and professional relationships that surrounds it. Like most works of scholarship, this book has accumulated more debts than I can conveniently acknowledge, some greater than I can repay. I nevertheless take pleasure in describing these acts of generosity and kindness, hastening to assume full responsibility for whatever flaws remain in this volume.

I began thinking about the children's troupes and their plays when Professor William Appleton asked a question one day in a graduate course on Jacobean drama that made me want to know more about the boy actors. I learned more about them—and about myself and the nature of scholarship—from writing a doctoral dissertation on the Children of Paul's under the benevolently rigorous direction of Professor S. F. Johnson. As a graduate student at Columbia University and a faculty member at the University of Illinois at Urbana-Champaign, I have had access to two splendid libraries and received assistance from several dedicated librarians, especially Miss Eva Fay Benton and Mrs. Charlene Renner.

At Illinois, I razed and rebuilt my earlier study of the Paul's boys and expanded it to cover the plays of all English children's troupes before 1613. With support from the Research Board of the Graduate College of the University of Illinois, I was able to accomplish much of this work during summers, and I recovered the energy I needed to complete the project while on sabbatical leave in Jerusalem. I am also grateful to the Board for partially defraying the cost of publication, and to Irene Wahlfeldt and Mary Knight for transforming my labyrinthine draft into a presentable manuscript. Many of my students, friends, and colleagues now or formerly at Illinois have responded to my work in a manner I can only characterize as bracingly constructive, but in three cases magnanimity of mind and spirit has transcended collegial responsibility: David Kay has shared with me so many of his rich insights into Renaissance drama that I fear I have appropriated some of them as my own, while Carol Neely and Richard Wheeler, who carefully read the entire manuscript, saved me repeatedly from rashness, inaccuracy, and clumsiness.

Another set of obligations lies beyond the walls of universities. The notes at the back of this volume record my use of previous scholarship, and I here apologize for the inadvertent, but inevitable, omissions. I have had opportunities to present my views on the children's troupes before other interested scholars, thanks to the Central Renaissance Conference and the Renaissance Drama Seminar of the Modern Language Association. Portions of this book have appeared in slightly different form in *Comparative Drama, Current Musicology, English Literary Renaissance, Notes and Queries, Theatre Survey,* and *Theatre Notebook,* and I wish to thank the editors of these journals for permitting me to use this material here. My work has benefited from the correspondence of other scholars, especially G. K. Hunter, from the comments of anonymous referees, and from the editorial acumen of William Bernhardt and David Diefendorf of Columbia University Press.

My deepest obligations are to my family. The love of my parents, my children, and my wife has sustained me through all phases of my work. To my children I must express gratitude for understanding—usually—why their own revels were sometimes overshadowed by those of mysterious rivals from the past. Finally, my wife sacrificed time from her own writing first to read many versions of this material, each one improved by her suggestions, and then to share with me the tasks of proofreading and index-making. These are her tangible contributions. For the rest, not even the dedication can suffice.

M.S.
Champaign, Illinois
July, 1976

Table of Contents

Abbreviations

IN referring to scholarly journals, I use the abbreviations listed at the front of the *MLA International Bibliography,* plus the following abbreviations for other journals, series, collections, and frequently cited books:

CA   H. N. Hillebrand, *The Child Actors, Illinois Studies in Language and Literature,* 11 (1926), nos. 1–2 (reprinted New York: Russell and Russell, 1964).

D&S   *Dramaturgie et Société,* ed. J. Jacquot (Paris: Centre National de la Recherche Scientifique, 1968), 2 vols.

ES   E. K. Chambers, *The Elizabethan Stage* (Oxford: Clarendon Press, 1923), 4 vols.

Materialien   *Materialien zur Kunde des älteren englischen Dramas*

MQ   *Musical Quarterly*

MS   E. K. Chambers, *The Medieaval Stage* (Oxford: Oxford University Press, 1903), 2 vols.

MSC   *Malone Society Collections*

MSR   *Malone Society Reprints*

PRMA   *Proceedings of the Royal Music Association*

ABBREVIATIONS

Revels	*The Revels Plays*
RN	*Renaissance News* (now *Renaissance Quarterly*)
RRD	*Regents Renaissance Drama*
S.R.	*The Stationers' Register*

Bibliographical Note

IN quoting from old plays and documents, one cannot avoid using a combination of modern- and old-spelling editions. To eliminate any feeling of quaintness, more than to achieve consistency, I have rendered all quoted material in standard American orthography. I have tampered as little as possible with capitalization and punctuation.

CHILDREN OF
THE REVELS

CHAPTER ONE

The Companies

EX nihilo nihil fit. The children's troupes that flourished in London at the end of Elizabeth's reign and the beginning of James's are the culmination of a long tradition. Throughout Western Europe in the later Middle Ages and the Renaissance, groups of grammar school students and choirboys performed plays in addition to pursuing their studies or attending at religious devotions. Because performing plays was a peripheral activity for them, they were regarded as amateurs, even though their masters often received remuneration for performances given to entertain nobility or royalty. This tradition of amateur children's troupes existed for over a hundred years before the boy companies of London achieved a quasi-professional status during Elizabeth's reign, when they began rehearsing for court performances in front of paying spectators at their own private theaters. The potential profitability of these "rehearsals" attracted investors, and by James's accession the two principal children's troupes of London were functioning as professional companies. Despite this drift toward commercialization they continued to style themselves as choirboy troupes—the Children of Paul's (i.e. the boy choristers of St. Paul's Cathedral) and the Children of the Chapel Royal (i.e. the boy choristers of the sovereign's private chapel), in order to foster the illusion that they were amateur children's troupes, the traditional purveyors of dramatic entertainment to the court.

Historically, there had been three distinct types of children's troupes—(1) students of grammar schools, (2) choirboys of private chapels, and (3) choirboys of ecclesiastical institutions. Chambers and Hillebrand offer a very full factual account of the English children's troupes, and I lean very heavily on their work for documentary evidence, having only a few facts to add to the wealth of material they have assembled.[1] I believe that most scholars have interpreted this evidence in a way that overemphasizes and needlessly denigrates the commercialization of the children's troupes.

Acting by children's troupes grew out of academic exercises and participation in mystery cycles and semi-dramatic forms of entertainment. During the Tudor period, however, boy companies began performing plays on a regular basis—first as social entertainment in aristocratic or royal banqueting halls, and later before paying spectators in their own theaters as well. The commercialization of the children's troupes did not terminate their court performances, but indeed depended on their reputation as purveyors of dramatic entertainment to the court and nobility.

Grammar Schools

The statutes and curricula of many English grammar schools in the sixteenth century provided for some type of dramatic production by the pupils. In order to make their students fluent in colloquial Latin, humanist educators of the Renaissance required their charges to act short dialogues and colloquies in Latin, and some, like Roger Ascham, recommended performing Roman comedies.[2] Moreover, the acting of plays could achieve one of the basic aims of humanist educators both in England and on the continent: the training of students in correct and elegant diction, poise, appropriate gesture, and graceful bodily movement. In a word, acting could help inculcate "eloquence," the art of effective public speaking. As a seventeenth-century schoolmaster explained, "This acting of a piece of a Comedy, or a Colloquy sometimes, will be an excellent means to prepare them to pronounce orations with a grace, and I have found it an especial remedy to expel the sub-rustic bashfulness, and unresistable timorousness, which some children are naturally possessed withall. . . ." [3] John Bale tells us that Ralph Radcliffe, a schoolmaster in Hitchen in the early sixteenth century, had his students act plays in order to "remove useless modesty" ("*inutilem pudorem exuendum*"), while Richard Mulcaster, first headmaster of the Merchant Taylors' School, used plays to teach his students "good behavior and audacity." [4] The emphasis on boldness in such pedagogical statements may help to explain the pleasure adult spectators took in plays acted by the children's troupes, especially those acted in the 1590s and 1600s, when audacity burgeoned into sauciness, parody, bawdry, and satire.

In England and on the continent, schoolboys not only performed Terence and Plautus but also presented original neo-Latin plays and even vernacular plays modeled on Roman comedies, such as Nicholas Udall's *Ralph Roister Doister*. The "Christian Terence" movement was created by Dutch and German schoolmasters to preserve the language and techniques of Roman comedies without exposing the schoolboys to a world of attractive courtesans, wily slaves, foolish fathers, and disobedient sons. [5] Most of these plays are moralistic treatments of the prodigal-son parable. The prototype, Gnapheus' *Acolastus* (pub. 1529), was translated into English by John Palsgrave, a chaplain to Henry VIII, and published as a school text in 1540. In England, several vernacular "Christian Terence" plays were written between 1550 and 1575. Like *The*

Disobediant Child (c.1560), they seem to have been performed by schoolboys, before audiences of children, and sometimes parents, who are warned against sparing the rod. The "Christian Seneca" movement also developed on the continent and spread to England.[6] In the 1540s, George Buchanan wrote Latin tragedies on both classical and Biblical subjects to be acted by his students in Bordeaux, while Dutch and German schoolmasters wrote plays for their pupils chiefly on Biblical subjects. Their favorites, Susanna and Judith, are the first of a long series of pathetic heroines in children's plays. Radcliffe's students at Hitchen also performed plays about Susanna and Judith, and Thomas Garter's dramatization of the Susanna story (1563–69), which requires eight actors, was probably written for a children's company.[7]

Although most of these Terentian and Senecan adaptations and imitations were primarily scholastic exercises, grammar school troupes sometimes performed in public—under municipal auspices, in the residences of great lords, and even at court. Pupils from the grammar school at St. Paul's, founded by John Colet in 1512, were among the first to bring academic theatrical productions to a wider and socially distinguished audience. The first headmaster, William Lily, had studied in Italy under Pomponio Leto (the first modern producer of Roman plays in Europe) and therefore probably accepted the pedagogical value of dramatic performance.[8] His son-in-law and successor, John Rightwise, apparently shared his views.

According to Anthony à Wood, Rightwise wrote a Latin play about Dido, a typical pathetic heroine, which his pupils acted before Wolsey, for whom they also performed *Menaechmi* in 1527 and *Phormio* in 1528.[9] During the season of 1527–28, they performed an anti-Luther play in Latin and French before Henry VIII, his court, and the French ambassadors. This latter play touched on matters of religion and international politics, with child actors impersonating Luther, the French Dauphin, and Wolsey, who was probably in the audience. Although the reaction of the Cardinal and the other spectators to the sight of child actors representing His Eminence and other living notables is not recorded, the play anticipates the saturnalian spirit that runs through many children's plays of the Elizabethan and Jacobean periods.

Nicholas Udall's students, perhaps somewhat less audacious than the troupe from St. Paul's grammar school, performed under equally distinguished auspices. His Etonians played before Cromwell in 1538, and by 1554 his pupils from Westminster had become particular favorites of Queen Mary, who ordered the Revels Office to supply his needs, because he had "at sundry seasons convenient heretofore showed, and mindeth hereafter to show, his diligence in setting forth of Dialogues and Interludes before us for our regal disport and recreation." [10] Participation in court revelry was, as we shall see, the gateway to the commercialization of the children's troupes.

Christmas Revels and the Chapel Royal

From late November until Candlemas or Shrovetide, the early Tudor court was diverted by a dazzling variety of entertainment: tilts, tourneys, and barriers; jugglers and minstrels; mummings, disguising, and masques; debates, pageants, plays, and interludes. Similar activities took place on an appropriately reduced scale in the great halls of castles, grammar schools, colleges, inns of court, and craft guilds. To furnish the court with this multifarious entertainment, the Lord of Misrule and later the more permanent Master of the Revels called upon courtiers, professional musicians, companies of adult actors, troupes of schoolboys like those from Westminster and St. Paul's, and of course choristers from the monarch's own private chapel.

During the late Middle Ages and early Renaissance, European sovereigns and nobles of every degree maintained chapels for their personal worship, which they staffed as well as their taste and vanity urged and their resources allowed. In addition to the usual complement of priests and canons, most private chapels included a choirmaster, an organist, possibly a few instrumentalists, and a choir of men and boys. These singers and musicians often performed for such festive occasions as coronations and weddings, and sometimes even participated in pageants and dramatic entertainment. Orlando di Lasso, for instance, *Kappelmeister* for the Duke of Bavaria from 1556 to 1594, supervised the music and participated in the dramatic entertainment for the wedding of Duke William of Bavaria and Renée of Lorraine.[11] In England, the chapels of the nobility were accustomed to playing and were often paid by their patrons for doing so, a sign that such performances were considered adjuncts to their regular duties. The Earl of Northumberland's chapel received 20 shillings each Christmas and Easter for giving a play written by the almoner, while the Duke of Norfolk's chapel received 6s. 8d. for playing at Christmas in 1564–65 and 1565–66, when their patron entertained the mayor and several burghers of Norwich.

The English kings maintained a private chapel at Windsor and another—the Chapel Royal—which moved with the court to the larger standing houses in and around London. For most of the sixteenth century, the Windsor Chapel had ten choirboys and the Chapel Royal twelve, and the masters of both chapels had the power to impress boys into service. As part of the royal household, both troupes frequently participated in the elaborate winter revelry at the Tudor court, for which their masters received extra compensation.

Although the Children of the Chapel Royal participated in numerous pageants and other semidramatic entertainments under the first two Tudors, we hear relatively little of their performing in plays. The Gentlemen of the Chapel seem to have presented plays as early as 1506, but the first play that can be safely assigned to the Chapel Children was *Troilus and Pandor*, written by William Cornish, the master of the troupe, and presented at Eltham on Twelfth Night, 1516, by "Master Cornish and other[s] and by the children of the chapel." [12] But accounts of their plays are rare before the accession of Elizabeth, and some plays and interludes we do know of, like *Love and Riches* (1527), were merely settings for tilts or disguisings. When Richard Edwardes became Master of the Chapel Children in 1561, he evidently encouraged the acting of plays. Edwardes himself was praised by contemporaries for writing many fine comedies, including *Damon and Pythias* (1564–65), the only surviving play by any of the Masters of the Chapel Children. Under his direction, the Chapel Children extended their theatrical activities, performing plays at court more regularly than ever before, and even participating in the Candlemas Feasts of Lincoln's Inn.

Choirboy Troupes

In addition to the Children of the Chapel Royal, choirboys from Westminster Abbey and St. Paul's Cathedral frequently entertained the Tudor court. Unlike the Chapel Children, however, choirboys from these and similar ecclesiastical institutions had appeared in dramatic and semidramatic productions long before they emerged as court entertainers. Indeed, the Medieval background of these choirboy troupes helps to explain their role in the Christmas revelry at court.

Throughout the Middle Ages, conventual and secular

houses of Christian worship had choirs of men and boys to assist in religious services. To insure a steady supply of choristers, the monasteries, cathedrals, collegiate churches, and even some parish churches supported choir schools, or song schools. The choirboys were generally maintained by alms, lodged in the almonry, called *pueri eleemosynariae*, or almonry boys, and supervised by the almoner, who was also frequently the choirmaster. Boys usually entered these schools at the age of seven or eight, and served as choristers until their voices broke, generally at thirteen or fourteen, although the change could sometimes be concealed for several years. The choir schools provided an excellent musical education, which included instruction in polyphonic singing and in playing such instruments as organs, virginals, viols, cornets, and recorders. The choirboys received their secular education from the almoner, from a special chaplain, or at the grammar school of the institution, if it maintained one, just as grammar school boys sometimes learned music at the choir school. Nevertheless, a clear distinction always existed between choristers and grammar school boys, and between the two types of schools. At St. Paul's, for example, the Cathedral statutes provided for eight *pueri eleemosynariae* in the fourteenth and fifteenth centuries and ten by the mid-sixteenth century to be trained at the song school in St. Gregory's parish church on the Cathedral grounds, but in 1584 the Dean of the Cathedral ordered them to attend St. Paul's grammar school "that they may learn the principles of Grammar." [13]

Once a year, as part of the general Christmas festivities in ecclesiastical institutions, as well as in some grammar schools and private chapels, choirboys performed the ceremony of the Boy Bishop.[14] This festival, which was known all over Western Europe, survived in England into Mary's reign, when the Boy Bishop from St. Paul's visited the court. Sometime before the ceremony the choristers selected one of their number to serve as Bishop on Innocents' Day (December 28), also called Childermas, the other boys to attend him as priests, deacons, and canons. On Innocents' Eve, garbed in the vestments of their offices, the choristers led a regular service in which the previously elected Boy Bishop preached a sermon and sometimes delivered the benediction, while the real clergymen, in place of the choristers, carried candles and censers. The service was usually followed by a dinner, at which the Boy Bishop and his entourage occupied the places of honor. Afterwards, the Boy Bishop and his retinue led a procession through the streets, singing hymns and providing an opportunity for great mirth on the part of the general public. On the following day, the Boy Bishop and his staff paid official visits to nearby religious establishments and residences of distinguished personages, demanding a small contribution from each host. At Vespers, the boys resumed their rightful places and the ceremony came to an end.

The festival of the Boy Bishop was essentially a saturnalia—a reversal of roles between master and servant, a licensed mockery of authority that at times surely involved mimicry of specific ecclesiastical officials. This ritualized type of saturnalian mockery may well have carried over into the plays which choirboys came to perform on or around Innocents' Day, for it is quite prominent in plays acted by later children's troupes, as we shall see in subsequent chapters.

True theatrical performances by choirboys arise not from the ceremony of the Boy Bishop but from tropes introduced into the Mass after the ninth century. From dialogues between two half-choirs, these tropes expanded into short scenes with clergy and choristers singing individual parts. In the earliest of these scenes, and in the later mystery plays, choirboys often took roles which naturally suited them:

angels; children, such as the Innocents; and sometimes women, such as the Maries. Choirboys continued to play these roles even after the municipal guilds undertook the production of religious plays in the fourteenth and fifteenth centuries. In smaller towns and villages, where the guilds were not large or prosperous enough to produce mystery cycles, religious plays remained under the auspices of the parish priest and choirmaster, who relied heavily on local choirboys. In the larger towns, there may have been some rivalry between children's troupes and craft guilds in the production of mystery cycles. As early as 1378, "the scholars of Paul's School," who are perhaps choristers or pupils of the pre-Colet grammar school, reputedly urged Richard II

> to prohibit some unexpert People from representing the History of the Old Testament, to the great prejudice of the said Clergy, who have been at great expense in order to represent it publicly at Christmas.[15]

The sneer at inexperienced players, possibly a crack at the guilds, suggests that some group of children at Paul's had presented this cycle many times before and resented poachers on its preserve.

In England during the fifteenth century, as these cycles developed into huge outdoor pageants and were shifted to the summer holidays of Whitsun and Corpus Christi, some of the responsibility for providing indoor plays during the Christmas and Easter seasons fell to the choirboys and other groups of children. These groups frequently presented plays on their traditional feast days of St. Catherine (November 25), St. Nicholas (December 6), and the Holy Innocents—usually before temporal or ecclesiastical lords. On Candlemas, 1413, for example, the almonry boys of Maxstoke played in the hall of Lord Clifton's castle.[16] Although itinerant adult troupes also played in aristocratic great halls, acting for them was obviously a vocation rather than the peripheral activity it was for the choirboys.

By the sixteenth century, indoor performances on festive occasions had become the choristers' main type of dramatic activity. Even when they presented religious plays on these occasions, such plays tended to be part of the evening's entertainment rather than a gesture of devotion. As early as 1487, for instance, the *pueri eleemosynariae* of St. Swithin's and Hyde Park Abbey performed *The Harrowing of Hell* before Henry at Winchester, but the social occasion for the play was the celebration of the birth of Prince Arthur. By the mid-sixteenth century, choristers from the London ecclesiastical institutions had become regular performers at the court's winter revels, along with troupes from the two royal chapels and nearby grammar schools. The choirboys of Westminster entertained Queen Elizabeth with some regularity between 1566–67 and 1575–76, and the choirboys of St. Paul's Cathedral, the Children of Paul's, appeared at court more often than any other boy or adult company during the first half of her reign.

Sebastian Westcote and the Children of Paul's

The Children of Paul's owed their prominence to two early choirmasters, John Redford and Sebastian Westcote, and to John Heywood, who probably assisted them both as actor, musician, or playwright.[17] Redford also held the posts of organist and almoner, and composed organ music and vocal motets. He is the author of *Wit and Science* (1531–47), the only extant play by a choirmaster at Paul's. After his death in 1547, he was succeeded by Westcote, the guiding spirit of theatrical activities at Paul's for the next thirty-five years, during which time the Children of Paul's performed plays at court practically every Christmas. Westcote may have produced two extant plays, which some scholars have placed in the repertory of the Paul's boys—*The Marriage of Wit and Science* and *The Contention between Liberality and Prodigality*. The titles of lost plays performed by the Children of Paul's suggest works in the pathetic-heroine tradition developed by humanist educators.

Under Westcote's mastership, the Children of Paul's evidently devoted considerable time and energy to playing, although it was still ancillary to their duties as choristers. Westcote's appointment provided for one or more deputies, perhaps in recognition of the troupe's theatrical activities or of the assistance hitherto rendered by Heywood. Westcote was also empowered to impress boys from any cathedral church in England, a privilege usually reserved for masters of the Chapel Royal or the Windsor Chapel, but which Westcote exercised in 1580 to "take up" a boy from Christ's Hospital.

The popularity of the Paul's boys at court gained Westcote influential friends, who usually managed to protect him from the troubles arising over his adherence to Catholicism. On more than one occasion, civil or ecclesiastical officials sought to have him removed from his post. Dr. Nicholas Sander, an exiled English Catholic, attributed Westcote's survival to Elizabeth's patronage: "He was such a favorite with Elizabeth, as to retain his place in that church, without doing anything schismatical." [18] Excommunicated in 1563, despite the Queen's protection and Leicester's intervention, Westcote retained his post at Paul's. In 1575 the Common Council charged him with remaining a Catholic, the very same year that the Privy Council concerned itself with the kidnaping of one of "his principal players." [19] Westcote's religious difficulties grew worse, and during the winter of 1577–78 he was briefly imprisoned in Marshalsea for recusancy. However, in December of the following winter, the Privy Council authorized the Children of Paul's, along with the Chapel Children and four adult troupes, to give public performances in order to prepare for their court appearances during the coming Christmas revelry. In short, while Westcote's Catholicism antagonized municipal and religious authorities, his theatrical activities secured for him the protection of the crown and some members of the aristocracy.

During Westcote's tenure of office, the Children of Paul's extended their playing to wider audiences. They provided music and perhaps dialogues or interludes at the election feasts of various guilds,[20] and, according to Stowe, performed in plays in their song school as early as 1569. Westcote's playhouse was clearly in existence by December 1575, when the Court of Alderman received a complaint that "one Sebastian that will not communicate with the Church of England keepeth plays and resort of the people to great gain and peril of the Corrupting of the Children with papistry." The same document records the appointment of one Master Morton "to go to the Dean of Paul's and to give him notice of that disorder, and to pray him to give such remedy therein, within his jurisdiction, as he shall see meet, for Christian Religion and good order," from which we can infer that the playhouse was probably somewhere on Cathedral property, although its precise location remains a mystery.[21] The Privy Council edict of December 1578 already mentioned classifies Westcote's troupe with professional adult companies, who evidently had their own theaters or regular places to play, and with the Chapel Children, who by this time were performing in their own playhouse in Blackfriars. Westcote's will mentions a small bequest to "one Shepard that keepeth the door of plays," [22] an indication that spectators paid admission to watch the Children of

Paul's rehearse for their court performances, a practice which marks the first step in the commercialization of the children's troupes.

The pupils of the Merchant Taylors' grammar school for a short time achieved a similar degree of commercialization. Richard Mulcaster, the headmaster from the school's opening in 1561 until 1586, introduced acting in the curriculum and brought his boys to court at least eight times between 1572–73 and 1582–83. The titles of lost plays attributed to Mulcaster's boys suggest that he shared Westcote's interest in plays featuring pathetic heroines. The troupe also gave public performances in the Merchant Taylors' hall until March 1574, when the guild's officers banished the company from the premises. The document recording this order complains that rowdy spectators usurped the best seats, reserved for the masters of the guild and their guests, and suggests the saturnalian atmosphere of these occasions "which bringeth the youth to such an impudent familiarity with their betters that often times great contempt of masters, parents, and magistrates followeth thereof. . . ." [23] We also learn of an admission charge of one penny, the earliest record of a boy company playing before paying spectators.

The First Blackfriars Theater

Like the Children of Paul's and the Merchant Taylors' Boys, the Chapel Children too edged toward increasing commercialization by acquiring their own playhouse. In 1576, Sir William More leased some rooms in the former Dominican Priory known as Blackfriars to Richard Ferrant, master of the Children of the Windsor Chapel and temporary replacement for William Hunnis as master of the Children of the Chapel Royal. Apparently, the two troupes merged into one under Ferrant's direction. According to More, "Ferrant pretended unto me to use the house only for the teaching of the Children of the Chapel but made it a Continual house for plays." Writing to the irate landlord in 1581 in support of Hunnis, who had returned to his post, the Earl of Leicester declared that Hunnis "means there to practise the Queen's children of the Chapel, being now in his charge, in like sort as his predecessor [Ferrant] did for the better training them to do her Majesty's service." [24] Ferrant's costs in the venture must have been considerable: he not only relieved Hunnis of the financial responsibilities for maintaining the Chapel Children and leased the Blackfriars property from More, but he had the premises converted into a theater, apparently by knocking out partitions to make a large rectangular hall. The court accounts for 1576–77 to 1579–80 show no increase in Ferrant's wages or rewards for court appearances, and Ferrant, like Westcote and Mulcaster, probably had to charge admission to these rehearsals simply to meet his expenses.

At what point these rehearsals became outright commercial productions is impossible to say, but I would suggest that the illusion of amateurism was accepted by many people as long as the children's troupes appeared at court. That service to the Queen was a motive behind the rehearsals is obvious, although it was equally obvious that money could be made in such a venture. The two motives are not mutually exclusive. Modern scholars tend to exaggerate the profit-motive. Westcote, it is true, died a fairly prosperous man, perhaps as a direct or indirect result of his theatrical activities. The reward for court appearance was usually ten pounds, no mean sum, and although Harbage calls it "the *vera causa* of juvenile professionalism," [25] it could rarely be earned more than twice a year. Moreover, any kind of service to the crown might lead to monopolies, lucrative positions in the royal household, or other opportunities for making money. John Lyly, for instance, aspired to the post of Master of Revels as a reward for his services as a court entertainer. On the other hand, service to the sovereign was an expression of loyalty, perhaps even a privilege for a subject. A vestige of this blending of profit and service survives today when certain British manufacturers and retailers proclaim—with a mixture of pride and astuteness— that they supply commodities to the royal household "by appointment to Her Majesty the Queen." [26] In the same fashion, the establishment by the children's troupes of their own theaters was in part a business venture, which though not directly subsidized by the crown exploited the prestige derived from the companies' association with Christmas revelry at court.

The commerical possibilities of the first Blackfriars theater attracted the attention of Henry Evans, who more than any other man envisioned the children's troupes as a business enterprise. A scrivener by vocation, Evans bought the lease to the Blackfriars theater sometime in 1582–83 from Hunnis and his partner, who had resumed control of the Chapel Children when Ferrant died in 1580 and subleased the theater from Ferrant's widow. Evans had had some association with Westcote and the Children of Paul's, for the choirmaster refers to him in his will as "my foresaid dear friend" and asks him to assist the "executor with his good counsel." [27] When Westcote died in 1582, Evans apparently brought the Children of Paul's into some sort of temporary union with the Chapel Children. The title pages of the 1584 quartos of *Campaspe* (1580–84) and *Sapho and Phao* (1582–84) state that the two companies together performed these plays at court. Evans' partners in leasing the Blackfriars theater included John Lyly and the Earl of Oxford, under whose name the combined troupe appeared at court in 1583–84 and, with Evans as payee, in 1584–85. But

Evans' project collapsed shortly after More regained his property in 1584 and evicted the children's troupes, who subsequently resumed their separate identities.

Very little is heard of the Chapel Children until they appeared at court in 1600–1. Most historians speculate that the troupe fell out of royal favor at this time, but there is virtually no evidence. Some scattered appearances in the provinces are recorded—Norwich and Ipswich in 1586–87 and Leicester in 1590–91 [28]—which suggest that the troupe may have acted outside of London when not serving in the Queen's Chapel.

The Children of Paul's, on the contrary, remained active for another half-dozen years after the closing of the Blackfriars theater, probably returning to the playhouse at the Cathedral used in Westcote's time. Lyly wrote a number of plays for the Paul's boys in the late 1580s, and may, like John Heywood, have assisted the master, then Thomas Gyles. Gabriel Harvey's taunt—that "he [Lyly] hath not played the Vicemaster of Paul's and the Foolmaster of the Theater for naughts"—is evidence of Lyly's connection with the theatrical activities of the Children of Paul's. The term "Vicemaster," probably meant as a pun, would have scored even more heavily if Lyly had assisted Gyles with dramatic productions, from which, Harvey implies, he expected some personal advantage. Further evidence of Lyly's involvement in the theatrical activities at Paul's is found in the "Ironical Letter" from Jack Roberts to Sir Roger Williams in December 1584: "I pray you take heed and beware of my lord of Oxenford's man called Lyly, for if he see this letter he will put it in print or make the boys in Paul's play it upon a stage." [29]

Under Gyles, and possibly Lyly, the Children of Paul's appeared at court no fewer than nine times between 1586–87 and 1589–90. The frequency of their appearances in these four seasons may partially explain why in 1585 Gyles, like Westcote, had been granted the unusual power to impress boys for the Cathedral choir. But after the season of 1589–90, the Children of Paul's did not appear at court again until 1600–1, and were probably suppressed because of their involvement in the Marprelate controversy, an exchange of pamphlets and dramatic satire between the supporters and detractors of Anglican episcopacy. The address of the Printer to the Reader in the 1591 quarto of *Endimion* (1587–88) merely says that "the Plays in Paul's were dissolved" (III, 18). Despite their suppression in London, the Children of Paul's performed in the provinces, playing at Gloucester in 1590–91 and perhaps at Archbishop Whitgift's palace in Croydon in 1592, where an unidentified children's troupe performed Nashe's *Summer's Last Will and Testament.* The troupe was still forbidden to use its own playhouse when Thomas Nashe wrote, in *Have With You to Saffron Waldon* (pub. 1596), that "we need never wish the Plays at *Paul's* up again" (III, 46).

Revival and Commercialization

Most scholars follow Chambers and Hillebrand in assuming that the Children of Paul's resumed playing in their own theater around 1599 or 1600, but evidence recently discovered suggests that the resumption of performances at Paul's occurred somewhat earlier, perhaps no later than the winter of 1597–98. This evidence is a passage in *Le Prince d'Amour,* the extended entertainment at the Middle Temple during Christmas, 1597–98. Midway through the published account of these revels, there occurs a list of "Offenses inquirable by the Jury" assembled for a mock-trial. According to this list, it is unlawful to point out the sources of lines which the authors of the entertainment have lifted from contemporary plays:

> If any man do appeal to any Play at *Paul's, Bishopsgate,* or
> the *Bankside,* upon any sentence given in any of his Ex-
> cellency's disports of Record; this is also Premunire." [30]

"Bishopsgate" undoubtedly refers to the theaters in the
Shoreditch area to the north of London. As the Theatre closed
permanently in mid-1597, the reference is probably to the
Curtain, which the Lord Chamberlain's Men reopened in October 1597. "Bankside" alludes to the theaters of
Southwark—the Rose, Henslowe's base of operations
throughout the 1590s, and possibly the Swan. "Paul's" un-
questionably refers to the theater on the Cathedral grounds
used by the Children of Paul's since Westcote's time. The
grouping of Paul's with theaters that were open and flourish-
ing suggests that playing had resumed at the playhouse by
this time. Moreover, even if *Le Prince d'Amour* is an older entertainment refurbished for the 1597–98 revels, the reference
to current theaters would have to be accurate, lest it elicit
derision from the fashionable young gallants of the Middle
Temple. In short, the resumption of playing at Paul's seems to
have occurred in the fall or early winter of 1597, between October, when the Curtain reopened, and Christmas, when *Le
Prince d'Amour* reigned at the Middle Temple.

The resuscitation of the Children of Paul's probably resulted from the familiar combination of profit and duty, but
one is intrigued by the possibility of a dash of aristocratic self-
display. A letter from Rowland White to Sir Robert Sidney,
dated November 13, 1599, links Lord Derby with the reactiva-
tion of the Paul's boys: "My Lord Derby hath put up the plays
of the children in Paul's to his great pains and charge." Lord
Derby (William Stanley, 1561–1642) may have wanted to emulate his father-in-law, the Earl of Oxford, in patronizing a

choirboy troupe, but there is no other evidence connecting him with the Children of Paul's. In fact, a letter from George Fanner dated June 30, 1599, describes him as "busy penning comedies for the common players," who were most likely the company of adult actors that had been performing under his name for many years.[31]

It is also possible that the resumption of playing at Paul's resulted from the appointment of Richard Mulcaster to the headmastership of the grammar school in 1596. The date of his arrival precedes by a year or so the reopening of the playhouse, just as his resignation in 1608 comes a year or so after the troupe stopped playing. What role, if any, he played in the activities of the Children of Paul's is unclear. His name appears in none of the documents relating to court performances by the troupe or to its legal and financial affairs. The Blackfriars troupe "impressed" one of Mulcaster's students, Nathaniel Field, along with several boy choristers from St. Paul's, which suggests that the headmaster encouraged his own pupils to act in performances by the choirboys, who were also part-time students at the grammar school, but there is no evidence of his having any official connection with the troupe known as the Children of Paul's. In Beaumont's *The Knight of the Burning Pestle* (Queen's Revels, c.1607), the grocer and his wife wonder if Humphrey belongs to Mulcaster's troupe, but the joke is probably on these middle-class interlopers, with their old-fashioned tastes in theater, for not knowing that "Master *Monkester's* Scholars" (I, 17), as the Merchant Taylors' Boys had been called, had been defunct for twenty years.

The safest assumption is that the revival of playing at Paul's was largely the work of the choirmaster, Thomas Gyles, and resulted from the usual blending of commercial enterprise and service to the crown. In mid-1600, Gyles was succeeded by Edward Pierce, formerly a chorister of the Chapel Royal, and it is Pierce under whom the Children of Paul's achieved their most brilliant success, rivaling the Chapel Children of Blackfriars for the role of the most fashionable theatrical troupe in London. Pierce appears to have brought his choirboys, his powers of impressment, and the prestige of his office into partnership with a theatrical speculator named Thomas Woodford. Although there is no record of a commission for impressment privileges granted to Pierce, he may have inherited Gyles's: several of the plays performed by the Children of Paul's after the resumption of playing in the late 1590s require more than ten actors, the number of choristers stipulated in the Cathedral statutes.

The increasing commercialization of the Children of Paul's is evinced by the frequent mention of admission fees. In 1589, shortly before the troupe was temporarily dissolved, prices recorded are 4d. and 6d., but around 1601 a character in William Percy's *Cuckqueans and Cuckolds Errant,* which the author intended for performance at Paul's, declares that "Paul's steeple stands in the place it did before; and twopence is the price for the going into a new Play there." [32] Similarly, the Prologue to Beaumont's *The Woman Hater* (Paul's, 1605–7) suggests that as late as that date the cheapest seat in the house cost twopence: "for I do pronounce this, to the utter discomfort of all two penny Gallery men, you shall have no bawdry in it." Finally, at the end of the Induction to Middleton's *Michaelmas Term* (Paul's, 1604–6), Michaelmas Term complains that the company has had "but sixpenny fees all the year long." If Beaumont's reference to twopence as the price of the cheapest seats in the house is accurate, sixpence probably purchased the most expensive seat and Michaelmas Term's plea of poverty is either ironic or else an allusion to the disparity between that sum and legal fees paid and received by members of the audience. In short, the evidence indicates that at Paul's the scale of prices after its reopening ranged from twopence to sixpence, which is only slightly more than the one to three penny scale at the public theaters. Obviously, someone in the directorate of the Children of Paul's hoped to make money out of the plays, but one must stress again that the basis for such a hope was the somewhat wider distribution of a product previously reserved for limited audiences of courtiers and aristocrats.

We can learn a good deal about the commercialization of the Children of Paul's from a libel suit over Chapman's lost play, *The Old Joiner of Aldgate,* which the troupe performed in February 1603. In his testimony, Pierce tried to minimize his connection with the choirboys' dramatic activities by denying that he did "at any time disburse any money for buying the plays which usually are acted by the Children of Paul's, but his care is otherwise employed for the Education of the . . . Children and to instruct them as appertaineth to his place and Charge." [33] Although Pierce's testimony was corroborated by his codefendants, Chapman and Woodford, the choristers probably could not have performed plays without their choirmaster's cooperation and more likely did so under his direction. Pierce was payee for most of the troupe's appearances at court, and later received a "dead rent" of twenty pounds from the managers of Blackfriars and Whitefriars "That there might be a Cessation of playing & plays to be acted in the said house near St. Paul's Church." [34] Pierce's testimony, if narrowly construed, merely denies that he was the troupe's business agent.

That function fell to Woodford. He admitted buying *The Old Joiner* from Chapman and acknowledged that the production came about through his "means & appointment." [35] The partnership between Pierce and Woodford may have been

complicated because the choirmaster was technically responsible to the Cathedral authorities. *The Old Joiner* was temporarily withdrawn from the stage when a "doctor White, one of
the Masters of the Church of Paul's," [36] objected to the libel-
ing of another clergyman. Friction between the partners, perhaps resulting from the suppression of Chapman's play or the
ensuing litigation, flared into violence on December 2, 1604,
when Pierce allegedly assaulted Woodford.[37] Around 1605,
Woodford evidently sold his interest in the troupe to Edward
Kirkham, a Yeoman of the Revels, through whom the company may have gained access to costumes and properties
owned by the Revels Office. Court accounts for March 31,
1606, list Kirkham as "one of the Masters of the children of
Paul's" and as payee for two plays performed by the company
at court.[38] Their last recorded appearance was a performance
of the lost play *Abuses* on July 30, 1606, before James and his
brother-in-law, King Christian IV of Denmark:

> the Youths of Paul's, commonly called the children of
> Paul's, played before the two Kings, a play called *Abuses:*
> containing both a Comedy and a Tragedy, at which the
> Kings seemed to take delight and be much pleased.[39]

The dissolution of the Children of Paul's is suggested by the
entrance of seven of its plays in the *Stationers' Register* between May 9 and August 6, 1607. The reasons for its dissolution are unknown.

Some of the members of the disbanded troupe may have
joined the children's company that played at Whitefriars in
1607 and 1608 under the name of "the Children of the King's
Revels," but both Chambers and Hillebrand discount that
possibility for lack of evidence. The Children of the King's
Revels was neither a nominal part of the royal household, like
the Chapel Children, nor a group of Cathedral choirboys, like

the Children of Paul's, but rather an enterprise designed to exploit and share in the success of the other two troupes. It was organized by Thomas Woodford, the entrepreneur behind the Children of Paul's, and Martin Slater, an actor, who was to serve as master of the children. Shareholders included the playwrights Lording Barry and John Mason, whose works the company performed. After two years, the troupe left London for the provinces and finally dissolved in 1616.

In late 1600, a few years after the Children of Paul's resumed playing in their playhouse, the Chapel Children were reactivated at Blackfriars. Once again, considerations of profit and duty merged. Nathaniel Giles, the choirmaster of the Windsor Children who succeeded Hunnis to the mastership of the Chapel Children in 1597, entered into a partnership with Henry Evans, the theatrical businessman who had been associated with the first Blackfriars theater. On September 2, 1600, Evans leased some property in Blackfriars from Richard Burbage. His father, James Burbage, had acquired it from William More in 1596 and converted it into a theater, but the residents of the neighborhood prevented its opening. This second Blackfriars theater was not the same property that Ferrant had converted into a theater in 1576, although it too was probably a large rectangular hall. Giles's responsibility was to recruit, by means of his power of impressment, enough additional boys to form an acting troupe. His charter provided for twelve boys, but some of the plays produced at the second Blackfriars shortly after 1600 require as many as twenty actors to be onstage at one time.[40] Late in 1600, Giles impressed eight boys. Three of them had been associated with St. Paul's Cathedral: Nathaniel Field, Mulcaster's pupil at the grammar school, and two choirboys, Alvery Trussel and Salomon Pavy, the subject of Ben Jonson's Epigram 120. Our information about Giles's recruiting comes from the lawsuit surrounding the impressment of another boy, Thomas Clifton, whose father appealed to powerful friends for his son's release and later brought legal action against Giles and Evans.

The organizers of the revived Chapel Children were apparently eager to exploit the success of the Children of Paul's, and to appear both at court and in their own theater as soon as possible. They were ready for their first court performance by Shrovetide 1601, and from various legal documents we know that they performed three times a week over a six-month season.[41] It was obviously hard to maintain that plays given at Blackfriars *after* a court performance were rehearsals, although one could advertise the productions, as publishers did printed texts, as having been performed before the King or Queen on such and such a date. Moreover, it appears from the prices charged for admission—probably ranging from sixpence to a shilling or shilling-and-a-half [42]—that the Blackfriars troupe was more commercially oriented than ever before. "Commercial" is not a dirty word; it implies not only that the managers desired to make money but also that the children's plays became accessible to more people.

Despite their initial successes, the troupe encountered legal difficulties. As a result of the Clifton suit, Evans was ordered to quit the Blackfriars management, but he evaded the decree by bringing new partners into the organization and leaving town. Evans' ploy initiated active speculation in shares of the operation. Among the many shareholders three deserve special consideration. The first was Edward Kirkham, the Yeoman of the Revels who would later invest in the operation at Paul's. The other two were literary figures. One of them, John Marston, joined the Blackfriars syndicate around 1603 and subsequently began to write plays for the Chapel Children rather than for the Children of Paul's, for whom he had previously written. The other, Samuel Daniel, contracted with the syndicate in 1604 to receive a salary for licensing the troupe's plays on behalf of the Master of the Revels and subsequently served as payee for court performance, until his own play, *Philotas* (Queen's Revels, 1604) brought royal displeasure on himself and the company.

The intense speculation in shares suggests that the venture was prospering. The Blackfriars children performed plays by Jonson, Chapman, Marston, and others, and according to a German visitor, offered an extensive musical prelude of high quality and attracted a large and respectable audience.[43] Like the Children of Paul's, the Blackfriars troupe was doing well enough to worry at least one of the adult companies. In the first quarto of *Hamlet* (pub. 1603), Gilderstone tells the Prince why the tragedians of the city have gone on tour: "I'faith, my lord, novelty carries it away; for the principal public audience that came to them are turned to private plays and to the humor of the children." [44] Curiously, this passage is omitted from the second quarto (pub. 1604–5), but is amplified in the folio (pub. 1623). I quote the most relevant portion:

there is, sir, an aery of children, little eyases, that cry out on top of the question and are most tyrannically clapped for't. These are now the fashion.

(II.ii.339–41)

In both versions of *Hamlet*, the Prince shows no surprise at the fickleness and perversity of public taste, observing that those who scorned Claudius when his father lived now offer extravagant sums for his uncle's "picture in little." Within the world of the play, these passages offer another example of corruption and debasement, but they may also reflect Shakespeare's own resentment of the success of his diminutive ri-

vals. Within a few years, his company would supplant one of
the troupes of "little eyases" in its "eyrie" at Blackfriars.

Despite their success, the actual choirboys of the Chapel
Royal seem to have been gradually withdrawn from theatrical
operations at Blackfriars. Because the plays acted there
frequently satirized James, his new Scots knights, his love of
hunting, and his silver mines, the King apparently no longer
wished to supply the troupe with choristers from his own
chapel. On February 4, 1604, James issued a patent to the
Blackfriars syndicate entitling them to the name "Children of
the Queen's Revels." Significantly, Nathaniel Giles is not
listed among the patentees. On September 17, 1604, James
issued a new commission to Giles in no way different from
those of earlier masters except in restoring the provisions for
sending ex-choristers to the universities. Perhaps James
wished to offer his former choirboys an alternative to acting.
Finally, on November 7, 1606, James took the unprecedented
step of issuing a new commission to Giles while his old one
was still valid. The new commission concluded with the following clause, which seems to be its *raison d'etre:*

> Provided always and we do straightly charge and com-
> mand that none of the said Choristers or Children of the
> Chapel so to be taken by force of this Commission shall
> be used or employed as Comedians or Stage players or to
> exercise or act any stage plays, Interludes, Comedies, or
> tragedies for that it is not fit or decent that such as should
> sing the praises of God almighty should be trained up or
> employed in such lascivious and profane exercises.[45]

With this, the Children of the Chapel Royal were completely
dissociated from the second Blackfriars theater, and the company acting there now styled itself the Children of the Revels

and was composed of boys taken on as apprentices and perhaps some ex-choristers.[46] By 1608, after further antagonizing King James, the troupe became known as the Children of Blackfriars. James was determined to dissolve the company and is said to have vowed that "they should never play more but should first beg their bread and he would have his vow performed." [47] In August of 1608, Evans dissolved the syndicate and returned the lease for the theater to Burbage, who immediately leased it to his own troupe, the King's Men, now eager to extend its operations to a private theater. The children's company was reorganized by Robert Keysar and Philip Rosseter, a royal musician, and moved to Whitefriars, vacant after the dissolution of the King's Revels. The Keysar-Rosseter troupe appeared at court as the Children of Whitefriars and, as the Children of the Queen's Revels, toured the provinces and finally merged with the Lady Elizabeth's Men in 1613, although companies playing under its name are mentioned in provincial records as late as the 1620s.

The history of the Children of the Chapel Royal, under its various aliases, parallels that of the Children of Paul's. One originated as part of the royal household, the other as members of the Cathedral song school. In the early part of Elizabeth's reign, both troupes brought plays to court during the extensive Christmas revelry. In the 1570s, when the adult companies too were then settling into their own theaters, the two children's troupes established their own playhouses, one at Blackfriars, the other on the Cathedral grounds, where they rehearsed for court performances before paying spectators. In the early 1580s, the troupes acted in combination at Blackfriars for a year or two under the aegis of Henry Evans. Thereafter their theatrical activities gradually petered out and may even have been suppressed by the government. In the late

1590s, the Children of Paul's resumed performances in its playhouse under a more commercially minded directorate, to be followed in 1600 by the Children of the Chapel at the second Blackfriars theater under the ubiquitous Evans. As both enterprises flourished commercially and artistically, they attracted sophisticated spectators and talented dramatists, and extended their repertories and their playing seasons. Whereas the operation at Paul's ceased abruptly in 1607 with the closing of the playhouse on the Cathedral grounds, the Blackfriars troupe faded gradually. It lost its connection with the Chapel Royal in 1606, was forced to move from Blackfriars to Whitefriars in 1608, and was eventually absorbed by an adult troupe in 1613. The reversals experienced by the two leading children's troupes evidently began when private-theater plays no longer appeared as courtly entertainments. The boy companies were less popular at court under James than they had been under Elizabeth, as the most fashionable form of court entertainment under the new sovereign became the court masque, which Jonson and Jones elaborated into dazzling spectacle.

The number and quality of extant plays performed by the Children of Paul's and the Children of the Chapel Royal as quasi-professional companies during the late 1590s and the early 1600s has dwarfed a much longer phase in which, as a sideline to their duties as choristers, the children's troupes offered entertainment for the court during the Christmas revelry, and rehearsals to paying spectators. Because of their long history as amateurs, they exploited their reputation as purveyors of dramatic entertainment to the court and nobility even after they became business enterprises, a reputation which accorded with the ritualistic nature of the theatrical occasions in which they participated.

🐾 CHAPTER TWO 🐾

The Occasion

TODAY, going to watch a play performed by children is not a glamorous occasion; it is a ritual of obligation. We squirm on hard chairs in the community hall or school gymnasium, we crane for a glimpse of our offspring and those of friends and relatives, usually the ones who have prevailed on us to attend, and we smile condescendingly at the inaudible diction and uncertain movements, all the while longing for the relief of the final curtain. It was not always so. During the late Middle Ages and Renaissance, children's performances, generally of high quality, were usually part of an elaborate program of seasonal entertainment, a ritual of festivity, a blaze of revelry against the mid-winter gloom. What did it feel like to watch a play in this ambiance? What were the physical conditions, the audience's expectations, the emotional climate? What was the nature of the theatrical occasion when a children's troupe performed at court or in its own private theater?

Banqueting Halls and Playhouses

We know that the London children's troupes established their own theaters in the 1560s and 1570s in order to rehearse the plays they would perform during these annual court revels. It seems reasonable to hypothesize that they tried to reproduce both the physical conditions and the festal atmosphere of such occasions, and continued to do so even after their complete commercialization after the late 1590s. Some scholars have suggested that the characterization of the children's performances in their own playhouses as rehearsals for court appearances was a legal fiction designed to protect the troupes from the municipal authorities who wished to abolish all professional theatrical activity in London. This may have been true after the late 1590s, but when the children's companies first established their playhouses twenty or thirty years earlier, the need to hold rehearsals was as real as the profit motive, and may even have preceded it.

Before a children's troupe, or an adult troupe for that matter, was invited to play at court, it had to perform before the Masters of the Revels. The first master, Sir Thomas Cawardan, used Blackfriars for such auditions from 1547 to 1559. In order to meet his standards and then to perform creditably at court, it was necessary to rehearse. This presented no problem to adult troupes, who were experienced and flexible enough to adapt their plays to all sorts of conditions and who could simply bring to court works from their repertories. For professional adult companies, the notion that their regular performances were rehearsals for court appearances was indeed a legal fiction. For the children's troupes, however, rehearsing the plays they hoped to bring to court was a practical necessity. In 1564, for instance, the grammar school boys of Westminster played *Miles Gloriosus* "in Master Dean's house," which probably refers to the banqueting hall in the residence of the Dean of Westminster, before "rehearsing before Sir Thomas Benger," the Master of the Revels, and presenting the play at court.[1] In similar fashion, Mulcaster, Westcote, and Ferrant prepared their troupes for auditions before the Master of the Revels and for subsequent court performance by holding rehearsals in the Merchant Taylors' guild hall, in the playhouse at Paul's, and in the first Blackfriars theater, respectively. Later, when the children's troupes had become somewhat more commercialized, they could encourage their audiences, as well as the municipal government, to regard performances in the private playhouse as rehearsals for court performance, for a facsimile of the occasion of the court play was precisely the product they were commercializing. When their playing seasons extended beyond Shrovetide, the time court revelry usually ended, they could then advertise their plays as having been performed at court, just as publishers did on title pages. People who would be or had been excluded from the Great Hall or Great Chamber by lack of space or by their own social status could see the same play in an ambiance that closely approximated that of the court production.

One way of recreating the courtly ambiance was to simulate the physical conditions of the Great Halls and Great Chambers in the royal palaces. The Tudor banqueting hall at Whitehall, which is typical, measured 45 by 100 feet, larger but otherwise scarcely different from any other Tudor great hall; in 1606 James replaced it with a new Banqueting House, 53 by 120 feet.[2] When such halls were fitted out for a dramatic performance, the actors might play either on the floor itself or on a slightly raised stage. The playing area was located either in the middle of the hall or more likely against the screen at the lower, or kitchen, end of the hall. The space behind this screen served as a tiring house and the openings in it allowed the actors to move easily between backstage and playing areas. Some screens supported a "minstrel gallery," which housed musicians or singers, and which might also serve as a second, elevated playing area. Light was supplied by torches, lanterns, candles, and candelabra. For court plays, which were probably somewhat more lavish than the typical banqueting hall play, the Revels Accounts after 1570 indicate the use of wood-and-canvas "houses," or booths, to represent dwellings, castles, temples, and other structures, although a similar effect could have been achieved by hanging a movable curtain from the gallery or over one of the openings in the hall screen. Spectators usually sat at tables on a dais at the upper end of the hall and along the side walls if a meal was in progress, or else in "degrees," i.e. tiered rows of benches like grandstand seats, or occasionally in temporary galleries. While servants stood wherever they could find suitable space, the aristocratic members of the audience sat on three or four sides of the hall, depending on whether the playing area was at one end or in the middle of the hall.

The private theaters evidently reproduced the physical conditions, perhaps on a reduced scale, of a Tudor great hall or royal banqueting hall on the occasion of a dramatic presentation. In the Prologue to *Antonio's Revenge* (Paul's, 1599–1600), Marston wonders if the spirits that breathe "within this round" and the hearts that "pant within this ring" are capable of responding to the tragic action that follows. Chambers regarded this passage as proof that the theater at Paul's was round, although prologues and epilogues of college plays produced in rectangular halls frequently use the words "round," "ring," "orb," and "circle" metaphorically to refer to the disposition of seats on three or four sides of a playing area, as does the Prologue to *The Family of Love* (Paul's, 1602–3? and King's Revels, 1607).[3] Without knowing the location of the playhouse at Paul's, we cannot speak with assurance of its shape, but most scholars assume it was in one of several halls on the Cathedral grounds. Even the parish church of St. Gregory, often mentioned as the site of this theater, could have been outfitted to reproduce the conditions of a rectangular banqueting hall with the audience seated on three or four sides of the playing area, as were university chapels in the 1560s. The extant plays that reflect performance conditions at Paul's after it reopened in the late 1590s require a raised stage, a second, elevated playing area containing a casement, and a curtained discovery space, and could easily have been performed in a banqueting hall arranged for dramatic production.[4]

If the picture at Paul's is blurred, our knowledge of other playhouses used by children's troupes confirms their physical similarity to royal banqueting halls. Mulcaster's troupe played in the guild hall of the Merchant Taylors, while the Whitefriars theater, used first by a children's troupe and adjacent to the office of the Master of the Revels, was located in the "great hall" or refectory of the former Carmelite priory, in a space measuring 35 by 85 feet.[5] Ferrant made his theater in Blackfriars by removing partitions added to a hall that had served the Dominicans as a refectory and later as a guest house. Irwin Smith concludes that Ferrant's playhouse occupied a rectangular space 26 by 46½ feet, about a quarter of the size of a royal banqueting hall, and that the seating area could accommodate 120 to 130 spectators, although other estimates run as high as 400.[6] The reference to a trap door in Peele's *The Arraignment of Paris* (Chapel, 1581–84) suggests a raised playing area, although we do not know if this was in the middle of the hall or against the tiring-house wall, which could have been adapted from a hall screen. Lyly's *Campaspe* and *Sapho and Phao*, the only other extant plays known to have been acted in this playhouse, require some sort of curtained discovery space. Assuming that these texts reflect actual performance conditions, this space could have been created by curtaining an opening in the screen or an area underneath the gallery, or if the playing area was in the middle of the hall, by a freestanding booth, somewhat like the mansions used in simultaneous staging. In short, the first Blackfriars theater probably resembled a typical Tudor great hall or royal banqueting hall fitted out for theatrical entertainment.

The second Blackfriars theater was constructed by James Burbage probably in what had been the Upper Frater, or Great Hall, of the Dominican Priory, a room large enough to have held meetings of Parliament. He bought the property in February 1596, and probably completed renovations in the same year. There is no evidence that Evans made additional renovations when he leased the theater from Burbage's son Richard in 1600 for the Chapel Children. James Burbage was a shrewd and far-sighted men. In 1576 he had built the Theatre, the first of the large, open-roofed playhouses in London. Twenty years later, one surmises, he intended to construct for an adult company the same kind of banqueting-hall theater that Ferrant had set up in Blackfriars. Being no less interested in profit than the choirmasters and their partners, and knowing that the members of an adult company earned their living from acting, Burbage made his banqueting-hall theater considerably larger than Ferrant's.

All three modern reconstructions of the second Blackfriars theater emphasize its derivation from the Tudor banqueting hall. One legal document refers to the theater as "the great hall." According to Smith, the theater occupied a space 46 by 101 feet, almost exactly the dimensions of a royal banqueting hall, with a partition across the width separating a backstage area from an auditorium that measured 46 by 66 feet. Other scholars argue that the entire theater measured 46 by 66 feet, which is still nearly three times the size of Ferrant's. The ceiling was high enough for galleries, to which there are many contemporaneous allusions, and estimates of audience capacity run roughly from 500 to 1,000.[7] Whether or not we accept

Smith's placement of the partition separating the backstage area from the auditorium, all recent reconstructions of the theater seat the audience on three sides of a raised playing area set against a tiring-house wall, which, as Richard Hosley argues, was directly or indirectly modeled on hall screens of the period. In short, the second Blackfriars theater was essentially a great hall adapted for dramatic entertainment, the adaptations probably having a more permanent and elaborate character than in halls used for a variety of purposes.

When the children's troupe left Blackfriars in 1608, Richard Burbage regained control of the playhouse and leased it to the King's Men, in which he was a shareholder. Despite some repair work required before the new tenants could move in, there is no evidence of major renovation and the theater probably retained its basic character until it closed in 1642. The three new theaters built between 1616 and 1642 were small indoor playhouses, as were the new theaters built after 1660, although the model of the traditional Tudor great hall was supplemented by other models, such as the English cockpit, the French tennis court, and the Italian amphitheater. As the adult troupes and their audiences favored the private over the public theaters, the latter falling gradually into disuse, the nature of the theatrical occasion in which they participated also changed. Even if the public theaters derived certain architectural features from the banqueting hall, their size and open roofs, to say nothing of their clientele and seating arrangements, recalled the bear garden and the inn yard rather than a royal Great Hall or Great Chamber. The intimate, artificially lit indoor playhouses, on the other hand, which the children's troupes had established in order to rehearse for court performance, reproduced the physical conditions and the atmosphere of a play at court.[8]

Courtly Ambiance

The court play was a token of esteem, a gift-offering to be laid at the feet of the royal patron. On at least two occasions, the grammar school boys of Westminster presented Elizabeth and members of her court with ornate copies of texts of their plays, perhaps to symbolize the oblatory function of such performances.[9] The reward bestowed on the performers, in turn, symbolized the patron's gratitude and magnanimity. Court plays were generally part of a larger program of revelry and spectacle—the debates, tournaments, pageants, disguisings, mummings, and interludes presented each winter at the Tudor court. Huizinga's remark on similar fêtes at the Burgundian court in the fifteenth century illuminates the ritualistic function of such entertainments: "They still preserved something of the meaning they have in primitive societies, that of the supreme expression of their culture, the highest mode of a collective enjoyment and an assertion of solidarity."[10] The analogy to rituals among preliterate peoples is particularly apt, for the courtly entertainments of the late Middle Ages engaged the spectator in symbolic action for the purposes of affirming communal values and strengthening social bonds. In addition to feeling the warmth of collective well-being, the spectator could also congratulate himself for belonging to such a body and attending such a ceremony. As part of such a ritualistic program of entertainment, court plays promoted and celebrated social cohesion, chiefly by affirming the virtues of the royal patron and the worthiness of his subjects. They generally accomplished this in complex rather than simple ways, that is, by balancing fear against wish, nightmare against dream. The strategy was to arouse and allay fears of social disintegration and to raise and dispel doubts about individual rank, to combine flattery and insult, the opposed but related impulses inherent in all festal celebration.

In *Shakespeare's Festive Comedy*, C. L. Barber applies to Shakespeare Cornford's suggestion that "invocation and abuse were the basic gestures of a nature worship behind Aristophanes' union of poetry and railing." [11] In hierarchical societies that no longer worship nature directly, the gestures of invocation and abuse usually become praise and insult of human figures of authority, and by extension of all those surrounding them—the audience of the court play and ultimately the society as a whole. Obviously such festal elements can be found in all comedy, for the impulses toward praise and abuse of authority figures can be generalized into sympathy for and ridicule of dramatic characters, emotions which Northrop Frye has called the comedic equivalents of pity and fear.[12] But the plays acted by children's troupes, linked as they were to a specific festal tradition, always redirect praise and abuse toward the audience. The genius of the children's plays was to reassure the spectator that he had achieved his own wishful view of himself by encouraging him to identify with attractive characters of high rank, and to scatter his doubts about his social status by inviting him to ridicule "others." These "others" are sometimes stock comic villains like pedants, puritans, and misers, but surprisingly often are foppish gallants, parvenus, court parasites, and similar deviants from aristocratic values, many of whom closely resemble court or private theater spectators as types and as individuals.

The particular forms which praise and abuse assume in the children's plays are rooted in the background and psychology of courtly and aristocratic audiences. Praise of individuals was a time-honored method of teaching virtue through examples.[13] Flattery of one's sovereign was not only tantamount to praise of the court, the audience, and even the entire nation, but had the same self-congratulatory and magical functions that Jonas Barish attributes to the court masque:

> The masque . . . represents a society not so much aspiring after as joyfully contemplating its own well-being, the possession of the blessings it considers itself to have achieved. The compliments to the king, so often dismissed as ignoble flattery, are one expression of this self-congratulation on the part of the community. To eulogize the king is to congratulate the society, of which the king is figurehead, for the communal virtues symbolized in him. To the extent that the actuality falls short of the ideal, the masque may be taken as a kind of mimetic magic on a sophisticated level, the attempt to secure social health and tranquillity for the realm by miming it in front of its chief figure.[14]

Whether the praise expressed in and by the court play was didactic, magical, or simply obsequious in intention, Tudor courtiers and aristocrats were surely human enough to enjoy it.

The presence of insults and abuse in children's plays intended for courtly and aristocratic spectators is a little harder to explain. To a certain extent it was simply traditional. From the time of Aristophanes, if not earlier, ritual mockery has been an integral part of comedy derived from festal ceremony. The late Middle Ages and early Renaissance were particularly fond of institutionalized forms of "misrule," such as the Feast of Fools and the Boy Bishop ceremony. Mimicry and ridicule of established authority was inevitable in these rituals, in which lower clerics, choirboys, and schoolboys exchanged roles with adult officials of their institutions, and the spirit of such licensed misrule gradually found its way into plays acted by the children's troupes.

Saturnalian abuse in children's plays may also have been licensed by the common belief that "children and fools speak truth." Quoted in three plays acted by children's troupes, this proverb meant that children and fools, as devoid of ratiocinative faculties as apes or puppets, were not morally responsible for their utterances, which at least in theory could not be considered malicious. Furthermore, Ascham's complaint about aristocratic parents who encouraged sauciness and scurrility in their own children suggests that spectators with a taste for cheekiness might have been even more pleased when the children in question were not their own but belonged to a troupe of schoolboy or choirboy actors.[15]

Under the dual protection of saturnalian misrule and juvenile impunity, the children's companies were free to insult their audiences. That spectators enjoy being insulted—up to a point—seems to have been as true then as in our own time, when a movie can be advertised as having "something in it to offend everyone" and a play can be entitled *Offending the Audience*.[16] The sources of this enjoyment are not altogether masochistic, for the intended victim can turn the insult to his own advantage by applying it to those around him while exempting himself. Since showing pain or annoyance would be admitting the validity of the taunt, it is in the spectator's interest to tolerate the abuse; if he can do so gracefully, he can even demonstrate his own poise and magnanimity, all the more so as the attacks increase in acerbity. A splendid illustration of this phenomenon comes from the early eighteenth century; the *Biographia Dramatica* (1764) records how Robert Walpole converted abuse to his advantage at a performance of Gay's *The Beggar's Opera* (1727):

Sir Robert, observing the pointed manner in which the audience applied the last line [of Air XXX, or XII of Act II] to him, parried the thrust by encoring it with his single voice; and thus not only blunted the poetical shaft, but gained a general huzza from the audience.[17]

Like a king applauding the taunts of his court jester, Walpole was or wished to appear so secure in his status that he couldn't possibly take offence.

In such situations, licensed festal ridicule gratifies both the mocker and the mocked, for while saturnalia may give the ruled an outlet for their discontent, every saturnalia is followed by the restoration of power to the authorities and so reaffirms the very order it has just inverted. Victor Turner explains this phenomenon from the perspective of an anthropologist:

> Cognitively, nothing underlines regularity so well as absurdity or paradox. Emotionally, nothing satisfies as much as extravagant or temporarily permitted illicit behavior. Rituals of status reversal accommodate both aspects. By making the low high and the high low, they reaffirm the hierarchical principle. By making the low mimic (often to the point of caricature) the behavior of the high, and by restraining the initiatives of the proud, they underline the reasonableness of everyday culturally predictable behavior between the various estates of society.[18]

Or as G. K. Hunter puts it, "One of the functions of 'Revels' was to engage in topsy-turvy activities and by allowing every dog his day to confirm him in his status as a dog."[19] The political conservatism inherent in festal abuse explains why those in power sometimes tolerate subversive mockery. For example, although King James smarted when the plays acted by the Children of the Queen's Revels ridiculed him, the troupe appeared at court during the Christmas of 1608–9, the season after he had vowed that the company "should never play more, but should first beg their bread."

Both the flattering and the mocking impulses inherent in the festal tradition find expression in the prologues and epilogues to plays acted by children's troupes at court and in the private theaters. These extradramatic addresses often praise the spectators directly for their taste and judgment, and apologize for daring to bring such unworthy entertainment before so discriminating an assemblage. In the Court Prologue to *Gallathea* (Paul's, 1585–88), Lyly writes, "Your highness hath so perfect a judgment, that whatsoever we offer, we are enforced to blush," and he turns the same compliment in the Blackfriars Prologue to *Sapho and Phao*:

> yet have we ventured to present our exercises before your judgments, when we know them [our exercises] full of weak matter, yielding rather ourselves to the courtesy, which we have ever found, then to the preciseness, which we ought to fear.

A retainer of the Earl of Oxford, Lyly strikes the pose of an amateur entertainer, a courtier-playwright, by exhibiting the courtier's virtue of *sprezzatura,* or nonchalance. Following Castiglione's model, he makes difficult achievements appear effortless and therefore displays no pride in them. Lyly employs this strategy in prologues and epilogues written for both court and private theater productions of his plays, flattering his audience as much as himself by tacitly acknowledging that they have the wit and grace to appreciate his courtly stance.

This gambit was revived when the children's troupes resumed playing in the late 1590s after a period of enforced dormancy. In the Prologue to *The Maid's Metamorphosis* (Paul's, 1597–1600), the author, Lyly or one of his imitators, figuratively kneels to lay the play at the audience's feet: "Then to the boundless Ocean of your worth, / This little drop of water we present." Similarly, the Prologue to *Cynthia's Revels*

(Chapel Children, 1600), Ben Jonson praises the audience by making invidious comparisons with public -theater audiences. He is pleased to present his play before "gracious silence, sweet attention, / Quick sight, and quicker apprehension," rather than "pied ignorance," and he scorns "popular applause, / Or foamy praise, that drops from common jaws." With unsavory zeal the Prologue to Marston's *Jack Drum's Entertainment* (Paul's, 1600) promises that the author's "industry should sweat / To sweeten your delights," while the Epilogue to Barry's *Ram Alley* (King's Revels, 1607–8) reveals the commercial rivalry among the children's troupes that lurked beneath the courtly surface:

> And for ourselves we do desire,
> You'll breathe on us that growing fire,
> By which in time we may attain,
> Like favors which some others gain:
> For be assured our loves shall tend,
> To equal theirs, if not transcend.

While most prologues and epilogues to children's plays praise the spectators, a few actually insult them, as in Marston's Prologue to *The Fawn* (Queen's Revels, c.1604), where he seems to exaggerate praise to the point of ambiguity, if not beyond.

> For we do know that this most fair-filled room
> Is loaden with most Attic judgments, ablest spirits,
> Then whom there are none more exact, full, strong,
> Yet none more soft, benign in censuring.
> I know there's not one ass in all this presence,
> Not one calumnious rascal, or base villain
> Of emptiest merit, that would tax and slander
> If innocency herself should write, not one we know't.
> O you are all the very breath of Phoebus.

Marston could transform praise into abuse with ease because some members of his audience were or felt themselves to be unworthy of such lavish tribute. A general rule operated at some level among audiences at court and private theater plays: the more extreme the praise the less likely that the recipients deserved it. When this rule applies, flattery becomes insult. In his Epilogue to *All Fools* (Queen's Revels, 1604), Chapman dispenses with ambiguity and insults his audience directly. He begins with the customary denial of "real worth" in the play, but ends by suggesting—through the implied final rhyme—that the spectators, like the characters in the play, are all foolish: "We can but bring you meat, and set you stools, / And to our best cheer say, you all are (   ) welcome." [20]

Praise and Abuse in Elizabethan Plays

Prologues and epilogues, mediating as they do between the play and its social context, help us to recreate the atmosphere surrounding court and private-theater plays, and to see the occasion as a complex ritual of festal celebration. Turning to the plays themselves, we should not be surprised to find that they also are attuned to the occasion and contain the festal impulses toward praise and abuse. In the simplest form, the court play praises or abuses royal figues of authority, and by extension their courtiers, councilors, and subjects, as the court masque was to do after James's accession. In the masque, such praise tends to be explicit, because the presence of the sovereign is acknowledged, is indeed an integral part of the action, and abuse is confined to the anti-masque; whereas in court plays praise and abuse are usually directed toward allegorical representations of the royal patron and possibly of other spectators of exalted rank. Many modern critics, still reacting against the rampant allegorizing of their colleagues, hesitate to acknowledge the presence of these allegorical parallels. Yet our aversion to reading plays as *romans á clef* should not blind us to the fondness of Elizabethan and Jacobean audiences for hunting such parallels, an endeavor they termed "application."

A case in point is *Sapientia Solomonis,* which the Westminster grammar school boys acted in Latin in 1565–66 before Elizabeth and her guest, Princess Cecilia of Sweden. The Prologue draws a parallel between Solomon and Elizabeth on the basis of their wisdom, and the Epilogue extends the correspondence to Sheba and Cecilia:

> The powerful Queen of Sheba was delighted to enjoy the countenance of Solomon. The illustrious Princess Cecilia, enduring much by land and sea, now at long last gladly, has looked upon her who is the rival of pious Solomon, and wishes to look upon her often.

Several other court plays performed by children's troupes revolve around royal figures who transcend ordinary human frailty—usually symbolized by love: Cyrus in *The Wars of Cyrus,* Alexander in *Campaspe,* Cynthia in *Endimion* and *Cynthia's Revels,* Sapho in *Sapho and Phao,* and the Prince in *The Phoenix.* The parallels with Elizabeth or James in these allegorical figures were probably not intended as point-for-point correspondences, which could no longer be deciphered with assurance even if they were present, but rather enrich the action at a given point with hints of topical relevance. Following the lead of Spenserians, critics are now beginning to appreciate the allusive subtlety of allegory in drama.[21]

To balance the impulses of the festal tradition, plays containing flattering allegorical parallels generally contain insulting parallels as well. Sometimes the plays abuse the sovereign's enemies—rivals, rebels, traitors, as in Lyly's *Midas* (Paul's, 1589–90), where the title character's foolish vendetta against the island of Lesbos recalls Philip of Spain's bellicosity toward England. Occasionally a playwright dares to attack powerful figures at court, as in *Godly Queen Hester* (Chapel, 1525–29), where Haman represents Cardinal Wolsey. Such attacks usually pleased the victims' enemies. Sir John Harington reports that when some of Elizabeth's courtiers urged the suppression of *A Game of Cards* (Chapel, 1582–83) "because it was somewhat too plain," Sir Francis Walsingham defended it on the grounds "that they which do that they should not, should hear that they would not." [22] Most daring of all are parallels which criticize the sovereign's own negative qualities, as in *Damon and Pythias*, where Edwardes deplores Elizabeth-Dionysius' susceptibility to parasitical councilors.

In creating insulting parallels the playwright may be magically destroying enemies, flattering partisans of a certain faction, providing his victims with a chance to display their superiority to such mockery, and impressing the neutral with his audacity in sailing ever closer to the wind. English audiences, especially those at court or in private theaters, evidently enjoyed identifying these allegorical targets of derision, and one indication that such "application" was not only prevalent but intentional is the force and frequency with which prologues deny its presence. As Edwardes says in the Prologue to *Damon and Pythias*: "talking of Courtly toys, we do protest this flat, / We talk of Dionysius' Court, we mean no Court but that." When not denying deliberate "application" in their plays, dramatists could justify the practice by citing classical authority. Aristotle had stated that drama began with praise and abuse of real persons, while Horace, Donatus, and Scaliger knew that satiric mockery of real persons was closely related to the festive mockery of Old Comedy. [23] In the Prologue to *All Fools,* Chapman speaks of "th' ancient Comic vein / Of Eupolis and Cratinus (now revived, / Subject to personal application)," identifying current practice with Athenian custom.

Until about the end of the sixteenth century, the children's plays balanced the opposing impulses toward praise and abuse fairly evenly. The two leading playwrights for the children's troupes during Elizabeth's reign—Edwardes and Lyly—praise allegorical sovereigns, those figureheads of political power and social stability who represent the Queen, but mock comic authority figures like Grim and Sir Tophas, who may not necessarily represent real personages but who caricature values associated with power and responsibility. Most of the attacks against these day-to-day figures of authority—comic dolts "dressed in a little brief authority"—are launched by the witty pages and maidservants, who were probably played by the smallest and youngest boys in the company. In contrast, the comic butts may have been played by adult actors, perhaps even by the choirmasters themselves, underscoring the saturnalian mockery of authority inherent in such scenes. Even in plays from the closing years of Elizabeth's reign—Marston's *What You Will* (Paul's?, c.1601), *Blurt, Master Constable* (Paul's, 1601–2), and Chapman's *Sir Giles Goosecap* (Chapel, 1601–3)—there are similar scenes in which one or more witty pages outwit a doltish authority figure.[24] Just as praise of the monarch flatters her attendants and subjects, so attacks against evil councilors, parvenus, and pedants indirectly insult the spectators, who thought of themselves as real or potential figures of authority, though we have seen how an adroit victim can turn insult to flattery.

The balance between praise and abuse begins to shift in two plays which Jonson wrote for the Chapel Children around the turn of the century—*Cynthia's Revels* (1600) and *Poetaster*

(1601). In these two works, Jonson follows Edwardes and Lyly in combining praise for an allegorical representation of the royal patron—Cynthia and Caesar—with abuse of the pretenders and parasites who debase court life. But whereas Edwardes and Lyly displayed the royal presences prominently throughout their plays, Jonson makes his monarchs remote and shadowy, and focuses instead on objects of abuse. Thus, in *Cynthia's Revels* the Queen does not appear until the final scene, then parts the "clouds of masque" and watches approvingly as the scholar-poet Crites sentences those drunk on self-love to acts of penance and purification. No member of the audience should take these punishments personally, for as Mercury had already explained:

> The better race in court
> That have the true nobility, called virtue,
> Will apprehend it [criticism], as a grateful right
> Done to their separate merit: and approve
> The fit rebuke of so ridiculous heads,
> Who with their apish customs and forced garbs,
> Would bring the name of courtier in contempt,
> Did it not live unblemished in some few,
> Whom equal JOVE hath loved, and PHOEBUS formed
> Of better metal, and in better mold.
>
> (V.i.30–39)

Whereas Lyly and Edwardes flatter the court or private theater audience chiefly by offering it a reflection of its own wit and elegance, Jonson—perhaps for reasons of temperament—praises spectators mainly by inviting them to jeer at "others," at the pretenders to courtliness that infest Cynthia's court. Similarly, in *Poetaster,* Caesar does not appear until the end of Act IV, at which time he heaps praises on true poets like Horace and Vergil and witnesses the purgation of the poetasters, Demetrius and Crispinus. To offset the remoteness of Cynthia and Caesar in these two works, Jonson used Crites and Horace to direct the audience in praising and mocking the proper targets. This innovation, as O. J. Campbell has argued, is the germ of "comical satire," a dramatic adaptation of formal satire.[25] In this type of play, the audience identifies with a blunt, plain-speaking adherent to old-fashioned virtues—frequently a scholar poet—and ridicules the "others"—usurers, merchants, *nouveaux riches,* fawning parasites, upstart courtiers, and puritans. Marston and Chapman also use satiric commentators to focus the audience's derision on the usual assortment of deviants from aristocratic values, but unlike Jonson they usually confine such ridicule to the sub-plot. Thus, the satiric commentator in Marston's *The Fawn,* the disguised Duke Hercules, encounters a jealous husband, a dissipated amorist, an effeminate courtier, a braggart and other stock fools and knaves. Chapman's sub-plots further restrict the ridicule to one major butt, three of his Blackfriars plays deriving their titles from such figures: *Monsieur D'Olive* (Chapel, 1601–2), where the title character ("the perfect model of an impudent upstart" [I.ii.194]) is mocked for squandering prodigious amounts of time, money, and energy in organizing an embassy to the King of France; *The Gentleman Usher* (Chapel?, 1602–3),[26] where the steward Bassiolo is made the butt of the jest for treating a nobleman with presumptuous familiarity; and *Sir Giles Goosecap,* where a trio of witty pages deride a trio of doltish knights, one of whom—Sir Giles—stands out for ineffectuality and malapropisms. Any spectator insulted by the attacks on such figures could flatter himself by identifying with the satiric commentators, figures perceptive enough to recognize folly and vice but poised enough to view them with Olympian detachment. In short, Jonson, Marston, and Chapman use the strategies of nondramatic satire to evoke the same festal impulses toward praise and abuse that all through Elizabeth's reign had informed plays acted by children's troupes at court.

Praise and Abuse in Jacobean Plays

Around the accession of James I in 1603, the children's troupes began performing plays less suited to courtly audiences of the ritualistic Christmas revels, before whom they still performed regularly, and more suited to audiences of their own private theaters. As we shall see in the next chapter, these audiences now included large numbers of students at the nearby inns of court and many provincial aristocrats or gentry sojourning in London during the sessions of the law court. The plays acted by the children's troupes around this time are much more personal in their "application" than the traditional court plays had been. Personal abuse was more common than personal flattery. The author of *Lingua* (pub. 1607), a Cambridge play, implies that such insults were expected in children's plays. In this work, a character called Communis Sensus, "a grave man in a Black velvet cassock like a Councilor (sig. D3)," is told he is to be ridiculed on the stage, evidently by a children's troupe, for he exclaims, "O times! O manners! when Boys dare to traduce men in authority, was ever such an attempt heard" (sig. D4ᵛ). When another character cites Aristophanes' ridicule of Socrates, Communis Sensus replies, "In those days it was lawful, but now the abuse of such liberty is unsufferable" (sig. E). In his *Apology for Actors* (c.1607) Heywood also blames the children's troupes for "the particularizing of private men's humors (yet alive) noblemen, and others," and attacks those who suppose "their juniority to be a privilege for any railing, be it never so violent." [27] In complaining of the "little eyases" in the private theaters, Rosenkrantz tells Hamlet "that many wearing rapiers

are afraid of goose-quills and dare scarce come thither"
(II.ii.343–44.)

Railing was never more violent than in Day's *The Isle of
Gulls* (Queen's Revels, 1606), which satirized James and his
Scottish favorites audaciously enough to provoke government
reprisal. In the Induction, the First Spectator asks for something "critical," hoping to find some "great man's life charac-
tered in't," but the Prologue, protesting too much, claims that
Dametas, a parasitic courtier resembling one or more of
James's favorites, represents not an individual but a type,
whose "villany may give the greater luster to the virtuous
dispositions of true-born gentility." Within the play, one character likens this type to "unnecessary worms, who . . . eat
into the credit of true born gentry, undermine and work out
the true nobility, to inroot & establish themselves" (sig. B2ᵛ).
Like the Prologue, the play as a whole flatters "the true nobility" while insulting Dametas and upstarts generally, whom the
spectators are free to identify with real persons. Naturally,
few spectators would be inclined to label themselves upstarts
by admitting that the proverbial shoe fit. If spectators felt
themselves to be targets of satiric "application," they generally had little choice but to apply the thrust to someone else
or to preserve a poised and dignified silence, thereby converting insult to flattery.

Not all such cases of "application" involved kings and their
favorites. Chapman's lost play, *The Old Joiner of Aldgate*, presented its audience with so recognizable a slice of middle-
class London life that the victims initiated a libel suit. The play
dramatized the plight of Anne Howe, a young heiress, who
had promised herself to one suitor, was sold by her father to
two others, and finally eloped with the Doctor of Laws to
whom her father had appealed for help. The audience at
Paul's probably had little trouble "applying" the characters in

the play to their counterparts in real life, for most of the figures on stage were clearly modeled after well-known merchants and stationers living or working near the Cathedral.
Two persons of higher social rank could also be identified:
one of the girl's suitors, known in the play as "Humphrey of
the Court," was Humphrey Rogers, Keeper of the Council
Chamber, while the Doctor who carried her off was John Mil-
ward, the well-known Preacher of Christ Church.[28]

In orienting themselves less toward their court than toward
their private-theater audiences, the children's troupes not
only heightened "application," most of it satiric, but began to
direct praise and abuse toward characters associated with the
legal profession. By any method of analysis, abuse outweighs
praise in the children's plays of the 1600s and much of it is
aimed at legal practices and practitioners, as anticourt satire
yields to antilegal satire. The high-water marks of this tendency are Day's *Law Tricks* (Chapel, 1604? or King's Revels,
1607) with its gratuitous profusion of legal jargon, and *Epicoene* (Queen's Revels, 1609–10) where Cutbeard and Otter,
disguised as a civil and canon lawyer, harangue Morose inter-
minably with legalistic jargon about divorce.[29] That such antilegal satire is aimed at the audience is clear from *Michaelmas
Term*, where the villain Quomodo thrice remarks that his im-
becilic son is a student of the law and, addressing the spectators directly, asks them to "Admire me, all you students at
Inns of Cozenage" (II.iii.441–42). Such pointed abuse undoubtedly appealed to the younger inns-of-court men—
dashing, brilliant young gentlemen like John Donne—who
could expect eventually to rise to positions of power and authority, but were presently at the bottom of a hierarchical
structure to which they were ideologically or pragmatically
committed. Their own revels, like *Gesta Greyorum* and *Le
Prince D'Amour*, abound in parody and mimicry of their insti-

tutions, and thus indicate a taste for saturnalian mockery. In response to the change in the character of their audiences around the accession of James, the children's troupes ridiculed not only the usual collection of pedants, parasites, and parvenus, but figures of authority resembling more closely than ever what the spectators were, might become, or thought themselves to be. As the satire became increasingly personal, spectators could either flatter themselves by maintaining an unruffled calm or by deflecting the mockery onto others, especially the fathers and father-surrogates in their own lives.

As the children's playwrights increased the "application" and antilegal satire in their plays, they also began to experiment with new dramatic forms. For example, Middleton's *The Phoenix* (Paul's, 1603–4) is a cross between the archaic semi-allegorical court play of Elizabeth's reign and the emerging Jacobean city comedy. The title pages to both 1608 quartos declare that the play was presented before James and at Paul's. It combines praise of an allegorical royal figure with ridicule of a collection of fools and knaves, several of whom belong to the legal fraternity. As in earlier court plays, the hero can be applied to the sovereign, now James I.[30] "Phoenix," an epithet applied to Elizabeth and to James after his accession, in the play is the name of the intelligent and virtuous son of the Duke of Ferrara. The parallel is underlined in two ways. First, the old Duke, who senses his approaching death, has ruled Ferrara for forty-five years, the exact length of Elizabeth's reign. Second, Phoenix expresses views on kingship borrowed from James's book, *Basilikon Doron,* and the prince's interest in correcting abuses of law and matrimony reflects the concern with those subjects already shown by the new monarch, and by extension his court. In the course of the play, his reforming zeal evinces his fitness to rule and justifies the glowing praise directed to him in the opening scene:

> Thou wonder of all princes, president, and glory,
> True Phoenix, made of an unusual strain!
> Who labors to reform is fit to reign.
>
> (I.i.135–37)

Despite this traditional allegorical resemblance between the Ferrarese Prince and the English sovereign, *The Phoenix* is largely satiric in tone and evokes the pungent urban atmosphere of London through allusions to the unsettled state of Ireland, the Irish monetary policy, and James's new Scottish baronets. In the main action of the play, Phoenix encounters and exposes a number of knavish intrigues, such as the schemes of Tangle, a lawyer, and Falso, a justice of the peace, the adulterous liaison between the impoverished Knight and the Jeweler's lecherous wife, and the treason of Proditor, a court councilor. Satiric attacks on these knaves probably struck uncomfortably close to home before the private-theater audiences of law students, lawyers, and litigants, as well as before the court audience of real or self-styled royal councilors. But Middleton balances the festal impulses of praise and abuse by reassuring his spectators of their moral superiority to the villains in the play:

> Admired Law,
> Thy upper parts must needs be sacred, pure,
> And incorruptible; they're grave and wise:
> 'Tis but the dross beneath 'em, and the clouds
> That get between thy glory and their praise,
> That make the visible and foul eclipse;
> For those that are near to thee are upright,
> As noble in their conscience as their birth.
>
> (I.iv.205–12)

Switching from the optative ("must needs") to the present ("they're," " 'tis," etc.), this passage encourages the nobly born representatives and upholders of the law of the realm to identify with the "upper parts" of the law, rather than with "the dross beneath 'em."

Middleton was fond of the prince-in-disguise framework but never again developed the parallel to James. In *Your Five Gallants* (Queen's Revels, 1604–7), Fitsgrave, a true gallant, poses as a scholar in order to expose the knavery of the five corrupt gallants, which threatens to obscure "the brightness of true gentry" (III.iii.149), while in *The Family of Love* (Paul's?, 1602–3), the romantic hero Gerardine disguises himself as a physician in order to reveal the corruption and hypocrisy of the other characters. Like Lyly's witty pages or Jonson's scholar-poets, the disguised prince or gallant is another device developed by the children's playwrights for evoking and controling the festal impulses toward praise and abuse. However, around 1603, these playwrights devised a new type of play, the satiric city comedy, which both flattered and insulted the spectators, as earlier children's plays had done. It did so by encouraging spectators to identify with a roguishly attractive young gallant locked in conflict with one or more caricatured figure of authority, with whom they might also identify, playing the spectators' wishful views of themselves against their fears of what they actually were.

In the typical satiric city comedy, a prodigal gallant endeavors to regain his land or his money or both from a usurous, miserly father-figure, as in Middleton's *Michaelmas Term*, or else contrives to acquire an advance on his legacy, as in Middleton's *A Mad World, My Masters* (Paul's, 1604–6), where his grandfather threatens to squander it all, or as in Jonson's *Epicoene*, where his uncle threatens to disinherit him. In all cases, the young man has a moral if not a legal claim to the land or money, a claim based on his consanguinity, his general attractiveness, and his implicit promise henceforth to avoid both miserliness and prodigality. The father-figures who possess the land or money when the play opens are usually masters of legal maneuver in league with the constituted authorities of the society, so that the hero's triumph over these paternal surrogates and their legal minions represents a saturnalian reversal of power and a victory of "true" justice over avarice entrenched in legality.

In addition to the sympathy he derives from playing David to these Goliaths of the law, the rogue-hero is more sexually vital than they are. Flirtations and affairs between young gallants and older citizens' wives are extremely common in satiric city comedy and constitute the main action of Webster's and Dekker's *Westward Ho!* (Paul's, 1604), while Chapman's *Bussy D'Ambois* (Paul's, 1604), is a tragic rendering of this motif. In Middletonian city comedy, the spendthrift-hero usually steals a young girl or rich widow from one or more rivals, or rescues her from the clutches of a father, uncle, or guardian who treats her like property, or wants to sleep with her, as in two of Middleton's plays—*The Phoenix* and *The Family of Love*. As these guardians and rival suitors are invariably older and wealthier than the prodigal rogues, Oedipal rivalry is abundantly clear. In *The Wisdom of Doctor Dodypoll*, *The Gentleman Usher*, and Barry's *Ram Alley*, where sons steal their fathers' girl friends, it is explicit, and it is treated ironically in Marston's *The Fawn*, where a father sends his bashful son to woo on his behalf but hopes the boy himself will propose to the girl. The impotence of these father-figures and rival suitors contrasts with the sexual vigor of the gallant heroes, especially in Middleton's plays. In *A Mad World, My Masters*, the hero's impotent grandfather, Sir Bounteous Progress, is flattered to hear that his mistress is pregnant; Gerardine's rival suitors in *The Family of Love* seek medical treatment for impotency; while Quomodo, who is both father-figure and rival suitor in *Michaelmas Term,* speaks of himself as "an old lecher, girt in a fur'd gown, / Whose mind stands stiff, but his performance down" (III.iv.10–11).

Despite these Oedipal overtones in the children's satiric city comedies, romantic intrigue is totally subordinated to satiric action and is usually presented in brief scenes and sometimes involves only secondary characters. In *The Phoenix,* the love between the Prince's companion Fidelio and Falso's niece is confined to two short scenes that together number less than eighty-five lines, and Phoenix's abbreviated marriage blessing is lost amid the judgments he issues in the final scene. In Middleton's *Michaelmas Term,* the romantic motif is doubled, though still subordinated to the saturnalian satiric intrigue. Easy, the prodigal hero of the main action, wins and marries Thomasine, the wife of the avaricious merchant, Quomodo, who has cheated Easy of his estate, while Easy's friend Rearage, the well-born hero of the subplot, steals Quomodo's daughter Susan from Andrew Lethe, a depraved Scottish upstart. The function of these brief romantic episodes is to heap further discomfiture on the father-figures and rival suitors, and to provide the all-but-eclipsed tokens of positive value in the satiric landscape. As Alvin Kernan has written, "Somewhere in his dense knots of ugly flesh the satiric author or painter usually inserts a hint of an ideal which is either threatened with imminent destruction or is already dead." [31] Like the church spire in the background of a painting by Bruegel or Hogarth, these romantic vignettes invoke a scale of values against which the satiric villains must be measured, and afford glimpses of a generous and fruitful mode of life which eventually triumphs over the sterile acquisitiveness of the corrupt figures of authority.

A Trick to Catch the Old One

Middleton's *A Trick to Catch the Old One* (Paul's, 1604–6) clearly illustrates the vitality of the festal tradition in a typical private-theater comedy of the early Jacobean period. It does so by playing the audience's fantasies against its fears, by praising and abusing the spectators. Through identification with Witgood, the prodigal hero, the audience is invited to ridicule several figures of authority, all of whom exploit the law for their own material advantage. Middleton allows Witgood to wear his reputation for prodigality and lechery like a badge of honor, encouraging the audience to dismiss these vices as the forgivable indiscretions of youth. Middleton also evokes sympathy for the lusty wastrel by blaming his impoverished condition on his avaricious uncle, Pecunius Lucre. As the play opens, Witgood laments that his estate, Longacre, is pawned to Lucre, who will use his mastery of the law to keep the property for himself:

> But where's Longacre? in my uncle's conscience, which is three years' voyage about; he that sets out upon his conscience never finds the way home again—he is either swallowed in the quicksands of law-quillets, or splits upon the piles of a *praemunire*.
>
> (I.i.7–11)

Appealing to Lucre's sense of kinship is as futile as fighting him with litigation, for Lucre's attitude, as Witgood informs us in the same speech, is "Let him that is his nearest kin / Cheat him before a stranger." Or, as Lucre himself later puts it:

> Upbraid'st thou me with nephew? . . . What acquaintance have I with his follies? if he riot, 'tis he must want it; if he surfeit, 'tis he must feel it; if he drab it, 'tis he must lie by't: what's this to me?
>
> (I.iii.29–32)

Middleton also makes Witgood attractive by portraying the Courtesan as a lively and intelligent girl. Unlike the other courtesans in Middleton's city comedies, she is not a common harlot, but Witgood's mistress, and was a virgin until he seduced her. She prevents Witgood from regarding their relationship in conventionally moralistic terms when he tries to dismiss her for causing his downfall:

> *Witgood:*   Hence, courtesan, round-webbed tarantula,
>   That dryest the roses in the cheeks of youth!
> *Courtesan:*   I have been true unto your pleasure, and all
>   your lands thrice racked, was never worth the
>   jewel which I prodigally gave you, my virginity;
>   Lands mortgaged may return and more esteemed,
>   But honesty, once pawned, is ne'er redeemed.
>
> (I.i.31–37)

Her rhymed couplet mocks Witgood's self-righteousness while her commercial metaphors and the word "prodigally" equate her status with his. She forces him to beg forgiveness, which she grants only after playfully parodying one of his earlier speeches:

> I that have been the secret consumption of your purse,
> shall I stay now to undo your last means, your wits?
> Hence courtisan, away!
>
> (I.i.42–44)

After the Courtesan ridicules his cant moralizing, Witgood acknowledges the similarity of their circumstances, recognizes their involvement in each other's lives, and accepts the "honest drab's" offer to help him regain his lost estate. By making Witgood abandon his homiletic posturing for a raffish gallantry, Middleton induces his spectators, of whom many were or had been urbane and sophisticated young rakes, to regard the prodigal hero with tolerant and amused affection. Like

Falstaff and Shallow, they too had "heard the chimes at midnight," or wanted to pretend that they had.

Middleton's handling of Witgood's successful intrigue against his uncle is characteristic of children's city comedy in general, if not of some of Middleton's other work in the genre. Whereas Follywit outsmarts himself at the end of *A Mad World, My Masters* and Easy triumphs over Quomodo in *Michaelmas Term* only because the villain overreaches himself and is betrayed by his wife, Witgood devises and executes an ingenious scheme to exploit his adversaries' cupidity. Resolving to rise by the very means of his fall, Witgood has his courtesan pose as the rich widow "Medler," uses her as bait to retrieve his estate from Lucre, and in the process marries her to another usurer named Hoard. When Witgood's plans come to fruition, the audience is invited to applaud his success and to enjoy the discomfiting of Lucre and Hoard. Although these two usurers are the comic villains of the play, and their predominant traits of avarice, bellicosity, and litigiousness spread to other characters, they are genial dotards by comparison with the satanic lawyer, Harry Dampit, in whom the same qualities rise to a diabolical level. In a brilliant monologue, Dampit describes the industry and unctuousness that led to his success in the legal profession:

Harry Dampit, a trampler of the time, say, he would be up in a morning, and be here with his serge gown, dashed up to the hams in a cause; have his feet stink about Westminster Hall, and come home again. . . . Then would I be here, I would trample up and down like a mule; now to the judges, "May it please your reverend-honorable fatherhoods"; then to my counselor, "May it please your worshipful patience"; then to the examiner's office, "May it please your mastership's gentleness"; then to one of the clerks, "May it please your worshipful

lousiness," for I find him scrubbing in his codpiece; then
to the Hall again, then to the chamber again—

(I.iv.42–55)

The spitefulness that surfaces at the end of the speech comes
back to plague him; our final vision of this self-made man
shows him on his death-bed, surrounded by erstwhile friends
who torment him as he drinks himself into a final stupor.[32]

In the play's romantic subplot, Witgood steals Joyce from
his doltish rivals and from the possessive guardianship of her
uncle Hoard, but this romantic action is handled with extreme
economy and functions more as a saturnalian discomfiting of
the rivals and uncles than as a celebration of young love. In
his opening speech, Witgood fears that his debts will keep
him out of London and hence cost him "a virgin's love," evidently an oblique reference to Joyce. When she vows her love
to Witgood, she notes that he is her uncle's "chiefest enemy"
(III.ii.7). Reports of his engagement to the "widow" arouse
her jealousy, but a note from the gallant dispels any doubt of
his constancy. Not until the end of IV.iv does Middleton finally bring the lovers together on stage, and even then Joyce
remains "above," physically separated from Witgood. The entire scene consists of the following four speeches and the delivery of another note:

> *Niece:* Master Witgood!
> *Witgood:* My life!
> *Niece:* Meet me presently; that note directs you
>   [throwing it down]; I would not be suspected. Our
>   happiness attends us. Farewell.
> *Witgood:* A word's enough.

This second note apparently contains plans for their elopement, according to Joyce's brief aside about preparations for
her uncle's wedding banquet: "though the feast be prepared

to you, yet it serves fit for my wedding dinner too"
(V.ii.17–18). Even the wedding of Witgood and Joyce takes
place off stage sometime before the final scene. Unless the
stage directions are incomplete, Joyce never reappears for the
final scene, in which Witgood makes only one slight allusion
to their marriage (V.ii.63). The main purpose of the scene is
not to celebrate the marriage of the young lovers, as in romantic comedy, but to discomfit the comic villain Hoard by
exposing the "widow," now his wife, as a courtesan.

To Lucio at the end of *Measure for Measure*, "marrying a
punk . . . is [equal to] pressing to death, whipping, and
hanging" (V.i.522–23), but Middleton's characters are generally less troubled. Follywit in *A Mad World, My Masters* easily
recovers from the initial shock of learning he has just married
his grandfather's courtesan. Hoard is at first appalled to find
himself married to "A common strumpet," but Witgood and
the Courtesan suggest another response. Witgood objects to
the adjective "common": "Excepting but myself, I dare swear
she's a virgin" (V.ii.148–49). The Courtesan herself reminds
Hoard that his abduction of her is tantamount to statutory
rape, that his deception results chiefly from his own greed,
that his shame will depend on how widely he publicizes her
past. She also advances the rather dubious proposition that in
marrying a sexually experienced woman he is less likely to be
cuckolded, for "She that knows sin, knows best how to hate
sin" (V.ii.140). Witgood appears to terminate his relationship
with the Courtesan, but the colloquial meaning of "aunt" and
the mock-reverence for kinship undermine his vows:

> . . . and now, by marrying your niece, I have banished
> myself forever from her. She's mine aunt now, by my
> faith, and there's no meddling with mine aunt, you
> know—a sin against my nuncle.
>
> (V.ii.149–52)

Finally, the Courtesan and Witgood kneel together, ostensibly to renounce and repent their past sins, but once again Middleton undercuts their sincerity: he pairs them off symmetrically, casts their proclamations of redemption in rhymed octosyllabic couplets, reminiscent of the Courtesan's earlier parodies of cant moralizing, and allows them to fondle the details of their past at great length and with nostalgic relish.[33] The Courtesan kneels and "repents" as follows:

> Lo, gentlemen, before you all
> In true reclaimed form I fall.
> Henceforth for ever I defy
> The glances of a sinful eye,
> Waving of fans (which some suppose
> Tricks of fancy), treading of toes,
> Wringing of fingers, biting the lip
> The wanton gait, th'alluring trip,
> All secret friends and private meetings,
> Close-borne letters and bawds' greetings,
> Feigning excuse to women's labors
> When we are sent for to th'next neighbors,
> Taking false physic, and ne'er start
> To be let blood, though sign be at heart,
> Removing chambers, shifting beds,
> To welcome friends in husbands' steads,
> Them to enjoy, and you to marry,
> They first served, while you must tarry,
> They to spend, and you to gather,
> They to get and you to father—
> These and thousand thousand more,
> Newly reclaimed, I now abhor.
>
> (V.ii.153–74)

In forsaking the stratagems and pleasures of adultery, the Courtesan renounces sins she has yet to commit, repenting in advance, as it were. Witgood's contrition is equally ironic. He kneels and confesses his follies:

And here for ever I disclaim
The cause of youth's undoing, game,
Chiefly dice, those true outlanders,
That shake out beggars, thieves, and panders,
Soul-wasting surfeits, sinful riots,
Queans' evils, doctors' diets,
'Pothecaries' drugs, surgeons' glisters,
Stabbing of arms for a common mistress,
Riband favors, ribald speeches,
Dear perfumed jackets, penniless breeches,
Dutch flapdragons, healths in urine,
Drabs that keep a man too sure in—
I do defy you all.
Lend me each honest hand, for here I rise
A reclaimed man, loathing the general vice.
                                        (V.ii.177–91)

The total effect of this richly ambiguous ending is indeed complex. On the one hand, Middleton suggests that the comic villains Lucre and Hoard have accepted their punishment with good grace and that social harmony has been restored now that Witgood has regained his patrimony, rescued and married Hoard's niece, and severed his liaison with the Courtesan. On the other hand, the ironies in the scene allow sophisticated spectators to question the stability of such a conventional resolution and congratulate themselves for recognizing a parody of the kind of ending that requires belief in miraculous fifth-act conversions. Combining the spectators' sympathetic delight in the triumphs of Witgood with their scorn for Lucre and Hoard, the ending, like the play as a whole, juxtaposes flattering and insulting images of the audience. It thereby evokes the twin festal impulses toward praise and abuse that animated plays acted by the children's troupes at court and in the private theaters throughout the Elizabethan and early Jacobean periods. In the next chapter we shall investigate the audience's role in creating and sustaining the notion that private-theater plays perpetuated the courtly and aristocratic festal tradition we have just traced.

CHAPTER THREE

The Audience

AS the ritualistic aspects of the children's plays come more clearly into focus once we recreate their social context, we must regard the audience as active participants rather than as passive spectators. Indeed, the very theatrical occasion casts them in flattering roles, as going to off-off-Broadway productions or their equivalent bestows membership in the avant-garde on the suburban bourgeoisie. Before considering how the plays themselves assisted spectators in sustaining their self-images, we must establish as carefully as possible just who these audiences were and what social forces drove them to use the children's plays as backdrops for their own performances.

Who Were the Spectators?

The children's troupes had two audiences: one at court and the other in the private theaters. The court audience, drawn from the highest-ranking nobility, "consisted of higher officials of government and their wives, officers of the royal household and their wives, suitors of the Queen, resident foreign ambassadors, ambassadors extraordinary, bachelor courtiers, ladies and maids of honor and other attendants and guests such as the Queen might desire." [1] If the children's troupes established the playhouses at Paul's and Blackfriars in order to commercialize the tradition of court revelry, one would expect these private-theater audiences to consist largely of aspirants to high aristocratic rank or those wishing to emulate the fashions of the upper nobility. Harbage describes them in detail, but implies that high admission prices guaranteed an exclusive audience:

> . . . they were the ones who could, or thought they could, afford to pay sixpence or a shilling to see a play. This eliminates all but a small fraction of the population. . . . Among the most available "gentry"—the younger sons in service, the students at the inns of court, the tutors or literary men associated with wealthy households, the inactive captains, the foreign tourists, the provincial gallants sojourning in London—those individuals with more than a few shillings a week to spend on luxuries must be considered exceptional.[2]

One can readily grant the aristocratic nature of these audiences, but it is difficult to accept the assertion that the "coterie" audience was drawn from so small a segment of the available aristocracy, a subgroup which Harbage characterizes as youthful, as well as parasitic and peripheral even to the main body of aristocrats. W. A. Armstrong and others have described the private-theater audiences as comprising chiefly aristocrats, lawyers, and members of the inns of court, as well as provincial gentry in London on legal business.[3] In other words, the private-theater audience was made up of actual, potential, or self-styled figures of power and responsibility who wanted and could afford vicarious participation in a courtly occasion. In order to understand the state of mind of these audiences, we need to recall some of the tensions and habits that characterized aristocratic life in the period.

In *The Crisis of the Aristocracy*, Lawrence Stone depicts upper-class English life between 1558 and 1641 as a constant struggle to maintain or acquire aristocratic status. Whether on the way down or on the way up, upper-class families felt "the moral obligations imposed upon a nobleman by society to live in a style commensurate with his dignity," although many no doubt hoped to attain a dignity commensurate with their style. In either case, such aspirations required that one act out an idealized conception of his social identity. A common form of such self-dramatization was conspicuous expenditure, and Stone provides an intriguing account of the ornate palaces and country houses, sumptuous banquets, luxurious clothing, reckless gambling, and elaborate funerals that characterized aristocratic life in Renaissance England.[4]

Self-dramatization has always been an integral part of European aristocratic life. Three pillars of the Renaissance aristocratic ethic—honor, reputation, and generosity—involve visible public gestures more than inner spiritual states. Castiglione and Machiavelli, diametrically opposed in so many respects, both urge their aristocratic readers to exploit the effects of their behavior on others. Many Renaissance aristocrats believed they were expected not merely to *be* noble but to *act* nobly, to dramatize their nobility. Just as the tournament allowed a combatant to enact the role of chivalric warrior, so the court play allowed those attending to enact the roles of wise ruler or sagacious councilor, perceptive critic, and magnanimous patron.

In the private theaters, opportunities for self-dramatization probably attracted members of the upper classes who felt their social status to be precarious: either old-line aristocrats struggling to maintain their standing; or gentry, *nouveaux riches,* and young men from the inns of court striving for higher status. Whatever its actual size, this group of spectators set the tone for private-theater audiences, a tone marked by condescension and exhibitionism, from the heyday of the children's troupes right through the Restoration period. Later in this chapter, we shall investigate the dramatists' efforts to prevent the audience from disrupting their plays. Whereas many playwrights addressed themselves extradramatically to this problem in prologues, epilogues, and inductions, others—like Jonson and Chapman—tried to elicit sympathetic attentiveness by manipulating the audience's responses within their plays.

Attitudes and Behavior

The two modes of self-dramatization most readily available to private-theater spectators were contemptuous silence and noisy disruption. If the spectator chose the first mode, he could preserve a haughty detachment, and, by refusing to allow the play to put him out of his own role, demonstrate that the illusion it offered was less substantial than the one which he himself projected. If the spectator chose the second mode, he could disrupt the play in any number of witty or childish ways, thereby manifesting his wit and critical judgment, and exhibiting the potency of his presence. Whether he chose to be ice or fire, the aristocratic spectator was actually giving a counterperformance of his own in order to assert his social worth.

Thomas Dekker, who wrote mainly for the public theaters and who was staunchly middle-class in outlook, ridicules such histrionic assertions of aristocratic standing in *The Gull's Hornbook* (pub. 1609), a parody of the conventional courtesy book. In Chapter VI, "How a Gallant should behave himself in a Playhouse," Dekker ironically advises his gallant to make himself the primary theatrical spectacle, and while Dekker may be overstating for satiric effect, the point would be lost were he not exaggerating a real phenomenon.[5]

To begin with, the true gallant waits until the last possible moment to enter the playhouse, rather than appear "when the belly of the house is but half full," or if he does take his seat early, he plays cards ostentatiously in order "to gull the *Ragamuffins* that stand aloof gaping at you." Naturally, the ideal place to sit is on the stage—the better to display one's person and clothing, and to publicize one's reaction to the play, and the evidence indicates that sitting on stools on the stage was particularly prevalent at Blackfriars.[6] One suggested reaction to the play is a show of detachment, for in that manner, Dekker advises, "You publish your temperance to the world, in that you seem not to resort thither to taste vain pleasures with a hungry appetite: but only as a Gentleman, to spend a foolish hour or two, because you can do nothing else." Or the gallant can simply walk out in the middle of the play, drawing "what troop you can from the stage after you." On the other hand, should bad weather or good company induce the gallant to stay through the play, he can assert his superiority by turning "plain Ape": "Take up a rush and tickle the earnest ears of your fellow gallants, to make other fools fall a laughing: mew at passionate speeches, blare at merry, find fault with the music, whew at the children's Action, whistle at the songs." As every heckler knows, such disruptive behavior is designed to upstage the actors: "It shall crown you with rich commendation to laugh aloud in the midst of the most serious and saddest scene of the terriblest Tragedy: and to let that clapper (your tongue) be tossed so high that all the house may ring of it." In short, the entire counterperformance was calculated to affirm the gallant's aristocratic status, if necessary at the expense of the play, and to show that he was more than a mere passive spectator.[7]

The private theater playwrights themselves attest to the prevalence of the kind of behavior Dekker is satirizing in their efforts to stifle it. To choose two from many examples, in the

Induction to *The Isle of Gulls,* Day mentions the gallant who, in rising to leave, cries "Mew!" or "By Jesus, vilde!" and in the Epilogue to *The Fawn,* Marston, referring to some "envious few," resolves to "let such adders hiss." In two plays which may have been written with upper-class audiences in mind, Shakespeare rebukes aristocratic characters who are eager to display their wit by disrupting amateur theatricals given in their honor. In *Love's Labor's Lost* (1594–96) Holofernes scolds the King and his friends for behavior which is "not generous, not gentle" (V.ii.629), while in *A Midsummer Night's Dream* (1594–96) Theseus tries to silence mockery by continually directing attention back to the mechanicals' play and by urging magnanimity ("The kinder we, to give them thanks for nothing" [V.i.89]).[8]

In order to prevent such disruptive behavior, private theater playwrights like Lyly, Marston, Jonson, and Chapman appealed directly to their audiences in prologues, epilogues, and inductions. Lyly, for example, mixes flattery with self-deprecation. He frequently acknowledges that his "exercises . . . full of weak matter" are only intended for mirth and deserve the contempt of such an intelligent and perceptive audience, to whose magnanimity he therefore appeals. In "the Prologue in Paul's" to *Midas,* Lyly hopes "that presenting our studies before Gentlemen, though they receive an inward mislike, we shall not be hissed with an open disgrace." Whether addressing a court or a private-theater audience, Lyly implies that no self-respecting aristocrat would debase himself by disrupting or even criticizing such well-intentioned trifles, and suggests that the proper way to assert one's nobility is to watch attentively and perhaps even to applaud. Whether the audience was flattered into silence, or kept still as a tribute to Lyly's skill in posing as a courtly entertainer, the result was the same.

Marston, who wrote some of the first plays performed by the reactivated Children of Paul's, repeated Lyly's blend of flattery and self-deprecation. In the Prologue to *Antonio and Mellida* (Paul's, 1599–1600) Marston offers "The worthless present of slight idleness, / To your authentic censure." In the Induction to *What You Will* (Paul's, 1601), he tried a more ingenious technique for silencing the potentially disruptive members of the audience. Three gallants—Atticus, Doricus, and Phylomuse—are seated like spectators on the stage before the play begins. Doricus is worried that the author may be upset by the jeers of *"Sir Signor Snuff, Monsieur Mew,* and *Cavaliero Blirt . . .* this threefold halter of contempt that chokes the breath of wit." Phylomuse, who expresses the defensive authorial viewpoint, replies that his friend is too high-blooded in spirit to be crestfallen if "Some boundless ignorance should on sudden shoot / His gross knob'd burbolt, with *that's not so good, / Mew, blirt, ha, ha, light Chaffy stuff."* Doricus, the audience's spokesman, denies that "these ingenuous breasts" seated around them would behave in such a manner, a stroke of flattery designed to cajole the audience into appreciative silence.

When Jonson wrote for the Children of the Chapel Royal in the early part of his career, he replaced the Lylyesque mode of self-deprecating flattery with a subtler type. He addresses his audience in the proud and manly tones befitting a humanist-poet whose alter egos—Crites and Horace—are beacons of virtue in their benighted societies. The child actor delivering the Epilogue to *Cynthia's Revels* claims that the author has forbidden him "to crave your favor with a begging knee," and therefore resolves to "speak what I have heard him say; *By (   ) 'tis good, and if you like't, you may."* Beneath this veneer of independence, Jonson is flattering his spectators by suggesting that they prefer forthrightness to servility.

To paraphrase Shakespeare's Decius (*Julius Caesar* II.i.207-08), when Jonson tells them they hate flatterers, they say they do, being then most flattered. However, when Jonson returned to the private theaters after nearly a decade, he reverted to the more direct mode of flattery. In the Prologue to *Epicoene* (Queen's Revels, 1609–10), he hopes "not to please the cook's tastes, but the guests," and in the play offers the audience a flattering image of itself, as we shall see.

Chapman's manner of addressing his private theater audiences was neither as brusque as Jonson's nor as obsequious as Lyly's and Marston's. In his Prologue to *All Fools*, Chapman pleads with the spectators seated on the stage to remain in their places, "for if our other audience see / You on the stage depart before we end, / Our wits go with you all, and we are fools." In an extradramatic passage inserted into the body of *Monsieur D'Olive*, Chapman deals more drastically with the same problem. After commenting on the ubiquity of fools, one character asks another, "and didst not see a pair of Gallants sit not far hence like a couple of Bough-pots to make the room smell?" and is told they have gone (IV.ii.155–57). Chapman's mocking of the fictive gallants in their absence is the playwright's revenge as well as a warning to real gallants of the cost of premature departure: Never turn your back on a playwright.

Dramaturgical Defenses Against Disruption

Just as "stand-up" comedians develop strategies to thaw frozen audiences and to silence boisterous ones, so dramatists writing for the children's troupes tried within the plays themselves to neutralize their spectators' counterperformances. Instead of allowing the audience's mockery to destroy their plays, dramatists simply built it into their work. For this reason, the plays acted by the children's troupes are largely satiric comedies, which channel the audience's derision toward "others"—upstarts, citizens, puritans, pedants, usurers, etc. By ridiculing these deviants from aristocratic norms of behavior, spectators ritualistically reaffirm their own claim to aristocratic status.

In *Summer's Last Will and Testament,* acted at Archbishop Whitgift's palace at Croydon in 1592,[9] Thomas Nashe sacrifices something more than a satiric victim or two to his audience's self-esteem: He invites them to ridicule a large part of the play itself. He does this by creating two levels of illusion: (1) a highly formalistic pageant about the passage of time, in which Summer, dying of the plague, searches among his servants for an heir, and (2) a number of episodes in which the court jester Will Summer—played by an actor named Toy—disrupts and ridicules this stylized pageant. As in the kind of *trompe l'oeil* picture where a fly is painted to look as though it has settled on the painted surface, Nashe used Toy–Will Summer to undermine the dramatic illusion of the main action. Even before the Prologue, he has the actor Toy enter *"in his fool's coat but half on,"* describe his role of Will Summer, refer to the prompter by name, and belittle "the Idiot our Playmaker." Throughout *Summer's Last Will and Testament,* Toy speaks directly to the audience, slipping in and out of character and offering a running attack on the main action, as he had promised to do: "I'll sit as a *Chorus,* and flout the *Actors* and him [the poet] at the end of every *Scene*" (III, 236). True to his word, Will Summer constantly interrupts the graceful and delicate pageant with asides, or speaks directly to the audience between scenes. In various ways he dissociates himself from the actors and identifies with the audience: *"Pergite porro,* my good children, and multiply the sins of your absurdities, till you come to the full measure of the grand hiss, and you

shall hear how we will purge rheum with censuring your imperfections'' (III, 253). At certain points in the main action,
especially in the songs, Nashe achieves a lyric poignancy that
can withstand Toy's satiric barrage, but in general the dramatic illusion of the stylized pageant is distanced, if not shattered, and in its place emerges the even stronger illusion that
Toy-Will is not part of some gossamer entertainment but
belongs—like the spectators—to life itself. Despite, or perhaps because of, his being a fool, he becomes the very incarnation of the audience's conviction that its own fragile social
identity is more vital and solid than mere art, while his ridicule of mutability and mortality encourages in the audience a
momentary illusion of superiority to the inexorable forces of
dissolution and death.

In *The Knight of the Burning Pestle* (Queen's Revels, 1607),
Beaumont complicates Nashe's strategy by establishing three
planes of illusion, all of which elicit derision: (1) the play
called *The London Merchant,* a spoof of middle-class comedy,
in which a humble apprentice falls in love with his master's
daughter, (2) an onstage audience of a grocer and his wife,
who are out of place among the gallants at the Blackfriars theater but nevertheless disrupt *The London Merchant,* and (3)
the chivalric exploits of the Knight of the Burning Pestle (actually the grocer's apprentice), which are performed between
scenes of *The London Merchant* at the insistence of the
grocer and his wife. Although modern audiences thoroughly
enjoy this three-ring circus, the play failed in its own time. As
the publisher explained in the dedication to the earliest
printed version, "The wide world, who for want of judgment,
or not understanding the privy mark of *Irony* about it (which
showed it was no offspring of any vulgar brain) utterly rejected it" (I, 7). In the absence of attractive aristocratic figures, the Blackfriars audience had to think of itself as the aris-

tocratic norm by which to judge the characters and action of the play, a task evidently beyond its capacity. However, some status-seeking spectators may have seen the grocer and his wife as insulting caricatures of themselves, while those who felt their status declining may have taken the intrusion as an unpleasant omen.

Most of the dramatists who wrote for the children's troupes avoided Beaumont's mistake. In addition to encouraging the audience to ridicule deviants from aristocratic standards, they offered the audience a flattering image of itself in the hope of engaging its respectful attention. The strategy is timeless: The wit and elegance of Lyly's plays appear to mirror the same qualities in his audience, Dryden's heroic plays create a mirror-image designed not only to "please by its likeness but also inspire by its nobility," and modern analogues—appealing to intellectual rather than social pride—come readily to mind.[10] However, in plays acted by children's troupes in the 1600s, flattery of the audience was blatantly obvious. In *The Fair Maid of the Exchange* (c.1602), one character denies flattering another and suggests that the latter's exalted view of himself will be confirmed by the chorister troupe in a private theater:

Me thinks a man so well reputed of,
So well commended for your qualities
In Schools of nimble activeness,
And places where divinest choristers
Warble enchanting harmony, to such
As think there is no heaven on earth but theirs:
And knowing yourself to be the *Genius*
Of the spectators, and the audience's hearts,
You wrong your worthy self intolerably,
To think our words savor of flattery.

(ll. 1592–1600)

Such expectations indicate that flattery had become a ritualistic celebration of the audience in private-theater plays, which perpetuated a courtly and aristocratic tradition. On the other hand, public-theater plays, which were ultimately derived from outdoor religious ceremonies, often involve the spectator in an ideal beyond himself, as the Elizabethan history play invites one to participate in the invincibility and social cohesiveness of England. In plays acted by children's troupes in the private theaters, by contrast, the audience *is* the ideal. When spectators fall short of this standard, idealized figures like the suave gallants of city comedy serve as models to illustrate appropriate speech, dress, and conduct, and thus eventually become or are thought to be reflections of the spectators.

Marston's *What You Will* is a fascinating example of such subtle and sophisticated flattery of the audience. In the main plot, adapted from an Italian play, a wealthy merchant named Albano is incorrectly believed to be dead, and his wife, Celia, is on the verge of marrying Laverdure, an itinerant French knight. Jachomo, another of Celia's suitors, conspires with Albano's brothers to block this marriage by disguising a perfumer named Francisco as Albano. Laverdure learns of the scheme and when the real Albano appears, the Frenchman mistakes him for an impostor, as do Jachomo, Celia, and Albano's own brothers. Albano even begins to doubt his own identity, but finally convinces Celia that he is her husband by alluding to intimacies that passed between them on the eve of his departure.

The subplot, which Marston invented himself, carries the burden of flattering the audience. Essentially a "comical satire," its structure and techniques derive from verse satire of the 1590s.[11] Here Marston invites the spectators to identify with Quadratus, whose name suggests "squareness" or honesty, and who directs their derision toward such conventional targets as the lovesick amorist, the effeminate courtier, the fashion-plate, and most of all, Lampatho Doria, the former scholar and professional satirist.

Quadratus himself is an accomplished courtier and a full-blooded hedonist, and whereas nondramatic satirists and raisonneurs of "comical satire" rail at fools or cultivate them for public exposure, Quadratus suffers them with tolerant amusement and shields them from Lampatho's satire. His principal objection to satire is that it inhibits "fantasticness," i.e., wit, imagination, and individuality. Quadratus advocates the adoption of any strikingly distinctive life-style—the more outlandish the better so long as one carries it off with aplomb. What Quadratus dislikes most in Lampatho is the conventionality of the satirist's posture and the obvious labor required to sustain it. To a detached observer of mankind like Quadratus, human identity is largely a matter of style and role, and Marston confirms this attitude by dramatizing the pathetic absurdity of Albano, the officially dead protagonist of the main action, who desperately tries to convince a disbelieving world that he is himself and not an imposter. In short, Quadratus' graceful superiority to the other characters in the play and his effortless enactment of his own chosen role were nicely calculated to produce sympathetic vibrations among the aristocratic spectators at Paul's, and thereby to prevent disruptive counterperformances.

The Widow's Tears

Spectators at Blackfriars also found wishful fantasies enacted in Chapman's *The Widow's Tears* (Queen's Revels, c.1605). By encouraging his audience to identify with Tharsalio, the audacious hero, Chapman allowed them to assert their social worth without disrupting his play.

Tharsalio's circumstances would have been familiar to the Blackfriars audience. He is the younger son of a venerable but languishing patrician family of Cyprus—"The ancient and most virtue-famed *Lysandri*" (III.ii.101)—and in both plots displays a traditional aristocratic concern for the state of his house. His marriage to the wealthy widow Eudora will repair the family's fortunes and bring advancement for all its members. As Tharsalio tells Lysander, "Alas brother, our house is decayed, and my honest ambition to restore it, I hope be pardonable" (III.i.48–49). Earlier Tharsalio had worried about Lysander's naive faith that his wife, Cynthia, would make good her promise never to remarry if she is widowed. In his doting trust, Lysander has made Cynthia his sole heir, thereby forcing the other male members of the family "to hang upon her pure devotion" so that "the ancient inheritance of our Family" will not pass out of the male line should she remarry:

> . . . he dead, and she matching (as I am resolved she will) with some young Prodigal; what must ensue, but her post-issue beggered, and our house already sinking, buried quick in ruin.
>
> (II.iii.69–73)

In short, Tharsalio's intrigues against both Eudora and Cynthia stem less from his desire to validate a cynical view of women than from patrilineal loyalty to his endangered clan.

Such loyalty is a positive virtue in Chapman's Cyprus, where unworthy upstarts—"a number of strange Knights abroad" (IV.i.25–26)—flourish at the expense of time-honored families, just as in England, at least to a Blackfriars audience of real or self-styled aristocrats. One of the upstarts in the play is

Tharsalio's rival suitor, Lord Rebus, "A Spartan Lord, dating himself our great Viceroy's Kinsman" (I.ii.16) but who, in Lysander's words, "for all his Ancestry would be much troubled to name you the place where his Father was born" (I.ii.25–26). Tharsalio refers to him as "a bagpipe; in whom there is nothing but wind" (I.ii.118), and as a "Calidonian Boar" (II.iv.182), associating him with James's newly minted Scottish knights, the Caledonian upstarts so often ridiculed in plays acted by children's troupes.[12] The play's other prominent arriviste is the Governor, a totally inept authority-figure incapable of resolving the play's complications without Tharsalio's intervention. Chapman even brings on a peripheral figure, the plain-speaking Captain, to describe the Governor in terms often applied by conservative satirists to Jacobean parvenus:

> He loves me not I know; because of late
> I knew him but of mean condition;
> But now by fortune's injudicious hand,
> Guided by bribing Courtiers, he is raised
> To this high seat of honor . . . and looks (as all
> Upstarts do) for most huge observance.
>
>   (V.ii.57–65)

Like the England envisioned by the audience, Chapman's Cyprus has countenanced the decline of its traditional aristocracy and is hence infested with incompetence, favoritism, bribery, and pretension. Reputation passes for true virtue, not only in Lord Rebus and the Governor but even in Cynthia. Since Fortune heaps rewards on the unworthy, Tharsalio is justified in transferring his allegiance to another deity—Confidence, "Sole friend to worth" (I.i.11). True to his name, which means "boldness," [13] Tharsalio has found the Goddess in whose worship he can express his innate *virtù*. While his rivals come to Eudora with "Titles and Authorities," Tharsalio boasts only "the liberal and ingenuous Graces—Love, Youth, and Gentry" (I.ii.77–79). Also among his graces is legendary sexual prowess. Eudora can not conceal her excitement, when the bawd Arsace tells her that she has "known nine in a night made mad with his love" (II.ii.85–86). Tharsalio, whose name also suggests "tarse," or penis, is a true son of Cyprus, where Venus is the reigning deity.[14]

In his wit, audacity, and perseverance, in his noble birth, in his sexual prowess, in his confidence in his own evaluation of people, and in his forceful rhetoric, Tharsalio is a comedic version of Bussy D'Ambois, a torrent of masculine energy. Whereas modern critics find Tharsalio's cynicism repellent, those members of the Blackfriars audience who were, or thought of themselves as, traditional aristocrats being displaced by upstarts, could readily identify with this explosive charge of male potency.[15] Instead of disrupting the play, they could enjoy the sight of a fellow gallant boldly and ingeniously rescuing his family's fortunes from a hypocritically venal society.

Epicoene

The most ambitious and rewarding attempt to control the audience's behavior is Jonson's *Epicoene* (Queen's Revels, 1609–10). Here Jonson provides his audience with a pleasing image of itself while directing its mockery to a gallery of deviants from its aristocratic ethos. In the Prologue, Jonson develops the metaphor of the play as a feast, where the audience "shall find guests' entreaty, and good room." Although the action of the play includes a broken feast, whose hollow revelry only amplifies the perversity of the celebrants and their community, Jonson considers the experience of the play a festal occasion for his spectators, who possess the harmony missing from the society of the play.[16] Nevertheless, some critics find the play's moral focus to be blurred. As Jonas Barish writes: "The total view of life expressed in *The Silent Woman* fluctuates uneasily between the two extremes, Ovidian and Juvenalian, between acceptance of the world and rejection of it, creating discords which are never fully resolved." [17] But the moral focus of the play becomes clear if we see Jonson as attempting to chart a middle way between acceptance and rejection of the world, and to identify that path with aristocratic detachment. Whereas Jonson's earlier private theater plays—*Cynthia's Revels* and *Poetaster*—attack perversions of aristocratic or courtly ideals, they offer no convincing positive image of those ideals, as G. K. Hunter has noted.[18] But in writing *Epicoene,* perhaps drawings on his recent experience as protégé of aristocratic patrons and maker of court masques, Jonson presented the three gallants—Dauphine, Clerimont, and Truewit—as coherent images of the way true aristocrats relate to a fallen world—despite their imperfections. Their kindred spirits are the noble men and women Jonson praises in his poems, although they lack the static perfection of the Wroths and Sidneys, because as figures in a dramatic action they move and change in time. From a didactic viewpoint, they are a miniature aristocratic community, whose members correct one another's deviations from the shared standards of nobility, and a model for the audience's behavior in ethics as well as in fashions, in life as well as in the theater.

In *Epicoene,* Jonson balances this positive image of aristocratic demeanor between a degenerate *beau monde* and a grotesque misanthrope. The fashionable society of the well-born and wealthy that flourishes in or near the court comprises a gaggle of hermaphroditic ninnies, while the ascetic critic of their mindless folly is neither a harmless antisocial crank like Libanius' Morosus in Jonson's chief source nor an impassioned if self-destructive idealist like Moliere's Alceste, but a malicious egoist. As in *Cynthia's Revels,* Jonson ridicules several varieties of frivolous vanity and modish decadence in the upper strata of society—Day's intellectual pretensions, La Foole's pride in his pedigree, Mrs. Otter's social climbing, her husband's vulgarity and pedantry, and the collegiate ladies' strident mannishness. But Morose, the chief adversary of these cacophonous worldlings, is no Crites, a humanist-scholar eager to restore court life to its pristine radiance, no Sir Robert Sidney, whose country estate seemed to Jonson a sanctuary for civilized withdrawal in "To Penshurst." He is, instead, a deliberate perversion of self-contained stability, a caricature of what T. M. Greene calls "the centered self," [19] and his aversion to noise is not a well-reasoned aloofness from fashionable vanities, but an involuntary loathing of life.

It is worth going over the familiar ground of Morose's pathological state in order to show how Jonson has made him the very antithesis of proper aristocratic conduct. Whereas Chapman's Tharsalio displays his aristocratic nature in his loyalty to his male blood-relations, Morose disclaims any responsibility to Dauphine Eugenie, his "next of blood, and his sister's son" (V, 171), and hopes by marrying to "thrust him out of my blood like a stranger" (V, 195).[20] Reducing his nephew's identity, first from "kinsman" to "your knighthood," he gleefully imagines the humiliations the well-born young man will suffer in his poverty, and then—regressing into baby-talk—he further diminishes Dauphine to "it" and "it knighthood":

> . . . no kinsman, I will now make you bring me the tenth lord's, and the sixteenth lady's letter, kinsman; and it shall do you no good kinsman. Your knighthood itself shall come on its knees, and it shall be rejected; it shall

be sued for its fees to execution, and not be redeemed; it shall cheat at the twelvepenny ordinary, it knighthood. . . .

(V, 195) [21]

As several critics have pointed out, Morose begins to suffer only when he forsakes solitude, for in seeking to enlarge his sphere of dominion to include a wife, he must thrust himself into the world he abhors. Yet Jonson makes clear that Morose's frenzied assertions of power, like his shrinking of his world to manageable dimensions, stem from a craving for absolute mastery, and some of the play's richest comic effects come from Morose's wild oscillations between self-immurement and self-assertion. For instance, at one point in the Fourth Act, we hear that "He has got on his whole nest of nightcaps, and locked himself up, i' the top o' the house, as high, as ever he can climb from the noise" (V, 219), but in the next scene he frantically asserts his phallic power, coming "down with a huge long naked weapon in both his hands" (V, 227). [22] Morose finally abandons the assertive mode as a temporary abberation by symbolically castrating himself. Desperate to have his marriage annulled, he falsely declares himself to be "no man, ladies. . . . Utterly un-abled in nature, by reason of *frigidity*, to perform the duties, or any the least office of a husband" (V, 265), and he even rejoices to learn that this wife is unchaste. However, as all possible grounds for annulment collapse, the futility even of his symbolic castration becomes the ultimate degree of impotence. He is now the complete opposite of Tharsalio and Dauphine.

When Dauphine offers to extricate Morose from the marriage, the latter crumbles into total dependency and offers complete capitulation for the privilege of resuming his isolation: "Make thine own conditions. My whole estate is thine.

Manage it, I will become thy Ward" (V, 268). Moreover, he symbolically castrates himself again when he forswears the legalistic trickery that might nullify the agreement. Like the fathers and father-surrogates who use the law to subjugate the attractive young gallants in Middleton's city comedies (nearly all of which were acted by children's troupes), Morose finally becomes weaponless:

> Come, nephew: give me the pen. I will subscribe to anything, and seal to what thou wilt, for my deliverance. . . . If there be a word in it lacking, or writ with false orthography, I protest before—I will not take the advantage.
>
> (V, 269)

Dismissing Morose with cruel nonchalance, Dauphine implies that the ultimate extension of his uncle's withdrawal is death: "Now you may go in and rest, be as private as you will, sir. I'll not trouble you, till you trouble me with your funeral, which I care not how soon it come" (V, 269–70). Behind Dauphine's morbid scorn is a truth which Morose still fails to understand, that human beings are social creatures and that life, as the saying goes, is with people.

Morose's rejection of kinship bonds, his abstention from communal festivity, and his repudiation of his own sexuality make him the perfect foil for Dauphine, Truewit, and Clerimont. These three are the true embodiment of aristocratic detachment in the play, and their stature is further enhanced by the contrast with the effeminate men and mannish women who aspire to aristocratic status in the play. Combining the urbane insouciance of Marston's Quadratus with the virile audacity of Chapman's Tharsalio, these three gallants constitute a small-scale model of an ideal aristocratic society, neither too detached from the world nor excessively involved in its vanities. Following Truewit's lead, they recognize the perversity and folly of their social world without repudiating it or withdrawing from it. Barish comments, "Truewit [is] an ideal of equivocal detachment, equally unable to commit himself wholeheartedly to the world and to let it alone." [23] For Truewit and his friends, however, "equivocal detachment" is not the involuntary ambivalence that Barish suggests so much as a deliberate aloofness which is based on keen moral perception of the world but which stops short of withdrawal. There is a good example of such distancing in the opening scene. Chastising Clermont for this reclusiveness, Truewit lists a number of fashionably insipid activities in answer to the question, "Why, what should a man do?" and then concludes, "These be the things, wherein your fashionable men exercise themselves, and I for company" (V, 165–66). Fully aware of the banality of the pursuits he has catalogued, he nevertheless participates in them for the sake of human fellowship. Those who are truly detached can enter into the world without fear of being contaminated and can even help others achieve the same detachment.

Like Crites, the three gallants in *Epicoene* perceive the absurdity of their own social world without the humanist-scholar's reformist zeal and self-righteous sobriety. Like Quadratus they are amused rather than outraged by folly, but like Macilente they hope to cure it by indulging it to the point of humiliating exposure, yet do so with playful competitiveness rather than savage envy, helping one another maintain the proper balance between detachment and engagement.

Playfulness—a blend of jest and earnest—is a reliable index of the kind of detachment that originates in benign superiority rather than snarling misanthropy. Truewit and his friends are playful not because they see life as meaningless or absurd, but because to them it "is neither more nor less serious than a game." [24] There is a kernel of truth in Truewit's mock-horror at Dauphine's half-ironic wish to "Maim a man forever, for a jest" (V, 239), for so sadistic an utterance betrays excessive commitment to one's own feelings. Like Hotspur's occasional churlishness, such a wish represents a mental departure from the chivalric rules by which an aristocrat like Dauphine has sworn to play the game of life. However arbitrary those rules may be, they are an index of self-mastery. They should therefore take precedence over emotions like rage, fear or hatred, and should dictate the style one uses in pursuing his goals, especially material goals like an income for life.

Truewit in turn nearly loses his detachment by an excessive commitment to the role of prankster. Several commentators have noted a compusive zeal behind his improvised jesting. Although he is not quite a professional entertainer, he does seem to feel that his social identity depends on his skill as a practical joker. He cannot admit that his warning to Morose against marriage was a mistake and claims that he knew all along it would have the opposite effect of strengthening the old man's resolve to marry, just as he peevishly refuses to let Clerimont help arrange the mock-quarrel between Daw and La Foole. Dauphine comments on the "extreme vanity" of Truewit's solicitude for his reputation as a trickster: "thou think'st thou wert undone, if every jest thou mak'st were not published" (V, 242). Truewit shows that he has finally corrected this tendency at the end of the play, when he pays graceful tribute to Dauphine and Clerimont for skillfully managing their own intrigues:

Well, DAUPHINE, you have lurched your friends of the better half of the garland, by concealing this part of the plot! But much good do it thee, thou deserv'st it, lad.

And CLERIMONT, for thy unexpected bringing in these
two to confession, wear my part of it freely.

(V, 270)

Far from being a jibe at the Whitefriars audience, as some
critics have argued,[25] Dauphine's outwitting of Truewit typifies the self-regulating interdependence of an ideal aristocratic community.

When not laboring to secure his reputation as a practical
joker, Truewit preserves the proper aristocratic spirit of playful detachment. His Ovidian defense of cosmetics against
Clerimont's celebration of unadorned nature indicates ironic
detachment, or superiority toward his own position, not the
confusion of values that Barish attributed to Jonson. In exaggerated pulpit rhetoric that recalls Falstaff's mock-preaching
to Hal, he delivers a Senecan homily to Clerimont on the
brevity of human life, but when his listener cuts him off, he
deftly changes topic and tone:

Truewit: . . . O, CLERIMONT, this time, because it is an
        incorporeal thing, and not subject to sense, we
        mock ourselves the fineliest out of it, with vanity,
        and misery indeed. . . .
Clerimont: Foh, thou hast read PLUTARCH'S morals, now,
        or some such tedious fellow; and it shows so
        vilely with thee: 'Fore god, 'twill spoil thy wit
        utterly. Talk me of pins, and feathers, and ladies,
        and rushes, and such things: and leave this *Stoicity*
        alone, till thou mak'st sermons.
Truewit: Well, sir. If it will not take, I have learned to
        loose as little of my kindness, as I can. I'll do good
        to no man against his will, certainly. When were
        you at the college?

(V, 166)

Once Truewit has therapeutically jolted Clerimont out of his solitary torpor, he can switch the conversation to the subjects Clerimont prefers—ladies, their fashions, and related trivia—and be confident of having a congenial and spirited companion. Such graceful tacking in his discourse suggests that Truewit wears his "stoicity" lightly, if not ironically. William Slights has recently described some of Truewit's exuberant, seemingly equivocal utterances as paradoxical encomia, that is, playful praise of that which is unworthy of praise.[26] Like Dauphine and Clerimont, Truewit exhibits a casual and unpedantic familiarity with classical authors, but preserves an ironic distance from their ideas even when he is paraphrasing them.

Unlike Morose or the denizens of the *beau monde*, the three gallants never entirely commit themselves to any intellectual position, not because they or Jonson are unsure of their moral standards but because Jonson deliberately created characters who define themselves by their style and who never allow their principles to delimit their identities. Their pervasive irony therefore signifies independence of all positions, values, and convictions, even—or especially—of their own. In their common attitude of playful detachment, their shared mode of ironic discourse, and their willingness to help each other preserve aristocratic superiority to the world around them, this trio is a flattering representation of the Whitefriars audience. Like other private theater playwrights, Jonson allowed his spectators to confirm their social identities by basking in the glow of the self-image he offered them, rather than by rejecting or disrupting his play.

Dramaturgical Defenses in Tragedy

Although comedies seem the most convenient vehicles for flattering an audience, certain tragedies—like Daniel's *Philo-*

tas (Queen's Revels, 1604) and Chapman's *Bussy D'Ambois* (Paul's, 1604) and his two-part play *The Conspiracy and Tragedy of Charles, Duke of Byron* (Queen's Revels, 1608)—occasionally do so too. In dramatizing the tragic downfall of a glamorous hero, these plays are the inverse of comedies like Chapman's *The Widow's Tears*, Jonson's *Epicoene* or Middleton's city comedies, where an attractive young gallant triumphs over corrupt and impotent figures of authority. Whereas these comedies are fantasies of success, tragedies of this type are nightmares of martyrdom, although the martyrdom brings with it a kind of victory, so that the fallen hero can still appear to the spectators as a heroic embodiment of their own real or imagined social identities.

More so than in the comedies, the protagonists of these tragedies are presented ambivalently. As modern critics have noted, their swashbuckling actions and heroic rhetoric are constantly undercut by flaws like arrogance, indiscretion, obtuseness, and naïveté.[27] The hero of Chapman's *Bussy D'Ambois* is accurately described by the oxymoronic phrase "glorious ruffi'n" (III.ii.62). He is on the one hand a natural force, an incarnation of prelapsarian "man in his native noblesse" (III.ii.91), on the other a vainglorious bully and adulterer. He is draped in the mantle of Herculean grandeur, with his victory in the six-man duel narrated in epic fashion by a Senecan nuntius, but he lacks the ethical discrimination to guide his valor. Like the bloody duel, his affair with Tamyra can be seen as an act of passion that either transcends or subverts conventional morality. While I have no doubt that such ambiguities are an important part of the play's total meaning, I don't think most of the spectators at Paul's would have taken so balanced a view. Spectators who could identify with figures like Witgood, Tharsalio, and Dauphine, probably stressed the facets of Bussy which they found congenial to their images of themselves.

Like Tharsalio, Bussy is a younger scion of ancient and venerable aristocratic stock, yet the French courtiers resent him as an upstart—"Fortune's proud mushroom shot up in a night" (III.i.98)—and mistake him "for some Knight of the new edition" (I.ii.111). But his rise, however swift, is merited by his valor, and his innate courage and dignity differentiate him from the corrupt high-ranking members of the French court. Monsieur, Bussy's patron, nurses secret designs on his brother's throne; the Guise we see in the play is an insanely jealous husband and a treacherous aspirant to political power, while the historical Guise was despised by the English for his role in the St. Bartholomew's Day massacre; and Montsurry is an impotent timeserver and a sadistic cuckold, who alienates the audience by torturing Tamyra. Bussy, unswervingly loyal to the king and to Tamyra, is their superior in everything but cunning and viciousness.

Chapman uses Tamyra to dramatize Bussy's superiority. When Monsieur propositions Tamyra with smutty innuendoes and lavish gifts, Montsurry advises her to endure those "opportunities almost to rapes" with politic forebearance: "Pray thee bear with him: / Thou know'st he is a bachelor, and a Courtier, / Ay, and a Prince" (II.ii.117–20). Her love for Bussy, by contrast, is neither purchased by bribery nor institutionalized by marriage, but rather springs from an overpowering passion which she knows is wrong but cannot control and which Chapman exalts through the language of courtly love. Unlike the craven Montsurry, Bussy will act as the public champion of Tamyra's reputation, despite the fact that he has compromised her honor in private. When he senses that Tamyra is in trouble, he must go to her. He cannot, as the Spirit Behemoth advises, "curb his rage, with policy" (IV.ii.138). He defies Behemoth's warnings of a trap, because he cannot imagine refusing Tamyra's summons: "Should not my powers obey when she commands, / My motion must be rebel to my will: / My will, to life" (V.ii.70–72). When he rushes to Tamyra's rescue, he discounts her warning, outfaces a crowd of assassins, killing one and sparing Montsurry only at Tamyra's request, before he is shot from offstage.

His death scene is magnificently theatrical—and something more than theatrical. Propping himself up with his sword, he vows to stand "Till death hath made me marble" (V.iii.145). With heroic magnanimity he forgives his killers and urges Montsurry to "be reconciled / With all forgiveness to your matchless wife" (V.iii.169–70). But in asking for Montsurry's pardon, Tamyra reveals her bleeding wounds, and the sight of this "killing spectacle" devastates Bussy. Seeing clearly for the first time the suffering he has caused his beloved, he perceives the "frail condition of strength, valor, virtue" (V.iii.188), and with his dying words renounces the claim to heroic stature he has just been laboring to assert. Chapman refuses to allow this expression of despair and self-doubt to be the final evaluation of the tragic hero, and concludes the 1607 version of the play with a eulogy by the Friar's ghost:

> Farewell brave relicts of a complete man:
> Look up and see thy spirit made a star,
> Join flames with Hercules: and when thou set'st
> Thy radiant forehead in the firmament,
> Make the vast continent, cracked with thy receipt,
> Spread to a world of fire: and th' aged sky,
> Cheer with new sparks of old humanity.
>
> (V.iii.268–74)

So much does his physical and moral heroism in the last scene redeem him from the shabby deceitfulness of his tangled affair with Tamyra that it is difficult to regard his death as moral retribution for adultery. Monsieur and Guise goad the cuckold Montsurry to murder Bussy, while they watch from above like "Fate's ministers" (V.ii.61). Their motive is purely political: Bussy's loyalty to the king protects Henry from their desire to control or depose him. At one point, Bussy vows to cleanse the land of all corruption. Sounding like a Crites or a Phoenix, he anatomizes three stock targets of satire: the great man who "rules so much more than his suffering King," the clergyman "that hath good living, and a wicked life," and finally the lawyer "that turns sacred Law / . . . Into a Harpy, that eats all but's own" (III.ii.29–54). This potential reformer of the realm is no match for Guise and Monsieur at political intrigue. Like many a political crusader, he is easily destroyed when his adversaries discover a vulnerable spot in his private life. He is not sufficiently suspicious of Monsieur and Guise, at least in the 1607 quarto, although he knows their natures thoroughly, and cannot anticipate that they will exploit his love for Tamyra to lure him into an ambush, or that she could ever be made their tool. To a certain extent he is the victim of his own naïveté, for he is unaware that the roles of courtly lover and political reformer are incompatible with each other or with his own primal innocence.

He left the rustic simplicity of his "green retreat" for a place in Monsieur's entourage almost on the dare that he could retain his virtue amidst the corruption of the court, if not purify it:

> I am for honest actions, not for great:
> If I may bring up a new fashion,
> And rise in Court with virtue, speed his [Monsieur's] plow.
>   (I.i.124–26)

Knowing he risks his own downfall by going to court, he chooses to accept the challenge on the grounds that death is inevitable in any case: "men that fall low must die, / As well as men cast headlong from the sky" (I.i.138–39). He does in-

deed fall from a great height and with a brilliance that illuminates the meanness of his enemies and dazzles the be-
holders.

Like Bussy, the hero of Daniel's *Philotas* is for all his flaws a
very attractive figure. At the outset, his pride, magnanimity,
and trust seem perilously close to arrogance, prodigality, and
naïveté, while at the end, though we admire his heroic bearing in the face of a rigged trial, false witnesses, and hideous
tortures, we regret his collapse to the point where "he was
more forward to / Confess, than they to urge him thereunto"
(ll.2037–38). Despite these flaws and instabilities, a Blackfriars
audience in the second year of James's reign would probably
have responded warmly to Philotas' criticism of Alexander for
assuming the title of Jove's son and converting the Greek
monarchy into an Asiatic despotism, with the traditional aristocracy reduced to abject servility. Like Bussy, he is the victim
of his own naïveté compounded with others' treachery, as his
enemies convince Alexander that his popularity and achievements are a threat to the crown, and that his failure to report a
regicidal conspiracy proves complicity in the plot. Philotas
does, as the Chorus comments, mar "all his former strains of
worth" (l. 2093) when he confesses to the charges against him
and, to please his accusers, invents new charges to confess to
and collaborators to implicate, but by this time he has been
tortured beyond human endurance so that he never completely loses the audience's sympathy.

Because of Philotas' resemblance to the Earl of Essex, Daniel was summoned before the Privy Council shortly after the
play was performed. Although the Essex rebellion had taken
place in 1600 and under a different sovereign, it was still a
sensitive issue. Many of Essex's prosecutors, like Robert
Cecil, Burghley's son, now held high offices under James. The
Essex case was probably very much alive among the members

of the upper classes who frequented the private theaters. Many aristocrats shared the impulses that drove Essex to defy his Queen. As Lawrence Stone has written, "In the 1580s and 1590s . . . there grew up a whole new generation of high-spirited young aristocrats in open rebellion against the conservative establishment in general and Lord Burghley in particular. Very many, like Oxford, Rutland, Southampton, Bedford, and Essex, had been wards of the old man and were reacting violently against his counsels of worldly prudence." [28] Moreover, in the early years of James's reign, many of the English aristocrats felt that James's new favorites had usurped their power, while the wholesale creation of new knights devalued their titles, and they therefore looked back on Essex as a champion of the traditional nobility against the arbitrary exercise of royal power. On the other hand, many aristocrats, especially those financially dependent on the crown, saw Essex's rebellion as a threat to the monarchy, the cornerstone of a political and social structure in which they occupied the most privileged positions. The divisiveness and sensitivity of the Essex question explains why Daniel, perhaps innocently, could write a play that appealed to one faction of aristocrats and find himself in trouble with another. His friend Fulke Greville avoided similar difficulties by destroying his play, *Cleopatra,* for fear some might take it as commentary on the Essex case.[29] In an Apology appended to the printed version of *Philotas,* Daniel claimed that he had started the play before the Essex rebellion, and protested against "wrong application and misconceiving"; he also hedged his bet by predicting that Philotas would have usurped the throne and plunged the state into ruin had it not been for the patriotic vigilance of Alexander and his chief prosecutors. Although Daniel escaped punishment, the whole situation must have been particularly awkward for him, as he was officially responsible for seeing that plays performed at Blackfriars contained nothing objectionable to secular or religious authorities.

In the Byron plays, Chapman used the Essex parallel with more discretion than Daniel had done, although these works managed to arouse official displeasure on another score. Chapman had once identified Essex with Achilles, the archetypal headstrong warrior, when he dedicated *Seven Books of the Iliad and Achilles' Shield* to the Earl, and he now developed an even stronger parallel between Essex and Byron. Elizabeth herself had commented on the resemblance between the two figures shortly after Essex's death, when the French ambassador told her of Byron's conviction.[30] In the second Byron play, *The Tragedy,* Chapman makes Byron himself refer to "the matchless Earl of Essex, whom some make / . . . A parallel with me in life and fortune" (IV.i.133–35), but he later tries to deny certain aspects of the parallel:

> The Queen of England
> Told me that if the willful Earl of Essex
> Had used submission, and but asked her mercy,
> She would have given it past resumption.
> She like a gracious princess did desire
> To pardon him, even as she prayed to God
> He would let down a pardon unto her;
> He yet was guilty, I am innocent:
> He still refused grace, I importune it.
>
> (V.iii.139–47)

Ironically, nothing could be more likely to underscore the parallel with Essex than this hope of Byron's that an impassioned assertion of innocence could magically erase the fact of his guilt.

Undoubtedly the resemblance between these two figures affected the Blackfriars audience in such a way as to engage those sympathetic to Essex in Byron's plight, to distance upholders of royal authority from the protagonist, and to divide the loyalties of still others, as Daniel had done in *Philotas*. But the Byron plays differ from Daniel's work and from Chapman's own *Bussy D'Ambois* in that there is no ambiguity about the hero's guilt. Rather than cloud the issue of the protagonist's moral culpability with an adulterous liaison or a "confession" extracted by torture, Chapman clearly involves the hero in treasonous conspiracy. That is, this involvement is clear to everyone but Byron, whose denial of what we have seen to be true verges on the psychopathic, and probably allowed the audience to take a more detached view of Byron than they could have taken of Bussy.

In *The Tragedy,* Byron insists on his innocence throughout, and when the evidence of his guilt can no longer be denied he pleads that he was bewitched. Whereas Bussy is complex and multifaceted, Byron seems mercurial, if not schizoid: "He alters every minute" (V.iii.187). In III.iii of *The Conspiracy*, Byron coaxes La Brosse to disclose a dire prophecy by threatening violence *only* if the man remains silent, and then promptly beats the astrologer when he utters the prediction. His changes in attitude toward the king are equally abrupt, for he sees Henry sometimes as his sovereign, sometimes as his client, and sometimes as his equal. These sudden shifts and inconsistencies prevent the spectator from identifying with Byron as closely as he could with Bussy or Philotas, and Chapman further complicates the response by making Henry not a devious tyrant, like Daniel's Alexander, but a capable and humane ruler, who prays to God for guidance and who overrules his counselors in insisting that Byron receive due process rather than a summary execution.

The conflict between Byron and Henry is as Oedipal as the

rivalries in the children's city comedies, but elicits a more balanced response. In *The Conspiracy,* Byron demands the cita-
del of Bourg as a test of the King's gratitude and trust; when
Henry refuses on grounds of policy, Bryon protests he is not
loved and rejects the King's argument by mocking Henry's
"grey beard" until the King reveals that he suspects Byron of
plotting with his enemies. Byron responds to this charge with
a long ranting recitation of his past services to the King, who
laughs in his face—presumably at the irrelevancy of the defense—and thereby nearly incites him to violence. But in the
following scene, Henry soothes the Duke's wounded ego and
then, like many a parent, blames Byron's rebelliousness on
bad companions. It is, he says, "no disease bred in yourself, / But whispered in by others" (V.ii.68–69). In *The Tragedy,* Byron discovers the limits of Henry's paternal love. "As
the kind father doth his riotous son" (III.ii.90), the King repeatedly begs him to confess and be pardoned, but Byron insists he has nothing to confess. He is troubled to hear that
Philip II of Spain actually executed his own son, but thinks
that Henry's threat of capital punishment is a bluff, and even
after his conviction expects a royal pardon. But in his determination to prove the insufficiency of Henry's gratitude, trust,
and love, Byron has pushed the King past the point of forgiveness, and must die.

Despite his delusions, there are moments when one feels
that Byron is not merely indulging himself in futile theatrics,
but is rather acting out his vision of reality, a vision which
casts him as a chivalric warrior of epic proportions and prelapsarian valor. When the poetry catches fire, as it does, say,
when he dominates the execution scene, it is hard not to
share Byron's vision of himself. Like the common soldier who
speaks out in his behalf, we marvel at the splendor of his

downfall, at the conquest of his own terror of death, and grant him a Pyrrhic victory over the father he forced to destroy him.[31]

A great many tragedies revolve around the headstrong warrior type, yet only in this handful of private theater plays do we feel the issues drawn in such a way as to speak to the private-theater spectators' immediate problems of social identity. Shakespeare's *Coriolanus* (c.1608) has a heroic and obstinate patrician as its hero, but his chief antagonists are the demogogic tribunes and the treacherous Aufidius, rather than a paternal sovereign. In *Troilus and Cressida* (c.1602), the conflict between Achilles and Agamemnon could have been developed along the lines of Chapman's Byron plays, but blends into a vast panorama of war and lechery. Moreover, the Byron plays present the conflict between rebel and king rather evenhandedly. When *The Conspiracy* and *The Tragedy* were performed before real, potential, or self-styled figures of authority, these works could not only divide the audience into factions but aggravate internal divisions within those spectators who, like Chapman himself, identified with both the flamboyant rebel and the sagacious monarch. Although the Byron plays have their weaknesses, they are an excellent example of the way a private-theater playwright could make tragic drama out of his audience's concern with its social identity.

Whether a dramatist writes under "coterie" or "popular" auspices, one of the inherent features of the theatrical occasion is a ritualistic celebration—however indirect—of the spectators themselves. In the theatrical situation under discussion, spectators sometimes celebrated themselves at the expense of the play. In extradramatic addresses, dramatists writing for children's troupes protected their work by explicitly reaffirming their audience's vision of itself. Sometimes they wove into their plays techniques for controlling their audiences' attitudes and behavior. Most effective was their double-edged technique, used primarily in comedy, of ridiculing unfashionable characters who deviated from aristocratic standards, while simultaneously encouraging spectators to identify with embodiments of these ideals. Even for tragedy, as we have just seen, the playwrights could secure a respectful hearing by manipulating spectators' conceptions of themselves. Understanding these tensions between audience and playwright helps to clarify the intent behind a number of private-theater plays, most notably *Epicoene* and *Bussy D'Ambois*, perhaps the two finest plays performed by the children's troupes in their brief but brilliant era.

CHAPTER FOUR

The Style

The truth is, that the spectators are always in their senses, and know, from the first act to the last, that the stage is only a stage, and that the players are only players.[1]

UNLESS they are naive or deranged, of course Dr. Johnson is right. But the problem is more complex, for if spectators know at all times that they are watching an illusion, are they always aware of possessing that knowledge? At what level of consciousness do they know that these people moving and speaking on the stage are really actors in a theater? I "always know" my telephone number, but only in special circumstances does that knowledge rise to my conscious attention.

Although we "always know" that the players are only players, we usually watch performances by little-known actors without much awareness of the actor behind the character, unless we are professionally involved in theater. However, when we watch a famous actor with a strong personality, we frequently find ourselves aware of that actor's identity, even while we concentrate on the character he is portraying. In such cases, we have what S. L. Bethell has termed a "dual consciousness of the player as player and as character,"[2] a state of mind in which we are highly aware of knowing what we "always know." A clear understanding of this fundamental principal of "dual consciousness" must underlie any discussion of the acting style(s) employed by the children's troupes.

Dual Consciousness and the Children's Troupes

As Bethell and others have argued, this dual consciousness was extremely common in the Tudor and early Stuart periods, when playwrights used a variety of devices to focus the audience's attention on the obvious fact that it was watching actors on a stage. Playwrights could make actors step out of character, address the audience directly, or refer to actors, plays, acting, stages, and theaters. Dramatists found it particularly easy to create dual consciousness in audiences watching boy companies perform, because of the obvious disparity between child actors and adult characters.

The members of a children's troupe ranged in age from ten to fifteen. According to Jonson's eulogy, Salomon Pavy was "scarce thirteen" (VIII, 77) when he died in 1603. Thus, he would have been nine or ten, the usual age of a novice chorister, when he was impressed into the Blackfriars troupe, and he may even have begun acting before than as "an apprentice to one Pierce" (Edward Pierce, who became master of the Children of Paul's in mid-1600). Similarly, the composer Thomas Ravenscroft (b.1588) served in the choir at Paul's from 1598 or 1599 to 1604, or from the ages of ten or eleven to fifteen.[3]

The visible disparity in age and size between child actors and adult characters exaggerated the same problem that adult troupes faced: how to control the audience's dual consciousness. The children's dramatists could solve the problem either by allowing the audience's awareness of the actor behind the character to remain latent, or by explicitly reminding the audience of what it "always knew" and playing upon its dual consciousness for a variety of effects. More often, they did the latter. In tragedies, as we have seen, the use of child actors afforded the spectator a detachment from material that threatened his own precarious social identity. The comedies acted by children's troupes, which comprise the lion's share of their repertories, are studded with various devices intended to remind the audiences of the actors behind the characters. The four most common of these devices are (1) the use of adult actors alongside the child actors, (2) bawdry, (3) self-reference, and (4) inductions.

The presence of an adult actor on the stage would have visually reminded the audience that the other actors, most of whom played adult characters, were children. Some of the records of payment for court performance suggest that adults occasionally acted with children in the early Tudor period. "Father" Grim the Collier in Edwardes' *Damon and Pythias* boasts, "I will sing in my man's voice, / Chave troubling bass buss" (11. 1659–60). He was probably played by an adult actor, perhaps by Edwardes himself, who was remembered in Hollyband's *The French Schoolmaster* (1573) not only as "the master of the Children of the Queen's Chapel" but also a "great player of plays." [4] While we have no evidence that Westcote himself acted with his choristers, his will indicates that seven former choristers, some of them between 16 and 30, lived with him at the time of his death, perhaps joining the regular choirboys for dramatic productions. [5] Hunter has speculated that one or two adult actors appeared in the subplots of Lyly's plays, which were performed by children's troupes in the 1580s and early 1590s, in the roles of the comic villains or comic butts who are always outwitted by the cleverer, smaller pages. [6] In plays by Lyly, and later in some by Marston and Middleton, pages are given names like Half-penny and Minutius and seem to be the smallest of the company, while the comic goons, perhaps played by older boys if not adults, usually comment on the pages' diminutiveness and youth.

These dramatists thus create a sort of Jack-and-the-giant situation, in which the audience's sympathies were clearly with the smaller characters. If, as seems possible, the adult actors who played the comic butts were often the masters of the children's troupes or their associates, the discomfiting of Lyly's pedantic dolts by their own children would have made more explicit the saturnalian impulses underlying the activities of children's troupes from the Medieval ceremony of the Boy Bishop to their temporary cessation of playing in 1591. There is, however, no evidence that adults acted alongside children during the boy companies' most prolific period, the ten or twelve years following their resuscitation in 1596 or 1597, but because the actors were usually between ten and fifteen years old the disparity between child actors and adult characters would have been obvious.

The use of bawdry in plays acted by children's troupes probably called the audience's attention to the prepubescence of most, if not all, of the child actors. For instance, in the Induction to *Cynthia's Revels,* two children forcibly attempt to stop a third child from presenting the argument of the play on the grounds that he will "stale the author's invention" (IV, 36); after what was supposed to be a violent tussle, the third child says, "I'd cry a rape, but that you are children" (IV, 38). This type of bawdry had the effect of heightening the audience's awareness that the actors were children, as bawdry of any sort would probably have done by underlining the incongruity between the erotic behavior of the characters and the sexual immaturity of the actors. In Lyly's plays, the songs sung by the pages and maidservants, who were played by the smallest and youngest actors, are full of bawdy puns and double entendres.[7] Marston too exploits this incongruity, most notably perhaps in *The Fawn,* a play which includes characters like Sir Amoroso Debile-Dosso, whose sexual athleticism has

weakened his back; Herod Frappatore, who boasts of prodigious sexual capacities; and Nimphadoro, who professes
lust on a grandiose scale.

The comic effect of the bawdry in children's plays depends
on the audience's sense of the actors' physical immaturity,
not on its presumption of their inherent innocence, a more
recent notion derived from Locke and Rousseau. Disturbed
by the incongruity between the characters' eroticism and the
actors' supposed innocence, Alfred Harbage and others have
found the sexual humor in plays acted by children's troupes
to be smutty and depraved, whereas they deem the bawdry in
plays acted by adult companies wholesomely ribald. However, the belief in childhood innocence, on which such a
judgment depends, would have been anachronistic in the
period under discussion.[8] While bawdry has for obvious reasons been an integral part of stage comedy since Aristophanes, its major function in plays acted by children's
troupes was not so much to titillate a decadent coterie audience as it was to encourage the audience to savor the disparity between the actors and their roles.

Instead of using bawdry to accentuate this disparity, the
1607 quarto of Chapman's *Bussy D'Ambois,* which is the version acted by the Children of Paul's around 1604, deemphasizes the sexual immaturity of the actor playing the title role.
In this version it is Tamyra, the heroine, who initiates the liaison with Bussy, as it is she who first speaks of her love and
who decides to use the Friar as a go-between. However, in
the 1641 quarto, which is probably the version of the play
revised for an adult troupe, Bussy is given a speech in which
he says that his love for Tamyra "hath long been vowed in
heart" (II.i.209c), and his conversation with the Friar in the
middle of II.ii implies that he is pursuing Tamyra rather than
being pursued by her.[9] Because of the early marriage age for

girls and the absence of actresses on the English stage, choristers could have played married women more convincingly than they could have played adult men and with far less chance of making the audience aware of the actor as actor. But when *Bussy D'Ambois* was performed by an adult company, there was no longer any need to distract the audience from the sexual immaturity of the leading actor, and Bussy was changed from the pursued to the pursuer. In the two-part Byron play, Chapman avoided the problem of the hero's sexuality by announcing in the opening scene that "his blood is not voluptuous, / Nor much inclined to women" (*Conspiracy* I.i.66-67). The first quarto of *Bussy D'Ambois* is the exception that proves the rule, for in most of the plays acted by the children's troupes, or at least in the bulk of the comedies, bawdry and erotic material is used to remind the audience of the obvious disparity between child actors and adult characters.

Self-referential discussions of actors, acting, plays, playhouses, and stages also heightened the audience's dual consciousness. Significantly, such discussions are far more common in plays acted by children's companies than in plays acted by adult companies. These discussions, like plays-within-plays, generally make the audience aware of three different levels of illusion: (1) the real world, which includes the audience and the actors as actors; (2) the world of the dramatic action, which includes the actors as characters; and (3) the world of play-acting within the world of the dramatic action. In plays acted by children's troupes, self-referential passages generally make the dramatic action seem artificial in comparison with the audience's world, or rather with the audience's conception of its own world. When one of these self-referential passages reminds spectators that they are watching actors on a stage, it also reminds them that they are spectators in a playhouse. Membership in a private-theater audi-

ence, as we have seen, carried with it the flattering illusion
that one was a participant, however indirectly, in a form of
courtly entertainment. This illusion was encouraged by the
notion that private-theater productions were rehearsals for
court performances and by the humble, supplicating prologues and epilogues scarcely different from those delivered
at court. From a commercial viewpoint, it hardly mattered
whether a spectator came to the private theaters to watch the
illusion created by the dramatic action or to nourish his own
illusions about his social status. Whereas self-reference in
adult plays can sometimes strengthen the illusion created by
the dramatic action, as in the players' scenes in *Hamlet* or
when Cleopatra fears that a child actor will mimic her ("I shall
see / Some squeaking Cleopatra boy my greatness / I' th' posture of a whore" [*Antony and Cleopatra* V.ii.219–21]), self-
reference in children's plays invariably exposes the artificiality
of the play world and emphasizes the reality of the spectators'
vision of themselves.

In *Jack Drum's Entertainment,* Marston makes four aristocratic characters comment patronizingly on the Children of
Paul's, the very company performing the play:

Sir Edward Fortune: I saw the Children of *Paul's* last night,
     And troth they pleased me pretty, pretty well,
     The Apes in time will do it handsomely.
Planet: I'faith I like the Audience that frequenteth there
     With much applause: A man shall not be choked
     With the stench of Garlic, nor be pasted

     To the barmy Jacket of a Beer-brewer.
Brabant Junior: 'Tis a good gentle Audience, and I hope
     the Boys

     Will come one day into the Court of requests.
Brabant Senior: Aye and they had good Plays, but they
     produce

Such musty fopperies of antiquity,
And do not suit the humorous age's backs
With clothes in fashion.

(III, 234)

Although the self-reference is less specific, the same mock-condescension toward chorister troupes occurs in Middleton's *Family of Love*, when two gallants returning from the theater express a decided preference for adult troupes over companies of "youths," such as the one performing the play:

Glister: And from what good exercise come you three?
Gerardine: From a play, where we saw most excellent
        Sampson excel the whole world in gate-carrying.
Dryfat: Was it performed by the youths?
Lipsalve: By youths? Why, I tell thee we saw Sampson,
        and I hope 'tis not for youths to play Sampson.

(I.iii.100–5)

Similarly, in one of the schoolroom scenes in Marston's *What You Will*, the Pedant tells how Holifernes Pippo, one of his pupils, nearly joined a troupe of boy actors:

I was solicited to grant him leave to play the Lady in comedies presented by Children, but I knew his voice was too small and his stature to low; sing, sing a treble, *Holifernes, sing.*

(II, 256)

The stage direction indicates that this passage is followed by "The Song," which underlines the irony of the schoolmaster's speech by demonstrating that the actor's voice was obviously not too small, nor his stature too low for him to join a troupe of boy actors.

The most complex example of self-reference in a children's play occurs in Chapman's *The Widow's Tears*, where Tharsalio uses theatrical imagery to describe his own deceptive strat-

agem and Cynthia's histrionic grieving. He congratulates
Lycus for playing his part in the intrigue so skillfully: "In
prose, thou weptst. So have I seen many a moist Auditor do at
a play; when the story was but a mere fiction: And didst act
the Nuntius well? would I had heard it" (IV.i.42–44). Interest-
ingly, Tharsalio casts Lycus not only as an actor, but also as a
spectator of Cynthia's performance, which he again describes
in theatrical terms later in the same scene: "This strain of
mourning wi'th' Sepulchre, like an over-doing Actor, affects
grossly, and is indeed so far forced from the life, that it
bewrays itself to be altogether artificial" (IV.i.96–98). As in a
children's play like *Summer's Last Will and Testament,* the effect of the theatrical terminology, like other examples of self-
reference, is to make one level of action seem closer to the
audience than another. Just as Toy-Will Summer mocks the
pageant-like main action of Nashe's play in order to substan-
tiate the spectators' self-esteem, so Tharsalio, a flattering reflection of the audience, exposes the artificiality of Cynthia's
grief to make the spectators identify with his own audacious
virility.

Most inductions to Elizabethan and Jacobean plays are self-
referential discussions of theatrical matters that supposedly
are unrehearsed and take place among actors, spectators, or
even tiremen. Although used in plays acted by both adult and
children's companies, inductions are especially prevalent in
the plays acted by chorister troupes in private theaters.[10] Like
other kinds of self-reference, these inductions were probably
intended to remind the audience of the presence of boy
actors behind the adult characters, the artificiality of the play,
and the substantiality of the spectators. In one type of induction, used by Jonson in *Cynthia's Revels* and by Marston in
Antonio and Mellida, the actors appear in what are supposed
to be their own persons and create the illusion that they are

not acting their parts but simply being themselves. In Marston's *Jack Drum's Entertainment,* a "Tireman" begins the Introduction by telling the audience that the author is trying to prevent the performance from taking place, but he is followed by "one of the Children," who explains, in what is really a conventionally obsequious court prologue, that the author "was loath, / Wanting a *Prologue,* & ourselves not perfect, / To rush upon your eyes without respect" (III, 179). The illusion of spontaneity within such inductions underscores the artificiality of the plays themselves. Like the self-referential passages already examined, these inductions remind the spectators that they are watching actors in a fashionable private theater, a fact which they "always knew," confirming their sense of participation in a courtly or aristocratic ritual.

In another type of induction, used by Marston in *What You Will* and by Beaumont in *The Knight of the Burning Pestle,* actors seated on the stage pretend to be members of the audience. When child actors are involved, this type of induction is an obvious self-reference, for there can be no mistaking the diminutive mock-spectators for real spectators, as there might be when an adult acting troupe employed the same device. This type of induction, like the other devices we have examined, underlines the artificiality of the play and reminds the spectator that he is watching actors on stage and sitting in a fashionable private theater among others of sophisticated taste and exalted rank.

Natural and Formal Styles of Acting

If dual consciousness of actors as actors and as characters was a fact of theatrical life in the Elizabethan and Jacobean periods, especially for the children's troupes, then any discussion of acting style(s) used by the boy companies must take this awareness into account, along with the dramatists' efforts to exploit or suppress it. Unfortunately, most writers on the subject fail to do so, and instead argue over whether the prevailing acting style for all actors in the period—children and adults—was "natural" or "formal," terms which are vague, imprecise, and wrongly thought to be mutually exclusive.[11] One can avoid this unnecessary dichotomy by proposing that companies of child actors used different styles for different plays and parts of plays, just as directors and actors do today, and that any style they used depended for its full effect on the audience's awareness that the actors were children.

A "natural" style, for example, is presumably illusionistic, an attempt to reproduce on stage the mannerisms of offstage behavior, although the inevitable selection and amplification of details make one question the degree of verisimilitude possible in such reproduction. Secondly, as Auerbach and Gombrich have argued for narrative literature and visual art, "natural" is a highly relative term: what is "natural" to one age seems stylized to another.[12] In spite of these theoretical objections to the term, the children's troupes seem on occasion to have employed a style of acting less conventionalized than other styles available to them and one which their spectators would have considered "natural." in his Epitaph on Salomon Pavy, Jonson is obviously exaggerating for poetic effect when he says that Pavy "did act . . . / Old men so duly, / As, sooth, the *Parcae* thought him one" (VIII, 77), but the effect would have been impossible if the boy, and presumably the other members of children's troupes, had never employed an illusionistic style of acting. A "natural" style was surely used in those inductions where the boys pretended not to be acting. One entire group of plays—the city comedies of Dekker and Webster, Middleton, and Marston—were probably acted by the children's troupes in a "natural" style. These plays are set in Jacobean London, abound in local and topical allusions, are written in extremely colloquial language, and portray familiar character types. It would seem likely then that these plays were presented in a style that was consistent with these other elements, a style that mirrored as closely as possible the traits of speech and gesture of these familiar character types and on occasion of recognizable individuals—in other words, a "natural" style.

The children's use of a "natural" style of acting, however, does not necessarily mean that their audiences were unaware of the disparity between boy actors and adult characters. Indeed, so obvious is this disparity, that in some contexts the more natural the acting the more comic the effect, for many actions natural in adults hardly seem natural when mirrored by children.[13] Consequently, the verisimilitude of the language, setting, and character types in these satiric city comedies probably heightened this incongruity, as in the saturnalian Boy Bishop ceremony, where the choristers wore the vestments and occupied the seats of their eccesiastical superiors. Mimicry of adults by children is at bottom a saturnalian attack on the adults being imitated, for mimicry is always derisive and is particularly so when the imitation is extremely close and when a reduction in scale is involved, exposing the behavior of adults as essentially childish. Ultimately, such mimicry is directed not only at the adults being portrayed on the stage but, in widening circles, at specific adults known to the spectators, at the entire adult world, and at the very principle of authority. Perhaps for this reason, the involvement of the children's troupes in the Marprelate controversy embarrassed the ecclesiastical establishment, whose side they took, as much as the antiepiscopal faction they satirized. Moreover, the boy companies also mocked their courtly and aristocratic audiences not only for being part of the adult world but also for being, or thinking themselves, real or potential figures of authority. At the same time, they invited the spectators to join the saturnalian mockery by deflecting it toward figures of authority in the plays, and sometimes "applying" it to similar figures in their lives. In short, when the children's troupes used a "natural" style of acting, the phenomenon of dual consciousness could readily transform it into ritualized festal mockery of the audience.

In *Epicoene*, Jonson transforms the "natural" surface of city comedy into such ritualized abuse with a single devastating stroke: the revelation that Morose's bride is really a boy. A shock to nearly everyone on or off the stage, this revelation publicly exposes the fraudulence of the gallants who claim to have seduced "her" and of the collegiate ladies who have admitted "her" to their sisterhood. At a deeper level, the revelation comments on the hermaphroditic quality of these and other fashionable pretenders, and then—because most of the actors were boys—it stresses the disparity between all actors and their roles, including those in the audience: "All are actors engaged in a masquerade, improvising various identities, sexual or professional, on the indeterminate basis supplied by nature." [14] Exploiting the audience's dual consciousness, Jonson brings to the surface the ritualized mimicry that was implicit whenever the children's troupes used a "natural" style.

On the other hand, some scholars argue that the children's troupes were obliged to use a "formal" style of acting because boy actors could not convincingly portray adult characters. Certainly the use of a "formal" style is consistent with the audience's awareness of the disparity between child actors and adult characters. To be more precise, however, there are two different "formal" styles—the first declamatory and the second parodic.[15] The paucity of external evidence makes it difficult to assess any conjectures about the acting style of the chorister troupes, but if one adopts as his criterion the suitability of a particular style to particular works, each of these two "formal" styles seems suitable to some of the plays or parts acted by the boy companies, as does a "natural" style, but none suits the entire repertory.

Declamatory Acting Style

Actors employing this style represent rather than impersonate characters, much the way opera singers do. That is, neither group attempts to achieve verisimilitude, but rather to express the thoughts and feelings of a dramatic character in an artistic medium—song for the opera singer, conventionalized speech for the player. A declamatory style would therefore be inappropriate for plays written in colloquial prose, like *Epicoene,* but would be better suited to plays or parts of plays written in stylized prose, like *Endimion,* in blank verse, like *Dido,* or in rhymed verse, like *Philotas.* This style of acting stresses rhetorical and poetic effects, and deemphasizes the idiosyncrasies of speech or gesture that individualize particular characters. The mode of delivery probably resembled that used by trained orators, and emphasized poise, elocution, vocal inflection and modulation, and graceful use of gesture. Whereas modern audiences accustomed to actors striving for verisimilitude are put off by the artificiality of the declamatory style, the children's troupes sometimes utilized this style for special effects.

Lyly's plays, with their balanced speeches and symmetrical grouping of characters around a central debate topic, seem ideally suited to declamatory acting, as do such Lylyesque works as *The Wisdom of Doctor Dodypoll,* and parts of *The*

Maid's Metamorphosis and *Cynthia's Revels*. Plays of this type usually employ highly stylized dialogue and present relatively static configurations of characters, rather than complex, individualized characters who develop in the course of the play.

Some children's plays invite a declamatory style of acting for reasons of decorum. Plays like *Damon and Pythias, Campaspe*, and *The Phoenix* revolve around a monarch who corresponds loosely to Elizabeth or James, thus creating a problem of style for the child actor cast in the role. In order to avoid making royalty appear ridiculous, dangerous even in licensed festal abuse, he could not use a "natural" style of acting, which would result in saturnalian mimicry, nor could he reproduce any of the real sovereign's idiosyncrasies of speech or gesture. He was, after all, creating a lucid and potent symbol of royal authority—an idealized reflection of Elizabeth or James and an icon for their subjects—not a convincing portrait of a human ruler, whose foibles and frailties would be embarrassingly puerile in miniature. To steer clear of these difficulties, the child actor playing the central role must have strived for a lofty, dignified, and unindividualized style—although the actual result was probably a bit stiff and wooden. Those players in close proximity to the royal figures would probably have adopted the same style, again to avoid making the sovereign appear ludicrous, although most plays with central royal figures have a few scenes or episodes of low comedy or bawdy usually involving servants—which call for a more "natural" style of acting. In these scenes of backstairs life, the disparity between actor and character could either be minimized if the characters were diminutive pages and maidservants, or emphasized as a satiric comment on the adult world. In a play like *The Phoenix*, the use of two such different styles may have sharpened the contrast of the moral gravity of the Prince and his followers with the corrupt behav-

ior of his adversaries. In Jonson's *Cynthia's Revels,* we can actually witness the shift from one style to the other, when Mercury tells Cupid how they must act now that they are
disguised as pages: "since we are turned cracks, let's study to
be like cracks; practise their language and behaviors, and not
with a dead imitation: act freely, carelessly, and capriciously"
(II.1.4–7). As lively and spirited as their dialogue is before they
don their disguises, Jonson evidently intended to contrast
their gravity as deities with their informality as pages, and to
have them do so by switching from a relatively declamatory,
or representational style to a relatively natural style that allowed close imitation of a familiar character type.

With its tacit acceptance of the audience's dual consciousness and its tendency toward representation rather than im-
personation, the declamatory style may also have allowed the
children's troupes to perform tragedy in a serious manner. It
is hard to believe that all of their tragedies were burlesques or
parodies. At the end of his Preface to *The Fawn,* Marston
proudly advertised the forthcoming publication of "a Tragedy," presumably *Sophonisba* (Queen's Revels, 1604–6), without any suggestion of burlesque or parody, while in a note
appended to the Epilogue of the latter play, he apologized for
"the fashion of the Entrances and Music" in his text on the
grounds that "it is printed only as it was presented by youths,
& after the fashion of the private stage," but he gives no indication that the performance was ironic. Chapman wrote
four tragedies for boy companies within six or eight years, all
of them intended and apparently received as serious plays.
Like *Sophonisba,* they are written in a lofty blank verse, with
complex aria-like sections of passionate utterance and philosophical reflection. As we have seen in Daniel's *Philotas* and
in Chapman's *Bussy D'Ambois* and two-part Byron play, the
spectators' dual consciousness gave them enough detach-

ment to consider the conflict between flamboyant rebel and sagacious monarch with cool objectivity. In short, the children's troupes probably used a declamatory style very effectively for specific purposes in some of their extant plays.

Parodic Acting Style

Because of the obvious disparity between child actors and adult characters, as well as the resulting tendency toward reductive mimicry, many scholars argue that most, if not all, of the children's plays are parodies or burlesques of adult plays, and were therefore acted in a corresponding style. Unfortunately, it is impossible to describe this style with any precision, as scholars can not agree on the acting style used by adult companies and so can not agree on precisely what style is being parodied. We can nevertheless gauge the general effect of such parody, for the obvious reduction in scale caricatured the theatrical behavior of adult players as effectively as the children's use of a "natural" style mimicked the behavior of adults in real life.

In its own way, parody flatters the spectator, for it assumes—or proclaims—that he is familiar with the object of parody and critically sophisticated enough to perceive its generic or particular defects. Parody, as many scholars have suggested, flourished in the private theaters because audiences there were eager to assert their sophistication. As we have seen, they often did so by ridiculing the actors, all or part of the play they came to see, and certain characters, who, like lightning rods, were intended to attract and neutralize this mockery. Parody too provides a target for the audience to ridicule, but locates it outside of the play rather than inside, in someone else's work, in this case in plays acted by adult troupes. It seems reasonable to suppose that such parodic scenes or plays were acted in a way that also ridiculed the style in which adult plays were performed.

The presence of verbal parody in plays written for children's troupes strongly suggests the use of a parodic acting style. Some children's plays, for example, parody specific plays from the adult repertories. In the Induction to Beaumont's *The Knight of the Burning Pestle,* Rafe replies to a request for "a huffing part" with a near-verbatim recitation of Hotspur's "By heaven, methinks it were an easy leap. . . ." (*1 Henry IV* I.iii.201ff.). The anonymous *The First Part of Hieronimo,* as John Reibetanz has recently argued, "is a full-blown theatrical burlesque of *The Spanish Tragedy,* written for and initially performed by child actors sometime between 1599 and 1604." [16] Reibetanz not only cites several references in *The First Part of Hieronimo* to the size of the actors, such as the protagonist's line "My mind's a giant, though my bulk be small" (iii.114) but studies numerous passages parodying the incidents, conventions, characters, and language of Kyd's play.

Some children's plays parody types of adult plays rather than specific works. In the absence of verbal parody of particular plays, readers seeking to demonstrate parodic intentions must rely on tact, sensitivity to tone, and judgment. The critical reaction to excessively zealous parody-hunters should not blind us to the presence of generic parody in plays acted by the children's troupes.[17] A common target for such parody is the tradition of moralistic plays based on the parable of the prodigal son. Dramatic adaptations of this parable had been popular with schoolboy and chorister troupes throughout the sixteenth century. Plays like *Nice Wanton* (1535–53) used it as a vehicle to preach respect for authority and to warn against the wages of sin. In the 1600s, moralistic treatment of the prodigal-son story is also found in a number of plays acted by adult troupes, such as *The London Prodigal* (King's Men, 1603–5) and *How a Man May Choose a Good Wife from a Bad* (Worcester's Men, c.1602). The writers of these public-theater prodigal-son plays deflect sympathy away from the protagonist by linking prodigality to other vices—lechery, gambling, despair— and by exploiting the pathos of his abandoned fiancée or wife, and sometimes his children. The forsaken woman always remains faithful to the prodigal, sometimes disguises herself as a page in order to be near him, and brings him to contrition and repentance by some overpowering display of her virtue. In Shakespeare's "comedies of forgiveness," this pattern becomes subtle and complex, but in the hands of lesser public-theater dramatists, it remains a simplistic formula: "a rake and spendthrift deserts his wife for gain or the love of a courtesan, maltreats the wife who remains faithful to him, and after he has sinned sufficiently, is taken into grace again and even rewarded." [18]

Two children's plays—*The Knight of the Burning Pestle* and *Eastward Ho!*—explicitly parody the homiletic variety of prodigal-son plays. In *The Knight of the Burning Pestle*, The Grocer's wife insists that Jasper Merrythought, the discharged apprentice, is a typical prodigal, although the play ascribes no such quality to him. Her error apparently is a conditioned response, the result of watching moralistic prodigal-son plays at the public theaters. Beaumont spoofs the prodigal-son tradition still further by celebrating old Charles Merrythought as a prodigal father, who meets every adversity with food, drink, and song. Beaumont also reverses the public-theater formula by making Merrythought's wife desert *him* and then allowing the old prodigal to convert the miserly shrew to his outlook before he takes her back. [19]

Eastward Ho! (Queen's Revels, 1605)—a collaboration by Jonson, Chapman, and Marston—establishes the prentice

Quicksilver as a prodigal in the opening scene. The younger
son of a gentleman, Quicksilver rebels against the authority of
his flat-cap master, the goldsmith Touchstone, and affects the
fashionable vices of a young gallant, which he supports by
stealing. His master's warning against prodigality recalls the
Biblical parable: "As for you, Master Quicksilver, think of
husks, for thy course is running directly to the prodigal's
hogs' trough; husks, sirrah" (I.i.98–100). His fellow prentice,
the obedient and industrious toady Golding, who betrays his
gentle birth, rises to the position of deputy alderman at the
end of the play and uses his authority to sentence Quicksilver
to jail. Here the play parodies a host of public theater plays—
notably the work of Dekker and Heywood—that end in miraculous conversion, sudden repentance, and instantaneous
contrition. In prison, the proud and hot-blooded Quicksilver
appears to have become a model of Christian humility and
selflessness, although it is clear that he plays the penitent in
order to gain his freedom. Initially skeptical of his former
prentice's "reformation," Touchstone is moved to forgiveness
by Quicksilver's recitation of his *Repentance, or Last Farewell*
in jangling octosyllabic couplets, like the following, sung to
the tune of "I wail in woe, I plunge in pain":

> Farewell, *Cheapside*, farewell sweet trade
> Of Goldsmiths all, that never shall fade:
> Farewell, dear fellow Prentices all,
> And be you warned by my fall.
>   (V.v.113–16)

The ludicrousness of this recitation of pious doggerel, combined with its enthusiastic reception by the bourgeois characters in the play, strongly suggests that Jonson, Chapman, and
Marston were parodying, among other things, one of the
most characteristic features of adult prodigal-son plays and

other works of middle-class homiletic literature—the sudden conversion or repentance and its concomitant rewards.[20]

Middleton appears to be mocking the same tradition not only at the end of *A Trick to Catch the Old One*, as we have already noticed, but in the subplot of *A Mad World, My Masters*, where it has not hitherto been pointed out. The very name of the protagonist of this subplot—Penitent Brothel— suggests the combination of piety and prurience so familiar in popular writing of a morally didactic character, and his self-righteousness, clearly indicated in Middleton's writing, surely invited and received parodic treatment on the stage. True to his name, Penitent Brothel is a lecher with a bad conscience. In his opening speech, he chastises himself for harboring "adulterous motions / And such an appetite that I know damns me, / Yet willingly embrace it" (I.i.94–96). He lusts after Mistress Harebrain, "the citizen's wife," whose husband is so afraid of being cuckolded that he regards all sins but adultery as inconsequential. To preserve his wife's chastity, Harebrain hires watchmen to guard her, contrives various tests for her, and spies upon her himself. Lest bad company lead her into sin, he deprives her of all companions save Lady Gullman, whom he takes to be a virtuous virgin of gentle birth. In fact, she is a courtesan and a bawd, who convinces Mrs. Harebrain to sleep with Penitent Brothel and then helps her do so by delivering a monologue on wifely fidelity for the benefit of the eavesdropping Harebrain, while his wife and Penitent Brothel make love off stage.

In the scenes that follow this tryst, Middleton shrewdly ridicules the facile conversions of many public-theater plays. Once having seduced Mrs. Harebrain, Penitent Brothel worries about the spiritual consequences of his behavior. Although he was aware from the beginning of the play of the sinful nature of his lust, he fails to act on this moral perception until after his desire has been gratified. His morality is little more than post-coital depression refracted as guilt. This phase of the play opens with Penitent Brothel, alone on stage, a book in his hand:

> Ha! Read that place again. "Adultery
> Draws the divorce 'twixt heaven and the soul."
> Accursed man, that stand'st divorced from heaven,
> Thou wretched unthrift, that hast played away
> Thy eternal portion at a minute's game
> To please the flesh.

$$\text{(IV.i.1–6)}$$

Unlike Macbeth or Beatrice-Joanna, who discover moral law by violating it, Penitent Brothel merely feels that sinful pleasures, once they have been enjoyed, no longer seem worth their price. He goes on to castigate himself, asking why he allowed his "nobler meditations" to abandon him to his own carnality. But self-flagellation blends into another familiarly hypocritical response—the debasement of the sexual partner, as he lashes himself for permitting his soul "To dote on weakness, slime, corruption, woman" (IV.i.18).

His resolve to break off with Mrs. Harebrain is immediately tested by the sudden appearance of a Succubus in her shape. Since the same actor must have played both roles, the audience probably needed some visual equivalent of Middleton's stage direction (*"Enter the devil in her shape"*) to help them distinguish the Succubus from the real Mrs. Harebrain, but to Penitent Brothel the distinction seems to be blurred. Because he regards Mrs. Harebrain as the cause of his sin, he has no trouble believing that she is the devil, while the spectators' dual consciousness gives them enough detachment to recognize the Succubus as a hallucinatory projection of his old lust, now congealed into remorse. In his mind, his paramour has become his seducer, and so the Succubus now pursues him with trochaic blandishments, mingled with taunts at his apparent impotence:

> Rouse thy amorous thoughts and twine me;
> All my interest I resign thee.
> . . . Once so firm, and now so hollow?
> When was place and season sweeter?
> Thy bliss in sight, and dar'st not meet her?
> Where's thy courage, youth, and vigor?
> Love's best pleased when't's seized with rigor.
>   (IV.i.46–59)

Striving to preserve his virtue, he finally banishes her by invoking "that soul-quaking thunder," and she *"stamps and exits,"* as the stage direction says, obviously disappointed. To Penitent Brothel, such virtuous resistance to temptation not only confirms his present innocence but *ex post facto* erases his previous sin:

> I am honest.
> When men's intents are wicked, their guilt haunts 'em,
> But when they're just they're armed, and nothing daunts
>   'em.
>   (IV.i.91–93)

To Middleton and his audience, however, this self-congratulatory crowing parodied the whole tradition of facile reformations in public-theater plays. His purity restored, Penitent Brothel first urges Mrs. Harebrain to be faithful to her husband, who has entered unnoticed by them just in time to overhear this request and his wife's vow of chastity. The lovers' contrition and restored purity do not require them to confess their adultery to Harebrain, who, unaware that he has been cuckolded, embraces them both:

Two dear rare gems this hour presents me with,
A wife that's modest, and a friend that's right.
Idle suspect and fear, now take your flight.
                                    (IV.iv.79–81)

The sleazy self-righteousness of Penitent Brothel's repentance, the concealment of the true facts from Harebrain, the
jingling of the couplets, and the sanctimonious senten-
tiousness of the entire action all suggest that Middleton is
parodying a theatrical convention familiar to the spectators
and perhaps the popular morality on which it was based.[21] In
performance these scenes undoubtedly parodied the style in
which adult companies performed plays that made repentance seem both effortless and profitable.

Middleton further parodies such plays in the main action of
A Mad World. In the scene that follows Harebrain's celebration of his "two rare gems," Middleton equates Mrs. Harebrain and Gullman, when the courtesan poses as a bashful
virgin in order to lure the young prodigal Follywit into marriage. Sharing Mrs. Harebrain's and Penitent Brothel's naive
faith in the power of repentance to erase past sins, Gullman's
mother sees this marriage as her daughter's redemption:
"Last, thou'rt made honest" (IV.v.139). However, unlike Harebrain, Follywit does not remain ignorant of his wife's past.
Gullman, he discovers to his momentary chagrin, has until
recently been his grandfather's mistress. Yet the courtesan
shows more courage than the heroine of the subplot, con-
fessing the truth about herself and begging forgiveness:

What I have been is past; be that forgiven,
And have a soul true both to thee and heaven.
                                    (V.ii.259–60)

Follywit has been the victim of a deception, but finds ample consolation in his grandfather's wedding gift of a thousand marks:

> By my troth, she is as good a cup of nectar as any bachelor
>   needs to sup at.
> Tut, give me gold, it makes amends for vice;
> Maids without coin are caudles without spice.
>   (V.ii.265–68)

His casual attitude toward his wife's past contrasts with Harebrain's obsessive fear of being cuckolded, just as the bawdry of the scene and the frankly expressed desire for money are at the opposite pole from the pious moralizing of the subplot, a contrast probably heightened by the use of a more natural style in the main action. Middleton's cynical faith in the power of money to eradicate the stigma of marrying a whore may be as facile as the convention of miraculously restored innocence he is parodying, but it probably pleased spectators who thought of themselves as virile enough to keep the love of a sexually experienced woman, worldly enough to accept hard cash as recompense for the shame of such a match, and sophisticated enough to laugh at the content and style of public-theater plays that preached the ease and profitability of repentance.

Juxtaposition of Styles: Marston's Antonio-Plays

Building on the proposition that the children's audiences were simultaneously aware of child actors and adult characters, I have suggested that the boy companies used three distinct styles which we might think of as segments of a continuum ranging from the least to the most formalized: (1) a natural style—mimicry verging on caricature, (2) a declamatory style—a stately but graceful oratorical style, and (3) a parodic style—a burlesque of the style(s) then or previously used by adult companies. Not only do different plays require different styles, but some plays, such as Middleton's *The Phoenix* and *A Mad World, My Masters,* or Nashe's *Summer's Last Will and Testament,* require two or even three different styles within the same work. In general, playwrights for the children's troupes invited the use of natural and parodic styles for satiric effects and employed the declamatory style to place a respectful distance between audience and action. Jonson's *Poetaster,* for instance, requires all three styles: (1) the natural style for scenes which satirize the fashionable follies of upper-class English life and which lampoon specific individuals like Marston and Dekker; (2) the declamatory style for scenes revolving around Caesar and the court poets—Ovid, Vergil, and Horace; and (3) the parodic style for the parts of III.iv where Tucca's pages burlesque passages from Kyd, Peele, and Chapman, presumably caricaturing the style in which adult troupes performed these works. Adult troupes too may have employed these three styles in a single play. *Hamlet,* for example, asks for a flexible declamatory style that ranges from the Prince's repartee to his meditative soliloquies to Laertes' grave-side ranting, but the gravediggers' scene demands a natural style and the players' speeches, when they are performing, demand a style which parodied the stiffer kind of acting that was old-fashioned by 1600. However, the children's troupes used these styles for somewhat different effects than their adult counterparts did, because of the obvious disparity between child actors and adult characters.

In the two-part Antonio play—*Antonio and Mellida* and *Antonio's Revenge* (Paul's, 1599–1600)—Marston can make particularly interesting use of different acting styles because he first rivets the spectators' attention to the disparity between actor and character. *Antonio and Mellida* opens with an Induction in which the actors appear in their own persons— "with parts in their hands, having cloaks cast over their apparel"—to discuss the roles they will play. Marston reinforces the audience's dual consciousness throughout the play by means of techniques discussed earlier in this chapter. The self-referential imagery that runs through both parts, such as Antonio's address to the "Most wished spectators of my tragedy" (*AM* V.ii.215), his refusal to "swell like a tragedian" (*AR* II.ii.105), or Pandulpho's comparison of himself to "some boy that acts a tragedy" (*AR* IV.ii.71), reminds the audience that it is attending a play and that the action on stage is an illusion created by child actors. The incongruity between the actors' physical immaturity and the characters' adult sexuality is underscored by bawdy details like Flavia's song—a "descant" upon the pages' names, Catzo and Dildo (both Italian for "penis")—or Balurdo's swaggering phallic pride ("As I am true knight, I grow stiff" [*AM* V.ii.260]). A stage direction requiring Balurdo to enter *"with a beard half off, half on"* (*AR* II.i.20.1) calls the audience's attention both to the actor's immaturity and to the artificiality of the action.

The audience's heightened dual consciousness adds an extra dimension to the interplay of the three styles which actually begins in the Induction. When the actors play themselves they must create the illusion that they are not acting but spontaneously exchanging shoptalk, an illusion best served by the natural style. This style must contrast markedly with the style(s) the actors use for those parts of the Induction where they step briefly into character. The actor playing Piero, who confesses "we are ignorant in what mold we must cast our actors," is instructed to use a style that parodies the type of acting found at the Globe:

Alberto: O, ho; then thus frame your exterior shape
   To haughty form of elate majesty. . . .
Piero: If that be all, fear not, I'll suit it right.
   Who cannot be proud, stroke up the hair and strut?
Alberto: Truth. Such rank custom is grown popular;
   And now the vulgar fashion strides as wide
   And stalks as proud upon the weakest stilts
   Of the slight'st fortunes as if Hercules
   Or burly Atlas shoulder'd up their state.

Similarly, the actor playing Matzagente, "a modern Brago-
doch," uses a style that parodies the one used by Edward
Alleyn in Marlowe's plays:

Matzagente: By the bright honor of a Milanoise,
   And the resplendent fulgor of this steel,
   I will defend the feminine to death,
   And ding his spirit to the verge of hell
   That dares divulge a lady's prejudice.
Feliche: Rampum scrampum, mount tufty Tamburlaine!
   What rattling thunderclap breaks from his lips?

Other actors seem to use a declamatory rather than a parodic
style. The actor playing Feliche gives "a draught of his spirit,"
a sample of "the old cut," when he describes his character as
being "so impregnably fortressed with his own content that
no envious thought could ever invade his spirit." The actor
playing Antonio is baffled not only by the Amazonian disguise
he must wear, but by the sudden emotional changes his part
requires:

   sometimes he must . . . possess his exterior presence
   with a formal majesty, keep popularity in distance; and
   on the sudden fling his honor so prodigally into a common arm that he may seem to give up his indiscretion to
   the mercy of vulgar censure.

The contrast between "formal majesty" and "common arm" suggests a shuttling between declamatory and natural styles to indicate Antonio's mercurial temperament. Generally, however, the Induction uses the natural style as a background against which the actors can display the parodic or declamatory styles demanded by their roles.

A word of caution is in order. In the Induction, as in the play itself, it is not always possible to know when declamation is so exaggerated that it becomes parodic. This is precisely the problem that has bedeviled critics of Marston's early work. Conservative critics prefer not to speak of a parodic acting style unless there is also evidence of verbal parody. In the Antonio plays, we have enough references to old-fashioned public-theater plays like *The Spanish Tragedy* (c.1587) and *Titus Andronicus* (c.1592–94) to indicate some parodic intention on Marston's part. Going a step further, R. A. Foakes suggests that virtually all passages of passionate rhetoric in the Antonio plays are ironic, and hence were acted in a parodic style, because such passages are either inflated, unrelated to the action, or undermined by farce. Most critics object to Marston's inconsistency or unevenness of texture. T. S. Eliot thought him dissatisfied with his medium, Ornstein called him incompetent, and Schoenbaum dismissed him as unbalanced. G. K. Hunter, however, has proposed that Marston resembles a modern absurdist in using the discontinuities in his work to reflect the discontinuities of life.[22] Indeed, these plays begin to seem less bizarre once we analyze the effects created by the juxtaposition of contrasting styles.

For whatever it is worth, Marston describes his intentions in the ironical dedication to "the most honorably renowned Nobody" that appeared in the 1602 quarto of *Antonio and Mellida*, published about two years after its initial production. Here Marston nonchalantly dismisses the play as "the worthless present of my slighter idleness," and confesses that "it hath flowed with the current of my humorous blood to affect (a little too much) to be seriously fantastical." In the context of humorousness and affectation, the most likely meaning of "fantastical" is "fanciful, impulsive, capricious, arbitrary" (*OED*, "fantastic" 4b), and it is this cluster of adjectives that also seems to describe the play's many sudden and surprising discontinuities. Moreover, the adverb "seriously" suggests that these discontinuities were deliberate and that Marston meant to do more than evoke gales of derisive laughter by mocking the tired war horses of the public theaters. While the play includes parodic elements, they seem to be part of a larger pattern of abrupt shifts in tone and style, and must therefore have been set off by contrasting elements. Performing the entire play in a parodic style, as Foakes suggests was done, would have reduced it all to farce, whereas Marston's aim was evidently to evoke a mixture of responses by combining elements of parody, Lylyesque comedy, "comical satire," slapstick, romantic comedy, and revenge tragedy. In theory, if not in practice, the total effect was to keep the audience off-balance, to dazzle it with contraries, to evoke amazement and wonder at the dramatist's novelty and virtuosity.

Assuming that the Children of Paul's were faithful to Marston's intentions, the mosaic of contrasting elements in the writing would have called for a mosaic of contrasting styles in performance. Whereas writers like Middleton and Jonson required different styles to delineate separate lines of action, Marston chose to juxtapose contrasting elements of tone and style at every level of the two-part play.

At the grossest level, the contrasting Prologues to the two parts of the play signal an abrupt change of direction; whereas the Lylyesque Prologue to *Antonio and Mellida* begs the indulgence of the "select and most respected auditors" for the trifle they are about to see, the Prologue to *Antonio's Revenge* challenges spectators "uncapable of weighty passion" to "hurry amain from our black-visaged shows." As the opening of *Antonio's Revenge* demonstrates, the reconciliations that ended part one in the conventional and satisfying manner of a romantic comedy could not restrain Piero's murderous ambitions. We learn, in fact, that Piero's forgiveness was feigned, that we had been deceived, and that the submerged "tragic idiom" of part one had been prophetic.[23] But we learn this primarily through the grotesque visual spectacle that opens the play: *"Enter Piero unbraced, his arms bare, smeared in blood, a poniard in one hand, bloody, and a torch in the other, Strotzo following him with a cord."* After this gory tableau, the first of several in *Antonio's Revenge*, we hear Piero exulting over the murders of Feliche and Andrugio, presumably in the exaggeratedly stiff "strutting" style described in the Induction. However comically parodic this style may have been, Piero's repeated references to "these hands" and "this warm reeking gore"—both visible to the spectators—inhibit the simple enjoyment of theatrical burlesque. But the horror of this spectacle and Piero's macabre celebration of his butchery contrast with the music-hall comedy routine that emerges within a dozen lines, when Strotzo tries unsuccessfully to break into Piero's monologue. Piero first ignores Strotzo's attempts to speak, then urges him to talk, scolds him for being incoherent, apologizes by begging him to utter his thoughts, bullies him into answering questions with no more than "yes" and "no," and finally chastises him for his reticence. For a final contrast, the scene ends with Piero's tenderly poetic description of the dawn:

> For see, the dapple-gray coursers of the morn
> Beat up the light with their bright silver hooves
> And chase it through the sky

followed by a renewal of his dedication to revenge:

> To bed, to bed!
> This morn my vengeance shall be amply fed.

The tensions among the grisly tableau, Piero's vengeful and bloody tyranny, the parodic acting style, the vaudeville comedy routine, and the imagistic lyricism are irreconcilable. The contrasting elements coexist rather than fuse, and similar effects, with these and other elements, are created by the discontinuities and incongruous juxtapositions that abound throughout the two-part play.

The next scene, for example, opens with Lucio's gallant attempt to comfort the noble widow Maria in stately blank verse, which is interrupted by Nutriche's report—in vigorous and earthy prose—of her dream of the joys of her wedding night. As Antonio and the courtiers enter, the scene modulates with Antonio's lyrical evocation of the dawn, followed by some coarse jesting involving Matzagente's nose and Balurdo's pretentiousness. Antonio then takes 24 lines of blank verse to describe an ominous dream of two ghosts clamoring for revenge, after which Balurdo reports his dream of "the abominable ghost of a misshapen Simile." Castilio and Galeatzo "salute the bride" by singing "one of Signor Renaldo's airs," and Maria and Antonio are reunited in a page or more of stately blank verse, before Antonio directs our attention to the curtain covering Mellida's window, which is drawn to discover not Antonio's "bright-cheeked love" but another grisly tableau—"the body of Feliche, stabbed thick with wounds." And so it goes.

This scene and a half (like the entire two-part work) requires the three acting styles we have isolated—natural, declamatory, and parodic—as contrasting elements in a constantly changing pattern. Any one style is set off against the other two, as well as against details of action, spectacle, and dialogue. Looking at the two-part work as a whole rather than at specific scenes, one can make some further observation about the use of the three acting styles.

The work demands the natural style for most of the anticourt scenes—that is, for the episodes revolving around Catzo and Dildo, the sharp-tongued Rossaline, or the self-styled social critic Feliche. Most of this satire ridicules the foolishness of the social-climbing bumpkin, Balurdo, and the extravagant manners and diction of courtiers like Castilio Balthazar, whose name reminds us of the author of *The Courtier*, Baldesar Castiglione. But the most unusual occasion for the use of the natural style occurs immediately after the lovers recognize one another in twelve lines of balanced and highly structured Italian verse. Although enough lines end with "Mellida" and "Antonio" to make the point of the scene clear to an English audience, Marston has Antonio's page step out of character to comment on the passage directly to the audience:

> I think confusion of Babel is fall'n upon these lovers, that they change their language. . . . But howsoever, if I should sit in judgment, 'tis an error easier to be pardoned by the auditors' than excused by the author's; and yet some private respect may rebate the edge of the keener censure.
>
> (*AM* IV.i.219–27)

As the natural style was the norm for the Induction, so the declamatory style is the norm for the dramatic action proper. In a play acted by children, this style is a tacit admission of the disparity between actor and character, makes the performance more representational than mimetic, and so affords the audience an extra degree of detachment from the action.

Like a Brechtian "alienation effect," it is useful when a playwright wishes the spectators to observe what is happening on stage with critical detachment. In the Antonio-plays, the declamatory style is especially appropriate for the many passages where characters expound their philosophical principles: Andrugio commits himself both to heroic and honorable action, as well as to a stoic endurance of adversity; Feliche asserts his contentment; Pandulpho explains his refusal to grieve for his murdered son; and Antonio swears allegiance to revenge.

The suspicion of an over-all parodic style is strong not only because of the disparity between actor and character, but also because of such broad, comic episodes as Pandulpho's imitating Kyd's Hieronymo or the stage tyrant Piero's boasting of his success and then quickly lapsing into incoherence or Italian. Marston was clearly not above cadging a few laughs at the expense of the adult players, but I think he resisted that temptation more than he is given credit for doing. Rather than mock his characters outright, he prefers to make a subtler point by dramatizing the collapse of their philosophical attitudes under the pressure of life. Thus, Andrugio's heroics lead to his grandly futile if not suicidal surrender, while his stoic principles break down the moment his servant mentions his troubles; the "content" Feliche erupts in a fit of jealous violence; Pandulpho discovers that "man will break out despite philosophy" (*AR* IV.ii.69) and forsakes stoicism for revenge; while the chief revenger Antonio emerges as another Piero, exulting over the blood of the innocent in a tableau that underlines his resemblance to the tyrant: "*Enter* Antonio, *his arms bloody, a torch and a poniard*" (*AR* III.ii.75.1–2). Moreover, the spectators' detachment would allow them to see the murders of Julio and Piero, not as the acts of ritual retribution that Antonio wants to make them but as deeds of sadistic slaughter.

As several recent critics have argued, in dramatizing the collapse of these attitudes, Marston reveals the inadequacy of the vision of life embodied in revenge tragedy, as he does with respect to romantic comedy, "comical satire," and other conventionalized representations of life.[24]

In short, Marston's studied capriciousness led him to use style as one of the many ways to complicate his audience's responses and to evoke wonder at the virtuosity that could create a work that is constantly surprising. Like all dramaturgical tactics, it had to be discarded when audiences learned to anticipate it, though not all critics agree that Marston achieved a greater consistency of tone in his subsequent plays. There, for better or worse, we find less straining to be "seriously fantastical," and hence less likelihood of juxtaposition of styles in performance.

In arguing that the children's troupes had as wide a range of possible acting styles as adult troupes, I hope I have not blurred certain crucial distinctions between the two kinds of companies. While both men and boys exploited the audience's dual consciousness and juxtaposed different styles, the children's troupes did so more often and for specific effects. In using the formal style they hoped to forestall mockery by tacitly admitting the disparity between actors and characters; in using the natural style, they hoped to deflect ridicule toward "others"—stock character types and real individuals; in using a parodic style, they hoped to deflect ridicule toward their own earlier plays, sacrificial parts of their own current plays, and plays performed by adult troupes; and in juxtaposing styles they succeeded in creating unusual effects and keeping their audience off balance. For the boy companies, acting style was intimately related to the entire theatrical occasion. It helped their spectators maintain the flattering illusion that they were participants in an aristocratic ritual, and it could also help the troupe defend itself and its plays against the ridicule which spectators felt obliged to offer because of their status and the festal tradition which lay behind the children's plays.

CHAPTER FIVE

The Plays (1)

AGAINST the background of the preceding chapters, we can now survey the repertories of the children's troupes. The repertories fall into two distinct phases. The later phase begins with the resumption of playing by the Paul's boys in 1596 or 1597 and by the Chapel Children in 1600 and ends with the extinction of the companies around 1607 and 1613, respectively. For this brief period, we have an abundance of texts and documents to help us analyze the repertories, and we shall do so in the next chapter. The earlier phase, our present concern, is much longer, beginning with the obscure origins of the children's troupes at the early Tudor court and ending around 1591, when the government evidently ordered the boy companies to cease playing. For this first phase, we have very few texts, but with the help of titles, records of the Revels Office, and fragments of documentary evidence, we can form some hypotheses about the four kinds of plays which the leading London children's troupes performed most often in this period: (1) plays influenced by debates, pageants, and other quasidramatic forms of court entertainment, (2) plays derived from Roman comedy, (3) plays about pathetic-heroines derived from Euripides and Seneca, and (4) Lyly's sophisticated comedies for the court and private theaters. Although this survey begins with early Tudor court revelry and ends with Lyly's work of the 1580s and early 1590s, I do not wish to regard these four categories as discrete phases in an evolutionary pattern, but to stress the tendency toward greater complexity and sophistication within each category.

Court Entertainment

Debates, pageants, and other quasidramatic forms of court revelry are not plays, but are worth considering because they indicate the range of the children's theatrical activities and because some playwrights made dramaturgical use of these materials. Participation by children's troupes in these quasi-dramatic entertainments began with the Chapel Children at the court of Henry VII and Henry VIII. According to Hall's account, one of the earliest recorded entertainments, *The Dialogue of Love and Riches* (1527), was little more than a debate used to introduce jousting at barriers:

> eight of the king's Chapel [entered] with a song and brought with them one richly appareled: and in likewise at the other side, entered eight other of the said Chapel bringing with them another person, likewise appareled, these two persons played a dialogue the effect whereof was whether riches were better than love, and when they could not agree upon a conclusion, each called in three knights, all armed; three of them would have entered the gate of the Arch in the middle of the chamber, & the other iii. resisted. . . .[1]

In the early sixteenth century, adult troupes performed plays by humanist playwrights like Medwall and Rastell, in which characters argued opposing positions on such topics as the meaning of true nobility, but formal debate is more prevalent in plays acted by children's companies. Although such fare appealed to educated audiences, it was not practical for professional adult troupes, whose livelihood came chiefly from cluded a debate or trial, probably before the "senate house" supplied by the Revels Office.[2] As late as 1601, the Children of Paul's or the Chapel Children performed *The Contention between Liberality and Prodigality*, which included a formal debate between Prodigality and Fortune before Fortune's throne.

Some of these debates and debate-scenes involved elements of visual spectacle, although the children's participation in court pageantry did not always involve disputation. According to Hall's account a dozen "children of honor," undoubtedly the Chapel Children, figured prominently in the triumphs of Shrovetide, 1511:

> The morrow being the xiii. day of February after dinner, at time convenient, the Queen with the ladies repaired to see the Jousts, the trumpets blew up, and in came many a noble man and Gentleman, richly appareled, . . . they and their horses in cloth of gold and russet tinsel: Knights in cloth of gold, and russet Velvet. And a great number of Gentlemen on foot, in russet satin and yellow, and yeomen in russet Damask and yellow, all the nether part of every man's hosen Scarlet, and yellow caps. Then came the king under a Pavilion of cloth of gold, and purple Velvet embroidered, and powdered with H. and K. of fine gold. . . . After followed his three aides, every of them under a Pavilion of Crimson damask & purple powdered with H. and K. of fine gold, valenced and fringed with gold of damask: on the top of every Pavilion a great K. of goldsmith's work; the number of the Gentlemen and yeomen attendant a foot, appareled in russet and yellow was C. lxviii. Then next these Pavilions came xii. children of honor [Children of the Chapel], sitting every of them on a great courser, richly trapped and embroidered in several devices and fashions, where lacked neither [em]broidery nor goldsmith's work, so that every

entertaining popular audiences in inn-yards, market-pl&
and eventually the public theaters.

The Chapel Children or some other children's troupe
formed Heywood's *Play of the Weather* (pub. 1533), whic
essentially a succession of formal pleas and disputations
fore Jupiter's throne, whereas Heywood's farces were pr
bly performed by smaller adult professional companies. In
first half of Elizabeth's reign, several children's troupes
formed plays which were often constructed around such
bate topics as the meaning of true friendship and which
up to climactic scenes of formal disputation. At the clima:
Edwardes' *Damon and Pythias,* for instance, Pythias orates
friendship to Dionysius and his court, thanking the g
"That they have reserved me to this passing great honor, /
die for my friend, whose faith, even now, I do not mistru
(ll. 1994–95). Before Dionysius can have him executed, h
ever, "entereth Damon running & stays the sword" (l. 202
and the two friends debate each other for the honor of s
sacrifice in the name of friendship. Such use of formal deb
seems to have been a tradition for the children's troupe
From versions of the story of Titus and Gisippus in Boccac
and Elyot, we suspect that the lost play about those tv
friends (Paul's, 1577) included another public debate
friendship, probably before the "two forms for the Senator
provided by the Revels Office. Other lost plays suggest a sin
lar use of debate scenes: *Ajax and Ulysses* (Windsor, 1571–7
was undoubtedly derived from the debate in Book XIII
Ovid's *Metamorphoses, Quintus Fabius* (Windsor, 1573–7
seems to be the story Livy tells (VIII.3–35) of Quintus' tri
before the Roman Senate in which he tried to justify his di:
obedience of authority, *Loyalty and Beauty* (Chapel, 1578–7'
was probably a debate on the claims or merits of the value
paired in the title, and *Pompey* (Paul's, 1581) evidently in

child & horse in device and fashion was contrary to other,
which was goodly to behold.[3]

Hall is describing a triumph—a procession of wagons or
chariots covered with canopies, a series of tableaux passing
before a stationary audience, as in our own float parades.
Children also participated in the opposite type of pageant, in
which a moving audience encounters tableaux placed along
its route. This second type of pageant was used well into the
seventeenth century for coronations, welcoming of distinguished visitors, and annual Lord Mayors' Shows, and
frequently involved schoolboys and choristers dressed in appropriate costumes and mounted on temporary platforms as
musicians, singers, orators, mute emblematic figures, or ex-
pounders of the allegory. Although adults sometimes appeared in these stationary pageants, children were generally
preferred for being less likely to crowd a scaffold or jeopar-
dize its stability. Children's troupes continued to appear in
such pageants even after they began offering plays at court
and "rehearsing" these plays in their own private theaters.

Lyly's plays, as G. K. Hunter has argued, absorbed a great
deal from both formal disputation and the court pageant.
Their debate-topic themes, flattering royal figures, mythological ornamentation, and emblematic staging clearly grew out
of a tradition of conventional court entertainment, but Lyly
molded these disparate elements into a coherent dramatic
pattern. More instructive for our purposes is *The Arraignment
of Paris* (Chapel, 1581–84), where Peele failed to unify these
same elements and so produced a series of discrete shows.
Critics who approach this work as a masque rather than a play
have argued persuasively for its integrity as a political allegory: the prelapsarian golden world destroyed by the Trojan
War is reestablished by Elizabeth, the ruler of the second

Troy. Critics who approach *The Arraignment* as a play, on the
other hand, regard it as a farrago of traditional forms of
courtly or aristocratic entertainment.[4] Peele offers, for example, mythological pageants like the opening scene, in
which the country gods and attendants carrying appropriate
offerings assemble to welcome the three Olympian Goddesses. The same scene includes Pallas' show, in which nine
knights in armor march to drum and fife and "tread a warlike
almain," a wealth of legalistic disputation and formal oratory,
and spectacular stage effects like Juno's rising and sinking
Tree of Gold, or the storm, perhaps created by the same "device in counterfeiting Thunder and Lightning" supplied to the
Revels Office for the lost play *Narcissus* (Chapel, 1571–72).[5]
The variety of metrical forms emphasizes the discrete quality
of the separate episodes, many of which contain or lead up to
songs or such complex musical effects as songs in Latin and
Italian, an artificial charm of birds, echo songs, and divided
choruses.

This aggregation of conventional ingredients provides a
great deal of variety of tone and mode, enriching parallels and
contrasts, and agreeable diversions from the narrative line,
but it offers little dramaturgical preparation for the final climactic scene, which is based on a static motif used often in
pageants and painting.[6] Here Diana offers the golden ball in-
scribed with the words *"Detur Pulcherrimae"* to her alter ego,
the real Queen Elizabeth, while Juno, Pallas, and Venus look
on approvingly, their identifying attributes selected as carefully as in a Jonsonian masque and perhaps with the aid of the
same mythographers. This emblematic tableau is followed by
another, in which the three Fates surrender to Elizabeth their
distaff, thread, and knife, so symbolizing her superiority to
the destiny of ordinary mortals. In short, the work's inadequa-
cies as a drama allow us to see even more clearly than do

Lyly's better unified works the influence of heterogeneous
court entertainments on the children's plays. A few adult
plays like *The Rare Triumphs of Love and Fortune* (Derby's
Men, 1582), also show this influence, but adult companies
generally transferred or adapted plays written primarily for
public-theater audiences when they played before the
Queen, whereas the children's troupes—especially before
1591—were offering their private theater spectators a preview
of, or vicarious participation in, the season's court revelry.

Fashions in entertainment as in all else must of necessity
constantly change. In the Prologue to *Midas* Lyly finds the
world "so nice . . . that for apparel there is no fashion, . . .
for plays no invention, but breedeth satiety before noon, and
contempt before night." Yet Lyly defied such contempt in *The
Woman in the Moon* (c.1590–95). Probably though not certainly acted by a children's troupe (no acting company was
mentioned in the *Stationers' Register* in 1595 or on the title
page of the 1597 quarto), it is more like a pageant or series of
shows than any of his other works and is the only one written
almost completely in verse.[7] In the opening scene, Nature
enters "with her two maidens, Concord and Discord," promising to reconcile their differences. Four shepherds "all clad
in Skins" enter and kneel before her to beg "A sure and certain means among ourselves, / To propagate the issue of our
kind" (I.i.41–42). Nature agrees to grant this request and they
leave the stage, "singing a roundelay in praise of Nature." Nature then orders her "virgins" to create a woman, with attributes from each of the planets, who complain that they have
been robbed of their "ornaments." After Nature overrules
their objections and leaves the stage, they plan one at a time
to exert their dominion over Pandora. The remainder of the
play fills in this design. Each of the planets in turn assumes his
place on an elevated playing area and announces the nature

of his influence, while the action below revolves around Pandora and illustrates her melancholy, disdain, churlishness, gentleness, amorousness, deceitfulness, or fickleness. While some of the middle episodes involve considerable intrigue on the human level, the bulk of the play preserves "its statuesque mode of tableau presentation," [8] and Lyly concludes the series of shows with a formal debate between Nature and the Seven Planets.

Into this sequence of animated pageantry, Lyly has inserted Gunophilus, Pandora's comic servant, who uses a coarse and bawdy prose and even speaks directly to the audience of "good people" (III.ii.208). His earthy presence is an implicit reminder of the artificiality of the play's mythological shows. Whatever the date and auspices of this play, Gunophilus represents Lyly's awareness that some spectators could be invited to laugh at the artificiality of court entertainment. As we shall see in the following chapter, the children's troupes often elicited mockery of their own work even in the period of their greatest success.

By the time Nashe wrote *Summer's Last Will and Testament* (1592), he could invite the audience to mock the kind of play which Lyly and Peele had so ingeniously assembled out of the traditional forms of court entertainment.[9] Will Summer scoffs that the pageant-like main action of the work is "no Play neither, but a show" (l. 75), and elicits and channels the audience's ridicule toward each tableau-like episode in turn. The first episode, for example, begins with the dignified entrance of Summer, Autumn, and Winter "attended with a train of Satyrs and Wood-Nymphs, singing" (l. 104), but when the satyrs and nymphs leave the stage after the song, Will Summer comments: "A couple of pretty boys, if they would wash their faces, and were well breeched an hour or two. . . . But let us hear what Summer can say for himself, why he should not be hissed at" (ll. 117–22). Will Summer interrupts or punctuates each processional episode with this sort of ridicule. When Sol, who enters "very richly attired, with a noise of Musicians before him" (l. 443), goes off stage after a long declamatory dialogue, Will shatters the illusion: "I think the Sun is not so long in passing through the twelve signs, as the son of a fool hath been disputing here about had I wist . . ." (ll. 583–85). The same treatment is accorded to Solstitium, who enters "like an aged Hermit, carrying a pair of balances, with an hourglass in either of them . . . brought in by a number of shepherds, playing upon Recorders" (l. 360). In sententious blank verse, he and Summer solemnly discuss the importance of maintaining a "just proportion" in all things, after which Will cracks: "Fye, fye, of honesty, fye: Solstitium is an ass, perdy; this play is a gallimaufry; fetch me some drink, somebody" (ll. 421–23).

Perhaps because of changing fashions, perhaps because of the closing of the private theaters around 1591, Elizabethan drama of the late 1580s and early 1590s assimilated elements of court entertainment that had retained more of their distinctive qualities in children's plays by Peele and Lyly. There is already a movement toward such assimilation in Nashe's and Marlowe's Dido (Chapel, c.1585–88), which unobtrusively includes mythographic details of classical deities, their wrangling disputations, and spectacular stage effects like the storm and the funeral pyre. Some of these effects seem to have become conventions in children's plays. Like the storm, the hunting scene was used in Narcissus, where it was enlivened, so the Revels Accounts tell us, by realistic offstage sound effects—"hounds, horns, and hallowing." [10] The producers of Narcissus were apparently imitating Richard Edwardes' lost play, Palomon and Arcite (Cambridge, 1566), which made a great impression on Elizabeth and her entourage during a visit to the university. Edwardes also used a funeral pyre, probably created by torches held below an open trap door, which we shall encounter again in *Dido*. In some ways, *Dido* was a harbinger, for when the private theaters reopened in the late 1590s, playwrights had learned how to create theatrical spectacles by weaving debates, masques, royal processions, ritualized combat into the design of their work.

New New Comedy and Prodigal-Son Plays

In chapter 1 we noticed that under the early Tudors, troupes of grammar school boys frequently performed comedies by Terence and Plautus at court or before Wolsey and Cromwell. Like university students and even some professional adult troupes, they began around mid-century to perform English plays written on the model of Roman comedy. *Jack Juggler* (c.1553–58), described on the title page as "a New Interlude for Children to play," is a reworking of Plautus' *Amphitruo*, while Jeffere's *The Bugbears* (c.1563–65), whose Epilogue refers to the actors as "we boys," shows the influence of Roman comedy filtered through Italian *commedia erudita*. Some of the children's plays of this type, however, reflect concern for the special talents of the boy actors.

Udall's *Ralph Roister Doister*, loosely based on Plautus' *Miles Gloriousus*, requires a large cast—ten or twelve actors are onstage during the battle scene, of which four are female characters, two are boys, and four are the members of Ralph's entourage who also serve as musicians (perhaps playing the lute, recorder, and gitterne mentioned in II.i). The musical effects in the play are rather complex. Dame Custance's servants sing twice in I.iii, and in I.iv one of them dances while Ralph's servants sing and play. In II.iii Ralph's page joins Dame Custance's page and two of her maids in a song that celebrates the harmonious union of the two households. Shortly after the mock requiem of III.iii, Ralph and his musicians perform "I mun be married a Sunday," while Ralph's "choir" sings a concluding song whose lyrics are lost. Dramatically as well as musically, Udall has divided the dramatis personae into two groups—Ralph and his entourage, and Dame Custance and her friends and servants, a division which leads to the zestful brawl in Act IV, where the two groups assemble behind "two drums with their ensigns." Ralph's military manner, his headpiece improvised from a kitchen pot, and the complete rout of his troops at the hands of their female adversaries suggest a possible burlesque of the ritualized combats of court entertainment.

Udall's inclusion of so many diminutive pages and maidservants is a departure from the Roman model, perhaps intended to replace wily slaves and seductive courtesans in Terence and Plautus. Whether or not Udall was the first to use these witty servants in this way, other writers of children's plays followed suit. The servants in *Jacob and Esau* (1550–57) and in Jeffere's *The Bugbears* prefigure the scenes in plays by Edwardes and Lyly, to mention only sixteenth-century playwrights, where pert, cheeky maids and pages ridicule and parody the attitudes and behavior of their betters. In Lyly's *Mother Bombie* (Paul's, 1587–90) these servants totally dominate the play.

The children's troupes of the sixteenth century also performed a number of plays derived from the "Christian Terence" tradition, particularly from the adaptations of the prodigal-son parable (Luke 15:11–32) to contemporary school life made by Gnapheus, Macropedius, and Textor.[11] In all of these plays, one or more naive, impressionable youth is deflected from the path of virtue into a life of riotous sin— represented dramatically by gambling, drinking, whoring, and—God help us—singing. Usually, the prodigal son sees his folly in time to repent and to be forgiven, but some plays omit the final stage of restoration to grace, and those plays having several prodigal-son figures punish some but reward others. One characteristic of this type of play is respect for authority—not only of sovereigns and magistrates, but also of schoolmasters and parents. The following speech by the Perorator of Ingelond's *The Disobediant Child* (c.1558–69) typifies the orthodoxy of these plays in tone and in its use of the biblical proverb—"He that spareth his rod hateth his son" (Proverbs 13:24), here attributed to Solomon and rendered in Latin for added weight:

> Wherefore take heed all ye that be parents
> And follow a part after my counsel,
> Instruct your Children and make them students
> That unto all goodness they do not rebel
> Remember what writeth Solomon the wise,
> *Qui parcit Virgae, odith filium.*
>   Therefore for as much as ye can devise
> Spare not the Rod, but follow wisdom.
>
>   (sig. C4ᵛ)

Playwrights for children's troupes not only dramatized the prodigal-son parable along Terentian lines, as Gascoigne did in *The Glass of Government* (1575), but also grafted it on to other biblical stories, as in *Jacob and Esau,* and blended it with morality plays, as in *The Nice Wanton* or *The Disobediant Child,* where the prodigal stands for all men and his corrupt companions for their vices. Adult troupes of the mid-sixteenth century occasionally performed a prodigal-son play, such as Fulwell's *Like Will to Like* (1558–68), also blended with morality techniques, but children's companies seem to have produced most of the extant plays of this type.

Although Roman comedies were presented before Henry VIII, we have no evidence that any of the later English plays derived from Terence and Plautus were ever performed at court. Because of Udall's reputation as a court entertainer under Mary, scholars have argued that *Ralph Roister Doister* was acted for her amusement by Udall's pupils from the Westminster grammar school, where he was headmaster from 1553 to 1556. But one can just as easily assign the play to his Eton period (1534–41), and while the Eton boys performed an unnamed play before Cromwell in 1538, we have no evidence that *Ralph Roister Doister* was that play. Some scholars list *Jacob and Esau*, *The Nice Wanton*, and *The Disobediant Child* as court plays merely because they end with prayers for Queen Elizabeth.[12] A recited or sung prayer for the sovereign and her councilors ends most court plays, but one also finds them appended to moral interludes printed for sale to schoolmasters and professional players for possible production under a variety of auspices but not necessarily at court. Such editions are clearly texts to be used, rather than records of past productions. The title pages advertise the plays as suitable for performance and often show schemes for doubling parts. Had these plays been performed at court, surely the title pages would proclaim that fact, as in the 1571 quarto of *Damon and Pythias*, which offers Edwardes' play as "newly imprinted, as the same was showed before the Queen's Majesty, by the Children of her Grace's Chapel, except the Prologue that is somewhat altered for the proper use of them that hereafter shall have occasion to play it, either in Private, or open Audience." The last song, really a prayer for "most noble Queen Elizabeth," is left in the text for subsequent performances. Printers of plays offered for sale to theatrical producers would have been foolish to include a prayer for the ruler that could only be used at a court performance. These prayers do not in themselves justify listing a play as a court production, for they appear to have been as much of a ritual between 1550 and 1580 as playing "God Save the Queen" is in English theaters today.

Although it is clear from title-page statements and the numbers of actors required that *Jacob and Esau, The Nice Wanton,* and *The Disobediant Child* were intended for children's troupes, they were probably performed, if at all, by pupils of provincial grammar schools rather than by the London schoolboy and chorister troupes who brought plays to court each Christmas. By Elizabeth's reign, these London children's troupes began to produce plays primarily for the entertainment of the Queen and her courtiers, and only secondarily as academic exercises. These particular companies—the Merchant Taylors' Boys, the Children of Paul's, and the Children of the Chapel Royal—developed their own private theaters and became more and more commercialized as the sixteenth century drew to a close. One must respect the distinction between plays which these children's troupes performed at court and plays which other children's troupes may have performed before their schoolmates and parents. The evidence reveals surprisingly little overlap. Except for Latin versions of Plautus and Terence, performed at court as late as 1564, when the Westminster schoolboys played Plautus' *Miles Gloriosus* and perhaps Terence's *Heautontimorumenus* before Elizabeth, none of the plays mentioned in this section—including *Ralph Roister Doister*—can be labeled with any confidence as a court play. Moreover, those few children's plays which blend Roman comedy, the prodigal-son play, and morality-play elements hardly seem suited to court performance. Their didactic tone, their advice to parents and children both, suggest performance under scholastic auspices, and their vaguely defined urban or academic settings offer little opportunity for the kind of visual spectacle that court audiences often expected.

The major London children's troupes, however, did not avoid moral interludes altogether—merely those derived from the "Christian Terence" tradition. Some of their moral interludes are extant—Redford's *Wit and Science* (Paul's, 1530–48), its revised version entitled *The Marriage of Wit and Science* (Paul's, 1567–68) and *The Contention between Liberality and Prodigality* (Paul's?, 1567–68).[13] The Revels Accounts also indicate some lost plays of the same type—*Truth, Faithfulness, and Mercy* (Westminster choirboys, 1573–74), *The History of Error* (Paul's, 1576–77), and *The Marriage of Mind and Measure* (Paul's, 1578–79). The extant moral interludes acted by children's troupes at court are very similar to plays of the same type brought to court by adult troupes, for whom this type of play was a more regular offering.

Neoclassic comedies, prodigal-son plays, and moral interludes influenced by the "Christian Terence" tradition never gained a foothold in the repertories of the leading London children's troupes. Partially as a result of this failure, English drama felt the wave of humanist influence without being totally swamped by it. Literary historians usually credit the professional adult troupes with saving English drama from the rigidities of neoclassicism and didacticism, but perhaps one ought to grant a portion of that honor to the London children's troupes who performed at court far more often than the adult troupes did in the first half of Elizabeth's reign. It is difficult to measure the influence of court plays on the development of English drama, but in Italy, by contrast, where the purveyors of theatrical entertainment to the courts and aristocracy favored neoclassical forms of comedy, written stage comedy was stunted for the next hundred years. The children's troupes directed by Mulcaster, Westcote, and Ferrant

barely acknowledged the revival of interest in Plautus and
Terence and completely rejected the "Christian Terence" tradition. Roman comedy and "Christian Terence" held no more
appeal for the children's troupes after their resumption of
playing in the late 1590s. Only Jonson's *The Case is Altered*
(Chapel, 1600–8),[14] a *"contaminatio"* of Plautus' *Captivi* and
Aulularia, and Chapman's *All Fools,* a blend of Terence's
Heautontimorumenus and *Adelphi,* descend directly from the
Latin comic playwrights. The influence of *commedia erudita*
appears only in Chapman's *May Day,* derived from Piccolo-
mini's *Allessandro,* and in Marston's *What You Will,* which is
partially based on Sforza D'Oddi's *I Morti Vivi.* The children's
prodigal-son plays by Middleton, Barry, Jonson, and Fletcher
would have shocked the sober schoolmasters who created
the "Christian Terence" to warn youths of the perils of the
world and the flesh.

Christian Seneca and Pathetic-Heroine Plays
Euripides, Seneca, and the "Christian Seneca" tradition, on
the other hand, had a considerable influence on the repertories of the leading children's troupes of London in the middle of the sixteenth century. The most popular plays of the
two classical authors seem to have been those with female
protagonists—Phaedra, Jocasta, Iphigenia, Alcestis, Medea—
and these works inspired a large number of neoclassical
tragedies about Sophonisba, Dido, Cleopatra, and other ancient heroines. All but one of Giraldi Cinthio's tragedies and
tragicomedies take their titles from a female protagonist.[15]
Among the protagonists of the earliest French classicial tragedies are Cleopatra, Dido, and Sophonisba. In the 1540s, after
adapting *Alcestis* and *Medea,* George Buchanan of Guinne
College in Bordeaux wrote two Latin plays—*Baptistes* and
Jephthes—the latter about the judge of Israel who sacrificed

his beloved daughter (Judges XI). German schoolmasters were particularly fond of writing tragedies about biblical heroines like Susanna and Judith. The popularity of female protagonists in the "Christian Seneca" tradition may also result from the scholastic auspices of so many of these productions, schoolboy-actors finding such roles more congenial than heroic male roles like Oedipus and Hercules.

English humanist dramatists perpetuated this tendency. As we noted in chapter 1, Radcliffe's pupils at Hitchen performed lost Latin plays about Susanna, Judith, and Griselda; Rightwise's pupils at Paul's grammar school performed *Dido* before Wolsey; and Garter's *Virtuous and Godly Susanna* (1563–69) and Phillip's *Patient Grissel* (Paul's?, 1558–61) are extant English works about two familiar heroines.[16] Political plays like *Godly Queen Hester* (Chapel, c.1528) and the morality *Respublica* (1553) owe something to the pathetic heroines of humanist plays who are threatened with death, dishonor, and imprisonment, and who lament their plight in eloquent declamatory verse or in musical complaints. Even William Cornish, hardly a humanist schoolmaster, led his Children of the Chapel Royal in a production of *Troilus and Pandor* (1515), which featured "Cressid inparaled [sic] like a widow of honor in black sarcenet." [17] By the middle of Elizabeth's reign, pathetic-heroine plays had become something of a speciality for the major London children's troupes, as well as for university and inns-of-court students.

In 1573–74, for example, Mulcaster's boys brought to court a lost play entitled *Timoclea at the Siege of Thebes,* which probably dramatized the tale of Alexander's magnanimity toward a female captive. Plutarch relates the story in his *Life of Alexander* and again in his *Moralia,* as does Painter in his *Palace of Pleasure* (1566), all three versions emphasizing the valor of the female protagonist within the following plot:

When Alexander conquered Thebes, some of his soldiers began plundering the city. One officer ravished a noble woman named Timoclea, and then ordered her to surrender her money and jewels. She led him outside to a pit or well, into which she said she had thrown her treasure when the city fell. As soon as the officer had gone down to seek the hidden wealth, Timoclea and her maids rolled large stones down on him, killing the varlet. Taken before Alexander for judgment, she proudly identified herself as sister of Theagenes, a brave warrior slain in battle, and she offered to die rather than suffer further humiliation. Alexander was so moved by her courageous and noble virtue, that he personally guaranteed her safety and that of her family.

The story of Timoclea is probably fairly typical of the pathetic-heroine plays. Usually the citizen of a conquered city or nation, the protagonist is subject to the will of her captors, whose sexual advances are sometimes subtle, sometimes violent. Whether through physical charm, adamantine integrity, or both, the heroine preserves her innocence and wins the admiration and respect of the leader of the occupation army, a gallant prince capable of controlling his erotic passions. Mulcaster's boys probably followed Plutarch and Painter in depicting Timoclea as the forceful, bold type of pathetic heroine rather than as the fearful, quivering type.

Lyly too stresses her courage in the opening scene of *Campaspe*, which dramatizes a related episode from Alexander's conquest of Thebes, but uses Timoclea merely as a foil for the title character. After a short introductory dialogue between two of Alexander's officers, Lyly has a procession of prisoners brought on stage. In graceful, euphuistic prose, Timoclea immediately asserts herself as the proud, valorous type of heroine, undaunted by captivity:

Fortune, thou didst never yet deceive virtue, because virtue never yet did trust fortune. Sword and fire will never get spoil, where wisdom and fortitude bears sway. . . . But destiny is seldom foreseen, never prevented. We are here now captives, whose necks are yoked by force, but whose hearts can not yield by death.

(l.i.29–38)

One of the officers assures her of Alexander's mildness and generosity as a conqueror, at which Campaspe steps forward, less defiant than Timoclea, offering to put her trust in Alexander's mercy. The contrast between Timoclea's resolute courage and Capaspe's delicate humility is underscored when Alexander asks the women to identify themselves:

Timoclea: Alexander, I am the sister of Theagenes, who fought a battle with thy father before the City of Chyronie, where he died, I say which none can gainsay, valiantly.
Alexander: [to Campaspe]. . . . what are you fair Lady, another sister to Theagenes?
Campaspe: No sister to Theagenes, but an humble handmaid to Alexander, born of a mean parentage, but to extreme fortune.

(ll. 64–72)

Timoclea never reappears, for Lyly's play, as the Prologue states, focuses on Campaspe: "we calling Alexander from his grave, seek only who was his love." Evidently the story of Timoclea was so familiar to Lyly's audiences at court and Blackfriars that he could quickly establish Campaspe's softer passivity by setting her off against the stalwart Timoclea in a few deft strokes.

The titles of several lost children's plays performed around the time of Campaspe also suggest works in the pathetic-heroine tradition. The Revels Accounts mention a tragedy of *Iphigenia* (Paul's, 1571–72), surely the story of Agamemnon's sacrifice of his daughter; *Perseus and Andromeda* (Merchant Taylors' Boys, 1573–74) was probably the myth of the enchained heroine's rescue from a monster, and *Alucius* (Chapel, 1579–80) must surely by the story of Scipio's returning a captive Celtiberean Princess unharmed to her fiancé. Gosson mentions a version of *Cupid and Psyche* (Paul's, c.1580–82), which may have been a dramatization of the myth in which the heroine suffers cruelty and humiliation at the hands of Venus before Cupid transforms her into a goddess and marries her. These titles, together with the evidence of the lost *Timoclea* and the beginning of *Campaspe*, suggest that the leading London children's troupes of the 1570s and 1580s often performed plays focusing on pathetic or captive heroines—either stalwart matrons or vulnerable maidens. Depending on the fate of the heroine in the source, such plays could take comic or tragic form.

The earliest extant pathetic-heroine play in the tragic mode is the anonymous, obscure, and neglected *The Wars of Cyrus* (Chapel, 1576–80?). The play was not printed until 1594, although the title page proclaims that it was "Played by the Children of Her Majesty's Chapel," who had ceased playing in the mid-1580s. A song by Richard Ferrant, however, found in a MS dated 1581, seems to be Panthea's lament for her dead husband Abradad (Abradates in the play), but unfortunately does not fit neatly into the extant text of the play. Most scholars believe that Ferrant's song was used in an earlier version of the play, probably written and performed between 1576, when Ferrant assumed the mastership of the Chapel Children, and 1580, when he died. The 1594 text, which contains echoes of Marlowe's *Tamburlaine* (c.1588?), may be a revision of the earlier work.[18]

Most of the material for the play comes from Xenophon's *Cyropaedia,* which appeared in English translation in 1567. The heroine, Panthea, Queen of Susa, combines the virtues of both Timoclea and Campaspe, the defiant matron and the vulnerable maiden. In the opening scene, three of Cyrus' officers in the Assyrian campaign open a tent to discover Panthea and her maid Nicasia in an affecting tableau: *"Nicasia* sings while *Panthea* sits and sighs, / But singing, sings of Panthea's wretchedness" (ll. 96–97). She identifies herself first as "a woeful dame" and then in more dignified terms: "I am a Queen, / And wife unto the absent Susan king, / My lord and heir, Assyrian Abradate" (ll. 124–26). Undaunted by her position as a captive, she maintains a stoic fortitude reminiscent of Timoclea:

> Victorious *Cyrus,* though I be his thrall,
> Shall know my honor is invincible. . . .
> Only this outward person is his thrall,
> My mind and honor free and ever shall.
> (ll. 152–58)

Two scenes later, the officer Araspas describes Panthea to Cyrus, stressing the poignant suffering of "this captive dame":

> She weeps and plays while both her handmaids sing,
> And sighs at every strain, using that note
> Which Orpheus sings for Eurydice.
> With wringed hands her waiting maids keep time
> Upon their mournful breasts, as were we flint
> We could not choose but melt to hear their songs.
> (ll. 305–10)

Araspas invites Cyrus to see Panthea for himself, but the conqueror refuses to risk exposure to her charms, and the two men debate whether or not the will can control love. Araspas, who believes that it can, soon learns "what a tyrant is this cruel love" (l. 411) and reveals his passion to Panthea, who cooly admonishes him to "perish in thy love" (l. 472) and walks away. Realizing that "against chastities no eloquence prevails" (l. 475), Araspas decides to use sorcery, for "nothing but Magic can obtain her love" (l. 480), and in the actual seduction scene conspires with a magician while Panthea sleeps on stage. The magician is confident in his art:

> Doubt not the operation of this charm,
> For I have tried it on *Diana's* nymph
> And made her wanton and lascivious.
> If *Panthea* be a Goddess, she must yield.
>   (ll. 766–69)

The magician instructs Araspas to place the charm "under the pillow of her bed" (l. 772), and both watch as Panthea, talking in her sleep, evidently dreams she is resisting someone's sexual advances. She wakes, and Araspas finds that the charm has had no effect, but nonetheless begins to woo her. Frustrated by her unyielding fidelity to her husband, he threatens first to rape her and then to torture her into submission, but backs down in the face of her resolute courage:

> *Araspas:* Nay then, if amorous courting will not serve,
>   Know whether thou wilt or no I'll make thee yield.
> *Panthea:* Though fortune make me captive yet know thou
>   That *Panthea's* will can never be constrained.
> *Araspas:* But torments can enforce a woman's will. . . .
> *Panthea:* I feel more torments than thou canst invent;
>   Who add the more shall ease that I sustain.
>   All torments, be they never so exquisite,
>   Are but ascending steps unto my end,
>   And death to *Panthea* is a benefit.
>   What are thy threats but sugared promises!
> *Araspas:* Then shalt thou live, and I'll importune thee.
>   (ll. 831–47)

Panthea then runs offstage to tell Cyrus of Araspas' villainy, while the magician explains that "Panthea's virtues frustrated all my art" (ll. 860).

After this highly charged presentation of the pathetic heroine's fortitude, the main action of the play begins to move toward the climax. Cyrus is angry that a Persian officer could be "so far misled with lust [as to] / Intend dishonor to a silly dame" (ll. 1274–75), and reminds Araspas of "your big and brave disputes / Wherein you pleaded love was voluntary" (ll. 1280–81). The dishonorable behavior of Araspas, an otherwise loyal officer, is one of a series of problems in moral leadership for Cyrus. His solution is to offer Araspas redemption through penitential service to the state: pretending to desert Cyrus, Araspas will spy on the Assyrians. Panthea urges Cyrus to fill Araspas' post with Abradates, who will surely repay Cyrus' magnanimous protection of her by deserting the Assyrian king, who once "affected *Panthea's* bed" (l. 1363), in favor of the Persian prince. Two scenes later Abradates appears and pledges himself and his 2,000 horsemen to Cyrus. The play subordinates his reunion with Panthea to his devotion to Cyrus by having Panthea arm him for battle practically as soon as they are reunited, just as it avoids the emotional complexity of Panthea's response when Araspas, the officer who tried to seduce her, enters to report to Cyrus the results of his spying mission. In this scene, the Persian prince remains the center of attention, as all the officers beg him for the honor of leading the army into battle, a privilege which falls finally to Abradates. In an episode not found in the source, Panthea and Nicasia decide to pray for a Persian victory, probably offering a vocal duet:

Nicasia: Madam, Bellona's shine is here at hand;
    O let us go to offer sacrifice . . .
Panthea: For Music is a sacrifice to her.

                    (ll. 1575–86)

Thrice Bellona turns her face away from Panthea, we are told, an omen which Cyrus tries to dismiss. But his reassurance is followed directly by the stage direction: *"Abradates borne in dead"*(l. 1613). A captain, an upgraded Senecan nuntius, narrates the circumstances of Abradates' death, and Panthea is then left alone with his body onstage. Although the text makes no provision for her to sing, Ferrant's lament was probably used somewhere in the course of the following speech, which ends with her suicide:

> Now Euphrates, whose sad and hollow banks
> Have sucked the sum of *Abradates'* blood,
> Which from his wounds did issue with his life,
> Now cease thy course of thy disdained tears,
> and let thy courage turn against the tide,
> Of mere remorse of wretched Panthea's plaints!
> Is this the hand that plighted faith to me?
> The hand that aye hath managed kingly arms
> And brought whole troops of mighty warriors down,
> Now sundered from the body of my lord,
> Clean void of feeling, sense, and vital breath?
> So Gods and cruel destinies command,
> Malignant of poor *Panthea's* happiness.
> Live, *Cyrus!* You Lords of Persia,
> Commend my honor to posterity,
> That ages hence the world report may make
> That *Panthea* died for *Abradates'* sake.
>
> (ll. 1643–59)

Nicasia, who doesn't even exist in Xenophon, enters, briefly laments her mistress' suicide, and then becomes a pathetic heroine in her own right by throwing herself into the Euphrates, whose "sedgy banks" (l. 907) probably concealed a trap door. Cyrus returns with his officers, eulogizes the dead couple, and orders an elaborate funeral.

The subplot furnishes the story of Alexandra, another pathetic heroine, and her page Libanio, neither of whom appear in the source. Xenophon merely records that the Assyrian lord Gobryas left a daughter behind when he deserted to the Persian side. The play, however, expands this nameless daughter into the pathetic heroine of a three-scene subplot, and in the process exploits the audience's dual consciousness more than the main action does, almost to the point of parody, if not beyond. The first of the three scenes opens with the stage direction: *"Enter Alexandra like a page, Libanio in Alexandra's apparel"* (II.iv). The characters describe these transvestite disguises with a theatrical metaphor:

> *Libanio:* Now, madam, carry a courageous heart,
>   And trust your page for *Alexandra's* part.
> *Alexandra:* A Tragical part, I fear, *Libanio.*
>
>   (ll. 627–29)

Pretending to be a "silly virgin," Libanio persuades the Assyrians to send his/her "page" as a messenger to Gobryas in the Persian camp. In the second scene of the subplot, Libanio finds that he is the prisoner not only of the Assyrians but also of his disguise, when Dinon, the captain guarding him, falls in love with this "captive maiden." However convincingly Libanio plays the pathetic heroine, the audience can surely see this scene as a sophisticated refraction of the scene in the main action that precedes it, where Araspas vainly attempts to seduce *his* female prisoner, Panthea. Libanio seems to be both foil and parody. He first protests immaturity and unfitness for love:

> *Libanio:* You know, my Lord, I am too young to love.
> *Dinon:* . . . Thy years are fit for love; so are thy looks.
> *Libanio:* How fit so e'er my years be and my looks,
>   I, Alexandra, am unfit to love.
>
>   (ll. 894–99)

Gently, Dinon presses his suit:

> *Dinon:* Love—may I call thee love? (Lo, she doth not
>   frown;
>   Her looks gives warrant for that Epithet)—
>   For thee I'll kneel before Antiochus. . . .
>   (ll. 917–19)

He offers to lavish his wealth upon his beloved, and Libanio appears to waver, mimicking girlish coyness, before finally capitulating:

> *Libanio:* If I should yield, your honor might suppose
>   That dignity and wealth should conquer me;
>   Therefore I blush to say I love my Lord.
> *Dinon:* And when thou blushes *Dinon's* heart is fired;
>   Therefore to quench it give a gentle grant.
> *Libanio:* My honor being preserved, my grant is given.
>   (ll. 933–38)

Dinon's triumph has apparently made him sleepy. He asks Libanio to "lull me asleep with sweetness of thy voice" (l. 942), but as soon as he is asleep, the page murders him with his own sword. The following soliloquy deliberately underscores the ambiguous sexuality of the boy actor playing Libanio playing Alexandra:

> Sleep, *Dinon!* Then, *Libanio,* draw thy sword
> And manly thrust it in his slumbering heart!
> . . . Now *Dinon* dies! Alas, I cannot strike!
> This habit makes me over pitiful.
> Remember that thou art *Libanio*—
> No woman, but a bondman! Strike and fly!
>   (ll. 944–57)

In the third and final scene of this subplot, Libanio arrives at the Persian camp "in woman's attire" (l. 1047) and is mis-

taken by Gobryas for "some shameless strumpet and lascivious trull" (l. 1052). When Libanio identifies himself, and
possibly removes a wig or some article of feminine clothing,
Gobryas praises him for saving Alexandra's life. Alexandra enters, Cyrus commands the "boy" to relate the means of his
own escape, and after he does so Cyrus praises the lad—still
largely in female garb—as "precedent of manly fortitude" (l.
1128), while Alexandra again speaks in theatrical metaphor:

> *Libanio,* now leave Alexandra's weeds—
> That part is played—and be yourself again;
> That part, poor boy, with danger thou hast played.
>
> (ll. 1131–33)

The author then returns to material supplied by Xenophon,
dramatizing the bizarre manner in which Gobryas chooses a
husband for Alexandra from among Cyrus' officers:

> *Gobryas:* Then wample both my eyes, that with this turf
>   I may be sure to hit a virtuous man.
> *Cyrus:* Shall she be his on whom this turf shall light?
> *Gobryas:* So that the man be good and virtuous.
> *Cyrus:* Then throw at random when you please, *Gobryas;*
>   You cannot miss a good and virtuous man.
>
> (ll. 1141–46)

Surely some spectators would have felt the deliberate playfulness of this passage. The stress on the manliness of Cyrus'
entourage becomes ironic through the presence of Libanio—
that "precedent of manly fortitude," still wearing Alexandra's
clothing. I doubt that the author or reviser is burlesquing the
main action of his play; more likely he is anticipating ridicule
by building into the play the spectators' dual consciousness
and their awareness of the conventions of the pathetic-
heroine play, which may even have been on the verge of ob-
solescence.

It is indeed possible that the self-conscious playfulness of
the Libanio-Alexandra episode owes something to a reviser influenced by Marlowe's and Nashe's pathetic-heroine play,
Dido, Queen of Carthage (Chapel, 1585–88?), which also appeared in print in 1594. As in *The Wars of Cyrus,* the playful elements in *Dido* creep in at the edges through minor episodes
not found in Vergil. Jackson Cope points to three such episodes, all of which mock romantic love by exploiting the audience's awareness of the actors as boys: (1) the Jupiter-
Ganymede Induction, which exploits what Cope calls "the
homosexual potential of the troupe," (2) the scene (III.i)
which ridicules love's absurdity by having Cupid climb into
Dido's lap and make her mad with love for Aeneas, (3) the
scene between Cupid and the nurse, another absurd boy-
lover, this time in the guise of an old woman.[19] Cope goes on
to argue that the entire play verges on parody, especially the
passages where a weak, vacillating Aeneas is manipulated by
the seductive, wily heroine. There is no need to assume, as
he does, that Dido was played by a larger, older boy than Aeneas, for in the plays performed by children's troupes, the
actors could usually portray female characters more convincingly than they could adult male characters. Audiences who
knew adult actors but had never seen actresses would have
found Aeneas a weaker dramatic illusion than Dido, regard-
less of the two actors' ages and sizes. H. J. Oliver, the most
recent editor of the play, reached this conclusion after seeing
a modern school production: "a schoolboy Aeneas, perhaps
no taller than his Dido and Anna, cannot be much more than
a puppet-like figure, no matter how good an actor he may be,
and is bound to seem somewhat artificial, and even stiff in
comparison."[20]
While Nashe and Marlowe may well be exploiting their audience's dual consciousness, I believe their playfulness stops

short of outright burlesque of the pathetic-heroine tradition, and functions rather as a foil for Dido's magnificent last scene. Here Dido's suicide receives less emphasis than in other dramatizations of the story, but Marlowe and Nashe build up to it with a remarkably rich portrait of the Carthaginian Queen that takes the better part of Act V. This last act is actually a single scene, which Dido completely dominates from the time she enters, about a quarter of the way through. Before she appears, Aeneas has been fantasizing about the country he will establish, when Hermes enters to deliver Ascanius and to chide him, on Jove's behalf, for being "too too forgetful of thine own affairs" (l. 30). Jarbas furnishes him with rigging and provisions, and he is now prepared to carry out his mission. At this point, Dido enters, demolishes Aeneas' arguments, if not his resolution to depart, and forces him to leave in what must be an exasperated and sullen silence. Her strategies for manipulating Aeneas demand considerable range and subtlety of feeling from the boy actor, as a close examination of the scene will show.

When Dido comes on stage she fears Aeneas' imminent departure, but decides to "try her wit" and demand that he explain his intentions, softening the demand with polite coyness:

> Aeneas, wherefore go thy men aboard?
> Why are thy ships new-rigged? Or to what end,
> Launched from the haven, lie they in the road?
> Pardon me though I ask; love makes me ask.
>
> (ll. 87–90)

There follow about 100 lines of formal disputation, in which Aeneas claims that Jove has ordered him to leave in spite of his love for Dido. Dido's rhetorical tactics are impressive, if ultimately unsuccessful. She first asserts that he cannot possibly mean what he says, that she will die if he leaves, and that they have exchanged vows:

These words proceed not from Aeneas' heart.   (l. 102)

I die if my Aeneas say "farewell."   (l. 108)

Thy hand and mine have plighted mutual faith!   (l. 122)

She then wonders if his refusal to "gainsay the Gods' behest" (l. 127) is due to the fact that "it is Aeneas calls Aeneas hence" (l. 132), and the debate reaches a crescendo of Vergilian verse:

> Dido: Si bene quid de te merui, fuit aut tibi quidquam
>   Dulce meum, miserere domus labentis; & istam
>   Oro, si quis adhuc precibus locus, exue mentem.
> Aeneas: Desine meque tuis incendere teque querelis,
>   Italiam non sponte sequor.
>
>   (ll. 136–40)

Dido reminds Aeneas of the political risks she accepted in loving him, compares him to the deceitful Paris, wishes she could bear his son, and, steamrolling over Aeneas' brief protest that words cannot move him, accuses him of Scythian cruelty, base ingratitude, and reptilian deceit. She tells him to go, hoping that rock and sea will avenge her betrayal, and finally dares him to desert her:

> Why starest thou in my face? If thou wilt stay,
> Leap in mine arms: mine arms are open wide.
> If not, turn from me, and I'll turn from thee;
> For though thou hast the heart to say farewell,
> I have not power to stay thee.
>
>   (ll. 179-83)

Once released from her gaze, he leaves without a word, while Dido's grand manner collapses into a wishful fantasy of his return:

> . . . he shrinks back, and now remembering me,
> Returns amain: welcome, welcome, my love!
> But where's Aeneas? Ah, he's gone, he's gone!
> (ll. 190–92)

The scene is still only about two-thirds done. Marlowe and Nashe bring other characters onstage to help Dido sustain and vary this bravura passage. First Anna calls Aeneas "wicked," provoking Dido to defend him and to send Anna to plead with him to return. When the nurse enters to tell her that Ascanius is gone, Dido fumes in violent rage, ordering this "cursed hag and false dissembling wretch" (l. 216) to prison. Anna returns to report the failure of her mission, and Dido wishes that she could follow Aeneas—either by swimming, like Triton's niece, riding a dolphin's back, or flying with "wings of wax like Icarus, / . . . That they may melt and I fall in his arms" (ll. 243–45). Watching his ships toss at sea, she fears for his safety and imagines his return, until, under Anna's prompting, she remembers who she is. She seems to regain her regal bearing, but in what must be an aside, determines to kill herself:

> Dido I am, unless I be deceived,
> And must I rave thus for a runagate?
> . . . What shall I do,
> But die in fury of this oversight?
> I, I must be the murderer of myself;
> No, but I am not; yet I will be, straight.
> (ll. 264–271)

She deceives Anna and Jarbus, however, into thinking that she plans to conquer her grief by burning Aeneas' mementos. As Jarbus helps her set up the ceremonial fire—probably in an open trap door that could emit some sort of flickering light, she speaks in distracted riddles, promising Jarbus that "after this is done, / None in the world shall have my love but thou" (ll. 289–90).

Alone on stage, she begins her ritual of self-destruction. First she solemnly throws into the fire Aeneas' sword, "that in the darksome cave / He drew, and swore by, to be true to me" (ll. 295–96). Then, as in Edwardes' *Palomon and Arcite,* she flings a cloak into the fire—"the garment which I clothed him in / When first he came on shore" (ll. 288–89); next his "letters, lines, and perjured papers all" (l. 300). Finally, praying for a future Carthaginian hero to destroy Aeneas' Rome, she leaps into the flames. When Jarbus and Anna return, they follow Dido into the fire, Jarbus for love of Dido, Anna for love of Jarbus. The ending appears so rushed and the suicides of Jarbus and Anna, not present in Vergil, so gratuitous, that some readers suspect a parodic intent here, though parody would seem highly unlikely after Dido's breath-taking scene. Perhaps, like Nicasia's suicide in *The Wars of Cyrus,* these two additional suicides supply faint echoes of the heroine's death.

Despite some awareness of the artificiality inherent in a boy company's pathetic-heroine play, Marlowe and Nashe place Dido squarely in the tradition we have been discussing. The last scene, indeed, may well be the culmination of English pathetic-heroine tragedy. Writing for the Chapel Children in the late 1580s, they could also include other traditional elements of children's plays, such as vocal music, formal disputation, and spectacular effects like the storm, the pyre, and the costumes, although in all these categories they were to be outstripped by Marston's *Sophonisba* (Queen's Revels, 1606),

an archaistic play about the suicide of another Carthaginian heroine.

Love Comedy

In plays where the pathetic-heroine motif is given a comic
treatment, the woman's distress is a dark and poignant interlude before her marriage, a structural necessity in romantic
comedy that provides "interesting suspense to progress along
the rough path of true love until the moment when the lovers
kiss and begin to live happy ever after." [21] Northrop Frye has
broadened and deepened our conception of the pathetic
heroine in romantic comedy by linking her to "the ritual
theme of the triumph of life and love over the waste land."
Frye writes, "In the rituals and myths the earth that produces
the rebirth is generally a female figure, and the death and revival, or disappearance and withdrawal, of human figures in
romantic comedy generally involves the heroine." Thus, romantic comedies usually contain a "ritual assault on a central
female figure": slander, exile, abduction, imprisonment, at-
tempted seduction or rape, rumored death, slumber or mock-
death induced by a potion or spell, a vaguely incestuous marriage to an older suitor who has parental endorsement, loss of
identity—often sexual identity—through metamorphosis,
disguise, or concealed birth. [22] In romantic comedies, the symbolic assault is unsuccessful: the heroine is always "re-
born"—i.e., cleared of slander, rescued, released, revived,
awakened, revealed *not* to be her lover's sibling, restored to
her own shape and sex; she then marries her lover or is reunited with her husband.

Many of the children's pathetic-heroine plays already discussed can be thought of as romantic comedies. Heroines like
Susanna, Griselda, and Esther are rescued from death or dis-

honor or both, and are restored to their good names, their husbands, and marital bliss. The lost plays about Andromeda, Psyche, and Alucius' fiancée probably ended with the lovers' reunion, following the heroine's rescue or release from captivity, and even the two *Wit* plays—*Wit and Science* and *The Marriage of Wit and Science*—are romantic courtship quests at the literal level, with the man enduring the ritual assault.[23] Under Richard Edwardes, the Chapel Children probably performed a number of romantic comedies, for in his Prologue to *Damon and Pythias*, his only extant play, Edwardes apologizes for departing from his usual drama of "young desires":

> But if your eager looks do long such toys to see,
> As heretofore in comical wise, were wont abroad to be:
> Your lust is lost, and all the pleasures that you sought,
> Is frustrate quite of toying Plays. A sudden change is
> > wrought.
> For lo, our Author's *Muse*, that masked in delight,
> Hath forced his Pen against his kind, no more such sports
> > to write.
> Muse he that lust, (right worshipful) for chance hath made
> > this change,
> For that to some he seemed too much, in young desires to
> > range:
> In which, right glad to please: saying that he did offend,
> Of all he humbly pardon craves: his Pen that shall
> > amend: [24]

Despite Edwardes' reputation as an author of love comedies, there is little evidence of this type of play in the children's repertories before Lyly. Yet literary historians like Harbage overstressed the children's dependence on love comedy and inaccurately characterized their handling of such material: "The theme by all odds dominant in the plays under survey is love—guilty love, frustrated love, love fantastically fulfilled." [25] Not only did the children's troupes perform other types of plays before 1591, as we have already seen, but what love comedies they did perform are far less perverse than Harbage asserts. Their plays about love were not swashbuckling adventures derived from popularized chivalric romances such as the adult troupes performed, but their treatment of love was essentially heroic in tragedy and romantic in comedy.

In *Campaspe,* Lyly creates a love comedy out of such conventional motifs as the pathetic heroine and the flattering allegorical royal figure. In addition to dramatizing the heroine's sad plight and Alexander's conflict between love and honor, Lyly has written a conventional story of romantic lovers, Apelles and Campaspe, painter and model, whose happiness is thwarted by Alexander's attachment to his beautiful prisoner. When Alexander perceives the mutual love of the young couple, he magnanimously renounces his claim to the girl, for he realizes that he "cannot subdue the affection of men, though he conquer their countries" (V.iv.128–29). He blesses their match and wistfully resolves to subdue his own affections in the future. In short, Alexander is a temporary obstacle to the fulfillment of young love in a conventional romantic comedy.

The leading dramatist for the boy companies in the 1580s, Lyly developed a particular type of romantic comedy and all of his plays except *Midas* and *The Woman in the Moon* fit this categorization. One of the unique qualities of Lyly's romantic comedies is an ambivalence toward the lovers. On the one hand, Lyly tries to make the audience feel superior to characters in the power of love (often described as a disease or an irresistible force), while on the other he is asking the spectators to admire these lovers for preserving sufficient poise, self-control, and detachment to articulate their feelings in witty and elegant ways. Beneath this semi-ironic treatment of romantic lovers, the main action in most of Lyly's plays follows the outlines of romantic comedy. In *Gallathea* (Paul's, c.1584), two virgins disguised as boys fall in love, each deceived by the other's attire. Diana's nymphs, tricked by Cupid, are also fooled by the disguise and fall in love with the two maids. When the girls' true sex is revealed, the nymphs resume their devotion to chastity, but the two heroines are permitted to fulfill their love when Venus transforms one of them into a boy. In *Mother Bombie*, where one pair of young lovers and their witty servants outwit the fathers who wish to match them with the idiot offspring of wealthy families, the witty servants spend more time furthering the romantic intrigue than mocking their masters. The second pair of lovers are a brother and sister who feel "affections beyond nature" (III.i.4), for one another, but even this seemingly insurmountable obstacle is removed by the conventional revelation that one of them was an exchanged infant. In *Love's Metamorphosis*, the heroine Protea uses her power to change her shape to escape from the Merchant and, in a reversal of the "captive heroine" motif, to rescue her lover from a Siren; the subplot deals with three coy nymphs, who are released from their transformations only after they agree to marry their lovers, the three foresters.

Even *Sapho and Phao* and *Endimion* are romantic comedies fused with royal flattery. In the former, Venus forces Sapho to fall in love with Phao, a ferryman, but then falls in love with him herself. This triangular relationship resembles the one in *Campaspe*, for Venus, like Alexander, controls the fate of the two lovers. But whereas Alexander's magnanimity in forgoing love serves as a vague compliment to a celibate ruler, Venus—a mere goddess—is free to love, refuses to step aside, and empowers Cupid to dampen Sapho's ardor for

Phao, although the ferryman retains his affection for her. In this play, it is Sapho rather than Venus who provides the parallel to the Virgin Queen and who therefore must not consummate an amorous relationship, particularly one with a lowly ferryman. Thus, the romantic drive in Sapho and Phao is resolved in an ideal relationship of subject and queen, instead of the usual marriage of hero and heroine. Sapho will "wish him fortunate" because she "once loved Phao" (V.ii.98–99), while Phao will be "ever kneeling before Sapho, my loyalty unspotted, though unrewarded" (V.iii.18–19). In *Endimion* the hero's passion for Cynthia is doomed from the beginning because she too, as Goddess of Chastity, is a parallel to Elizabeth. Although Cynthia is more aloof than Sapho, she does deign to rescue Endimion from his forty-year sleep and to restore his youth. Once again the final relationship is that of subject and ruler:

> *Endimion:* Such a difference hath the Gods set between our states, that all must be duty, loyalty, and reverence; nothing (without it vouchsafe your highness) be termed love. . . .
> *Cynthia: Endimion,* this honorable respect of thine, shall be christened love in thee, & my reward for it favor.
>
> (V.iii.168–80)

Thus, in *Sapho and Phao* and *Endimion* Lyly uses the structure and expectations of romantic comedy, but substitutes an idealized relationship of courtier and queen for the conventional union of young lovers.

Throughout his plays, Lyly uses short colloquial servant scenes, as Edwardes did in *Damon and Pythias,* to add a satiric counterpoint to the lofty and rhetorical romantic actions. A large dose of romance spiced with satire or low comedy is, of course, the general formula of nearly all Elizabethan comedy, particularly Greene's and Shakespeare's, but several of their plays of the early 1590s seem to appropriate the Lylyan mode of the children's plays for the adult troupes. Greene's *Friar Bacon and Friar Bungay* (c.1589), which ends with a prophecy of Queen Elizabeth's birth, resembles Lyly's *Campaspe* in testing magnanimity in the crucible of passion; like Lyly's Alexander, King Edward gallantly steps aside when he finds that Margaret, the keeper's daughter, really loves the Earl of Lincoln. Shakespeare's *Two Gentlemen of Verona* (1594–95) is a romantic comedy constructed around a debate between the claims of love and honor, here represented by friendship, and the play contains servant scenes and disputations of rivals and lovers, which project the same idealized wit and elegance that Lyly claimed was reflected from his courtly and aristocratic spectators. Possibly written for an aristocratic wedding, *A Midsummer Night's Dream* (1594–96) uses balanced groups of characters, introduces them serially, and keeps them in separate compartments for most of the play. This work too is built on a debate subject—imagination versus rationality, which is developed by every group of characters in turn. The most Lylyesque of all Shakespeare's plays is *Love's Labor's Lost* (1594–96), which was performed both at court and at the Globe.[26] An obvious parallel is Armado's similarity to Tophas of *Endimion:* both are Spanish braggart-soldiers and pedants, both are mocked by pages who are wittier than they, and both pursue ludicrous mates. *Love's Labor's Lost* also has balanced groups of characters of different social levels, the same debate subject (will versus affects), and courtly wit-combats with ingenious word play of every sort. Like most of Lyly's plays, *Love's Labor's Lost* presents noble lovers who are endowed with the social poise to shape life into patterns of wit and elegance, although the play ultimately criticizes poise achieved at the price of genuine human feeling.

Where these Shakespearean romantic comedies differ considerably from their Lylyan models, they do so partly because of differences in the dramatists' artistic skill and breadth of vision, partly because of the type of actors and audiences for whom they wrote. Shakespeare's poetry suggests depths of emotion, complex states of mind, and facets of personality beneath the surface of his characters, whereas Lyly's figures are rarely more than glittering but static incarnations of attitudes. Furthermore, Lyly compliments his audience by persuading them that *they* are the ultimate reality behind the illusory action, as in a court masque, whereas Shakespeare, even in plays that may have been performed under aristocratic or courtly auspices, constantly juxtaposes different levels of illusion and even suggests that the spectators' "reality" is merely another illusion. One asks the unanswerable question: what would Shakespeare's plays be like if he had written them for a boy company?

Growing out of the festal tradition of ritual abuse, satiric servant scenes had been an important element in children's plays throughout the sixteenth century, and such abuse could be generalized—as in the servant scenes of Edwardes and Lyly—or could touch on personalities and issues—like *Godly Queen Hester* and *Midas*. In the late 1580s, one or both of the London choirboy troupes jumped squarely into the Marprelate controversy, committing itself heavily to personal and topical satire. The evidence is unclear and none of the plays in question is extant, but it seems that the Paul's boys attacked the Puritan Martinists on behalf of the ecclesiastical establishment, but in doing so aroused the ire of religious or secular authorities. Whether it was because of the virulence of their satire or the fact that the child actors made their friends as well as their foes appear ridiculous, the Children of Paul's, unlike the adult troupes that campaigned on the same side, were banished from court and forced to close their playhouse.

Although this first phase of the children's troupes ended with a flurry of pointed satire and although satiric elements had traditionally been an important part of children's plays, satire as a genre forms a surprisingly small part of the pre-1591 repertories. For most of the sixteenth century, as we have seen, the principal children's troupes performed pageants and debates, Latin comedies, pathetic heroine plays, and love comedies. Each type of play seems to have had its own era of particular prominence—the early Tudor period for pageants, debates, and Latin comedies, the 1570s for pathetic-heroine plays, and the 1580s for love comedies, but it is impossible to confine these subgenres to precise periods within the century. Instead of trying to view them as sequential though overlapping stages of development, one can more profitably observe that a similar trend occurs in all categories—a tendency toward the more self-conscious use of conventional materials. This tendency probably resulted from the pressure of sophisticated audiences who came into being after the children's troupes of London established their own theaters in the 1560s and 1570s. Unlike the troupes of provincial schoolboys, who amused their friends and parents with neoclassic comedies and didactic prodigal-son plays, the major boy companies of London met the challenge of more demanding audiences by handling familiar types of plays with increasing complexity, self-awareness, and sophistication.

୫ CHAPTER SIX ୫

The Plays (2)

THE second and more brilliant phase of the boy companies began in late 1596 or early 1597, when the theater in Paul's reopened. In 1600 the children's troupe at Blackfriars was reactivated under a more commercially minded directorate than the Paul's boys. As we shall see in Appendix C, scholars have had some success in establishing the repertories of these two children's troupes, as well as that of the third boy company, the short-lived Children of the King's Revels. The distinguishing characteristics of these repertories, however, are more difficult to discern and await further study. In this chapter, I propose the preliminary step of grouping together plays performed by all children's troupes, in order to consider the principal kinds of plays they acted and to trace patterns of development within their repertories.

In his discussion of the fifty-five or so plays of this second phase, Alfred Harbage notes "the overwhelming preponderance of satirical comedies, all but about a dozen being classifiable as such." [1] Given their tradition of festal abuse and their need to deflect their audiences' ridicule, the children's troupes of course were inevitably drawn to satirical comedy. Harbage's classification can serve as a rough generalization but it needs considerable refinement, as there are important differences among the forty-odd plays in question. The earliest plays of this second phase seem, not surprisingly, to be plays of the type performed late in the first phase, that is, plays by Lyly or his imitators, in which satire, if present at all, is a subordinate element. A few years after the boy companies resumed playing, there is a gradual shift toward satiric comedy, but this category needs to be subdivided if we are to appreciate the various techniques and modes of satiric comedy and how they combine with other elements in the children's plays. In the repertories of the children's troupes, there is great richness and variety to be found under the general rubric of "satirical comedy."

Lylyesque Comedy

In 1596 or 1597, when the chorister troupes resumed playing after their dormant period of the mid-1590s, their initial impulse was to pick up where they had left off, to perform plays or types of plays which they had performed successfully before their enforced closing—comedy in the manner of Lyly and perhaps even by Lyly himself. Printers show a renewed interest in Lyly's plays about this time: in 1597, the Widow Brome acquired the rights to *Campaspe* and *Sapho and Phao*, and William Jones printed *The Woman in the Moon*, which Robert Fynche had registered in 1595, while in 1598 Cuthbert Burby published a second edition of *Mother Bombie*. This sudden traffic in Lyly's texts may have resulted from recent stage production of one or more of his plays. The most likely play to have been produced at this time is *Love's Metamorphosis* (S.R. 1600, pub. 1601). The dates of composition and performance of this play remain uncertain, although it is the only one of Lyly's plays not already in print by 1595.[2] There is also some evidence that Lyly himself returned to writing plays, perhaps even acting in them, around the time the Paul's boys were resuscitated. In a letter to Cecil dated December 22, 1597, Lyly wrote: "I will Cast my wits in a new mold, & turn the water Course by a contrary Sluice, for I find it folly that one foot being in the grave, I should have the other on the stage." [3] Scholars have interpreted this statement as a refusal to return to the stage in the future rather than as a resolve to abandon it in the present, because they assumed that the Paul's boys did not resume playing until 1598 or 1599. Recently discovered evidence, however, which may move the resumption of playing in Paul's back to 1596 or 1597, places a different construction on Lyly's statement: "I will try something new, for I find it folly to be writing plays now, at this stage of my life." By 1596, Lyly had moved back to London from Mexborough and taken up residence in St. Bartholomew's Hospital, not far from St. Paul's, a move which may have been prompted by the reopening of the theater on the Cathedral grounds. His statement to Cecil, his abrupt return to London, combined with the publishers' renewed interest in his plays, suggests that Lyly was once again involved with the Children of Paul's in some way. It is tempting, though not necessary, to speculate further that he wrote or revised *Love's Metamorphosis* during this time.

Whether written or revised for the Children of Paul's, performed by them before 1591 or after 1596, the play passed to the Children of the Chapel, sometime shortly after Blackfriars reopened in late 1600. When William Wood entered *Love's Metamorphosis* in the Stationers' Register on November 25, 1600, he described it as "played by the Children of Paul's," but the title page of Wood's quarto advertises it as "first played by the Children of Paul's, and now by the Children of the Chapel." [4] If trustworthy, this statement suggests that the Chapel Children wished to emulate the Children of Paul's in reclaiming their role as courtly and aristocratic entertainers and did so by performing a play—possibly one recently written, revised, or revived—by the man whose works the children's troupes had frequently performed at court, Blackfriars, and Paul's throughout the 1580s and early 1590s.

In *Love's Metamorphosis,* as in some of his earlier plays, Lyly uses an Ovidian pastoral fable to illustrate various attitudes toward love. The characters, who are virtually allegorical representations of specific attitudes, are grouped symmetrically according to their allegiance either to Ceres or to Cupid. If Ceres and Cupid must respect one another's claims, as the Gods do in *Gallathea,* then mortals must surely abandon absolute devotion to a single ideal, learn to fuse or balance opposing impulses, and achieve union through the give-and-take of ordinary human relations. These compromises are necessary because the powers of the gods are more limited in *Love's Metamorphosis* than in Lyly's other plays. No single deity has absolute jurisdiction and the nymphs refuse to yield to love, defying Ceres' entreaties as well as Cupid's threats to transform them a second time, and then consent only on condition that their lovers accept some responsibility for the nymphs' human imperfections.

The presence of such graceful but pragmatic balancing of conflicting claims is not a new element in Lyly's dramatic work; what is new is the resolution of the play in so precarious a compromise with an absolute ideal. His earlier love comedies generally end with a greater sense of stability: characters renounce love for some higher ideal, as in *Campaspe, Sapho and Phao,* and *Endimion;* deities impose solutions through edict, as in *The Woman in the Moon,* or through some miraculous transformation as in *Gallathea;* even in *Mother Bombie,* where the union of lovers is achieved through the servants' intrigue, the lovers retain their idealized perfection. But *Love's Metamorphosis,* though similar to the earlier plays in many ways, ends in tenuous reconcilement rather than confident celebration of an absolute ideal.

Accustomed as we are to seeking the influence of Lyly on Shakespeare, a late dating of *Love's Metamorphosis* introduces the possibility that Lyly was following Shakespeare when he made the lovers in this play mortal enough to achieve union through forgiveness. With so clear a representation of flawed humanness, one hardly misses the usual satiric subplot, which may or may not have ever existed, where the servants' conventionalized cynicism contrasts with their masters' high-minded idealism. This undercurrent of mild cynicism in *Love's Metamorphosis* may reflect Lyly's growing disillusionment with the course of his life in the 1590s— suspension of the Children of Paul's, exile from court, lack of a patron, fading prospects of appointment to the Revels Office, reduced if not desperate economic straits—the sum total of which makes all the more remarkable his ability to control cynicism with the customary wit and elegance. Yet how else but by such control, such *sprezzatura*, could Lyly hope to regain the role of courtly entertainer and win Elizabeth's patronage?

The passage of time, however, thwarted such hopes, for by 1596 or 1597 his courtly manner must have seemed quaintly old-fashioned. "Cynthia" was nearing death, the uncertain succession aroused fears of civil war, inflation racked the economy, and a mood of melancholy and pessimism prevailed. The euphuistic prose style, a hallmark of an earlier, sunnier era, had by then passed out of fashion, at least for aristocrats. Greene and Shakespeare parodied euphuistic prose for its excessive use of alliteration and symmetry, while Lyly's prose fictions achieved popularity with bourgeois readers.[5] In private-theater plays of 1599 or 1600, Jonson and Marston use euphuistic speech to label pretenders to courtliness like Asotus and Amorphous in *Cynthia's Revels*, Sir John Puffe in *Jack Drum's Entertainment*, and Castilio Balthazar in *Antonio and Mellida*. Although *Euphues* continued to be reprinted in the late 1590s and early 1600s, euphuism and the mode of life it implied had passed into history and were now safe targets for the sophisticated to ridicule.

Always sensitive to prevailing tastes, the Children of Paul's never returned to Lylyesque comedy in its pure form. Although several of the plays performed at Paul's shortly after the reopening are indebted to Lyly's work, the authors go out of their way to assert their independence of the man who had once been the most prominent playwright for the children's troupes. One such work, the anonymous *The Maid's Metamorphosis* (1596?–1600), illustrates this ambivalence by both imitating and parodying Lyly's work.[6]

The main action of this fairly obscure play is conventional Lylyesque comedy: Prince Ascanio seeks his beloved, the low-born Eurymine, a fugitive from his father's court. When he finds her, he discovers that she has been transformed into a boy, but their marriage is assured when Apollo restores her to her own sex and reveals her to be of gentle birth.

This play is so much in Lyly's manner that Bond included it in his edition of Lyly. Its plot is taken from the story of Iphis and Ianthe in Book IX of Ovid's *Metamorphoses*, Lyly's favorite source. The play has the pastoral-mythological setting that Lyly often borrowed from the Roman poet, and the title may allude to Lyly's *Love's Metamorphosis*. *The Maid's Metamorphosis* also resembles Lyly's dramatic work in using such conventions as the mantic authority-figure, the interceding deities, and the countermetamorphosis, which removes the final obstacle to the marriage of young lovers. Moreover, *The Maid's Metamorphosis* employs other typically Lylyesque devices, such as patterned speeches, singing contests, a fairy chorus, rival suits by a shepherd and a forester, and a group of witty pages, who sing, ridicule their masters, complain of fatigue and hunger, utter bawdy *double entendres,* and celebrate drink and sex.

But the play also conveys an awareness of the artificiality of these conventions. For example, one of the pages, Joculo, appears outside the servant scenes, often standing aloof from the action and commenting on it directly to the audience. When his master lies down to sleep, Joculo bids him farewell and then in accordance with the stage direction (*"He speaks to the people"*) addresses the audience:

> Well, I pray you look to my master: for here *I* leave him amongst you: and if *I* chance to light on the wench, you shall hear of me by the next wind.
>
> (II.i.61–63)

The author makes Joculo, like Will Summer in Nashe's *Last Will and Testament,* establish an independent relationship with the spectators by mocking the stylized main action. In IV.i, Joculo clowns with the Echo, ridiculing the sagely Aramanthus for, among other things, not being able to "transform this tree into a tart"(l. 189). Later he advises his master, who is aghast that his "love's transformed into another kind," to "take her aside and prove" (V.i.71–73). Earlier in *The Maid's Metamorphosis* Joculo belittles Ascanio's grief and exposes the child actor behind the romantic hero by criticizing his master for "crying up and down after your wench, like a Boy had lost his hornbook" (II.i.19–20).

Joculo's bawdy, tongue-in-cheek manner spills over into the fairies' scene (II.ii). As in *Endimion,* they sing a choral song or two, dance, and behave in strict accordance with standard fairy lore—except for one, whose name is "little, little *Prick.*" Joculo points up the joke: "you are a dangerous Fairy, and fright all the little wenches in the Country, out of their beds" (ll. 81–82). The first two fairies speak of tripping

among flowers and dew drops, but the activities of the third
are in keeping with his name, as Joculo suspects:

> *Third Fairy:* When I feel a girl asleep,
>   Underneath her frock I peep,
>   There to sport, and there I play,
>   Then *I* bite her like a flea:
>   And about *I* skip.
> *Joculo:* Aye, I thought where I should have you.
>
> (ll. 93–98)

The leering tastelessness of this passage illustrates how *The
Maid's Metamorphosis* parodies the use of fairies, a convention which the children's troupes had employed playfully but
without mocking irony not long before.

When Ben Jonson wrote *Cynthia's Revels* for the Chapel
Children shortly after Blackfriars reopened in the fall of 1600,
he too used Lylyesque conventions both ironically and
seriously. The conception of Cynthia as a female sovereign
reforming her court imitates Lyly's compliment to Elizabeth in
Endimion, the opening scene of the play specifically recalls
Lyly's use of the Ovidian-pastoral setting, and the witty pages
Mercury and Cupid descend from Lyly's pert servants. Despite the indebtedness to Lyly, *Cynthia's Revels* has more and
different kinds of satire than any of Lyly's plays, as G. K.
Hunter has argued.[7] When plays like *Endimion* contain anticourt satire, it is usually generalized and conventional, anal-
ogous to the antimasque of a court masque. Indeed, such
plays resemble the court masque in stressing the restoration
of the court to its essential state of virtue. *Cynthia's Revels,*
on the other hand, emphasizes the negative qualities of the
courtiers, almost as if it were nearly all antimasque. While the
primary concern of Lyly and Edwardes was to evoke admiration for the royal figure and by extension for her courtiers,

the primary concern of Jonson in *Cynthia's Revels* is to evoke judgment of foolish pretenders to the title of courtier. Moreover, in making some of these pretenders, Asotus and Amorphus for example, addicted to Lylyesque modes of expression, Jonson is parodying an ideal, already antiquated, that had been presented seriously in the chorister plays of the 1580s and early 1590s, and in revivals and imitations of those plays after 1596. Such plays, one of the children in the Induction explains, are inappropriate for a fashionable private-theater audience:

> they say, the *umbrae*, or ghosts of some three or four plays, departed a dozen years since, have been seen walking on your stage here: take heed, boy, if your house be haunted with such *hobgoblins,* 'twill fright away all your spectators quickly.

Sharing his audience's ambivalence toward Lyly, Jonson grafted on to the traditional Ovidian pastoral stock a new species of play—the "comical satire," whose characteristics we shall discuss in greater detail further on in this chapter.

If *Cynthia's Revels* was performed in the winter of 1600–1, as is generally believed, it must have been on the boards the same season as the Chapel Children's production of *Love's Metamorphosis,* a play which the Paul's boys had abandoned (perhaps rather recently) and which is probably one of Jonson's "*umbrae,* or ghosts." But Jonson's parody of euphuism and the ironic use of other Lylyesque conventions surely signified the end of an era, and may have hastened it as well. Some on the periphery of the theatrical world were slower to hear the news. In the early 1600s, an amateur dramatist named William Percy submitted a play entitled *The Fairy Pastoral* to the Children of Paul's. This play employs such typical Lylyesque conventions as a mythological-pastoral setting, balanced trios of fairy hunters and huntresses, and a group of witty pupils who mock and discomfit their doltish schoolmaster. As far as we know, the play was never performed. Percy may not have been the only one speculating on another wave of interest in Lyly's plays, for on August 23, 1601, George Potter acquired Widow Brome's rights to publish five of Lyly's plays, but never printed them.

The closest the children's troupes came to returning to the Lylyan mode was Fletcher's *The Faithful Shepherdess* (Queen's Revels, 1608–9), which Greg describes as "a conscious attempt to adapt the Italian pastoral to . . . the English stage." [8] The main action of Fletcher's play involves the shepherdess Amoret, whose reputation is tarnished when her rival assumes her shape and behaves wantonly with her lover, Perigot. Appalled by this conduct, the chaste Perigot later wounds the real Amoret, but she remains faithful to him, is cured of her wounds and her bad name, and is reconciled with him. In addition to its Italianate pastoralism, the play has several features of the Lylesque mode of pastoral drama: The characters are nearly all static and stylized representations of various responses to the power of love, such as shyness, chasteness, eagerness, and wantoness, and all of them are purified by the controlling figure of Clorin, who is chastely devoted to the memory of her late lover. Like Mother Bombie, Sybylla, and other mantic authority-figures in Lyly's plays, Clorin inhabits a curtained central structure, in this case a bower. The prefatory verses to the first quarto (c.1609) indicate that the play failed in performance. In 1608 or 1609, the figure of Clorin would no longer suggest a flattering parallel to a virgin queen, as it might have done in Lyly's day. By this time the private-theater audiences had become accustomed to satiric comedy and were no longer interested in romantic comedy, at least in the rarified pastoral atmosphere of the

Lylyesque variety, which they had laid to rest by 1600. A generation later, however, these old-fashioned plays could appeal to a nostalgic longing for the lost innocence of the Elizabethan age. In 1632, when Blount published a collection of Lyly's plays under the title *Six Court Comedies*, he advertised them on the title page as "Written by the only Rare Poet of that Time . . . The Witty, Comical, Facetiously-Quick and unparalleled: John Lyly, Master of Arts."

New Romantic Comedy

Seeking for a new type of play to replace the antiquated comedies of Lyly and his imitators, some of the writers for the children's troupes turned to plays performed successfully by adult companies during the 1590s. Except for Marston's *Antionio's Revenge* and Chapman's *The Revenge of Bussy D'Ambois*, they ignored revenge tragedy as they did chronicle history, but discovered a type of play suitable for the talents of the children's troupes—the romantic comedies of Greene and Shakespeare, which had themselves been influenced by Lyly's earlier plays. This "New Romantic Comedy," as I shall call it, differs from Lylyesque comedy in several ways. It usually takes place in remote Medieval England or in some exotic continental dukedom rather than in an Ovidian pastoral setting, is more often written in prose than in verse, has low-comic or farcical subplots instead of satiric episodes involving witty pages, and is inspired directly or indirectly by continental novelle and prose romances like Sidney's *Arcadia* rather than by classical sources. Above all, Lyly manipulates allegorical counters to illustrate a debate topic, whereas New Romantic Comedy dramatizes the intrigue of figures with enough pyschological complexity to be recognizably human. Two anonymous plays acted at Paul's, *The Wisdom of Doctor Do-*

dypoll (1596?–1600) and *Blurt, Master Constable* (1601–2) indicate the shift from Lylyesque comedy to New Romantic Comedy.[9]

The Wisdom of Doctor Dodypoll seems closer to the robustness of New Romantic Comedy than to the delicacy of Lylyan tableaux in style, tone, and characterization, and close verbal parallels with *A Midsummer Night's Dream* suggest that the author of this obscure work set out to imitate the kind of play that had been successfully produced by adult troupes—usually before public-theater audiences but in some cases before aristocratic spectators under private auspices or at court. Despite some superficial Lylyesque touches, the play belongs to the category of New Romantic Comedy. In exotic Saxony, Lassingbergh, an earl disguised as a painter, is secretly married to Lucilia, his subject, a situation which initially recalls the love of Apelles for the heroine of *Campaspe*. Lassingbergh's identity and the marriage are discovered, his father-in-law, Flores, is enraged at the deception, and the Earl flees from his wife in a fit of melancholy. Lucilia eventually catches up with her husband, but the two are bewitched by a group of fairies and an Enchanter, who binds the Earl and tries to rape the girl. Flores arrives in time to save his daughter and to release Lassingbergh, but the Earl dashes off once more, again pursued by his faithful wife. Tired from his flight, Lassingbergh lies down to sleep, whereupon Lucilia finds him and watches over him. She reveals her plight to Duchess Katherine of Brunswick, Lassingbergh's aunt, who somehow helps bring about the couple's reconciliation, in scenes perhaps cut from the extant version.

In another plot, Flores hopes to match his other daughter, Cornelia, with Prince Alberdure of Saxony, who is in love with Hyanthe, his own father's beloved. Flores gives the prince what he thinks is a love potion, but which induces madness and causes romantic complications.

In a low-comedy subplot, Doctor Dodypoll and a merchant compete for the hand of Cornelia, and in so doing furnish most of the low comedy in the play. Two pert Lylyesque "cracks"—Motto and a "petit Jack" (l. 565) named Hauns—appear in vestigial form. On a single occasion, Motto mocks Alberdure's love-sick yearning for Hyanthe as one of Lyly's pages might have done:

> Madam dispatch him then; rid him out of this earthly purgatory; for I have such a coil with him a nights; grunting and groaning in his sleep; with O *Hyanthe;* my dear *Hyanthe;* and then he throbs me in his arms, as if he had gotten a great jewel by the ear.
>
> (ll. 252–57)

In Act I, Hauns speaks directly to the audience, like Joculo or Will Summer:

> But we have such a wench a coming for you (Lordings) with her wooers: Ah, the finest wench: wink, wink, dear people, and you be wise: and shut, O shut your weeping eyes.
>
> (ll. 80–84)

But this potentially privileged relationship with the audience never develops any further. On the whole, there seems to be less self-conscious sophistication in *The Wisdom of Doctor Dodypoll* than in *The Maid's Metamorphosis,* a play that casts a parodic glance backward at the antiquated conventions of the Lylyesque pastoral. *The Wisdom of Doctor Dodypoll,* on the other hand, a "straight" comedy of love intrigue set against an exotic background and interspersed with interludes of magic and farce, attempts to establish a new mode.

The author of *Blurt, Master Constable* follows Edwardes and Lyly in spicing his main action—a story of romantic love—with the mischief of pert, witty servants—Doit, Dandyprat, Trivia, etc. One page mocks his master, a bragging pedantic Spaniard reminiscent of Sir Tophas in *Endimion* and Don Armado in *Love's Labor's Lost,* and pokes fun at Blurt, a clownish officer modeled after the Constable in *Endimion* and Dogberry in *Much Ado About Nothing.*

The maidservants sing a bawdy song ("In a fair woman what thing is best?"), provide a number of ribald puns, and join with the pages in the saturnalian discomfiting of the Spanish pedant and an elderly lecher. These satiric elements are far more prominent than in Lyly's plays and rather than balance or complement the romantic main action they threaten to overwhelm it.

The main action itself is closer to New Romantic Comedy in tone, style, and characters than it is to Lyly's work. Camillo, a Venetian warrior, presents his beloved Violetta with a recently captured French prisoner, Fontinelle, as a tribute to her beauty, but he becomes jealous when they fall in love with each other and returns Fontinelle to prison. The usual romantic solution to this problem—the prisoner's escape and elopement with his beloved—is complicated when Fontinelle offers to repay the courtesan, who engineered his escape and sheltered him, by sleeping with her. In order to preserve his innocence, Violetta contrives to take the courtesans's place in bed—a device Shakespeare used shortly thereafter.

The children's troupes continued to perform love comedies of this type but when writers like Day attempt the genre, their work is so laboriously contrived that one suspects them of writing deliberate parody. Mindful of Richard Levin's warning that not all bad plays can be salvaged by this gambit, I suspect that Day may have decided to write parody because he was incapable of animating the conventions of New Romantic Comedy and perhaps fearful that his audience had wearied of them. So familiar had these conventions become that Beaumont, in his Prologue to *The Woman Hater,* casually assures his spectators of finding at least two of them: "A Duke there is, and the Scene lies in *Italy,* as those two things lightly we never miss." Plays like Day's *The Isle of Gulls, Law Tricks,* and *Humors out of Breath* are a potpourri of familiar elements from Sidney, Greene, and Shakespeare, but used without imagination.

The framework of *The Isle of Gulls,* for example, is the main plot of Sidney's *Arcadia.* Pestered by his daughters' suitors, the Duke of Arcadia abandons his court and comes to an island fortress, challenges worthy princes to try to win the girls from him by "wit and active policy" (sig. A4). Two pairs of suitors attempt the task, in a series of intrigues too complicated to summarize. Suffice it to say that they all disguise themselves—one as a shepherd/woodman and another as an Amazon princess, "Zelmane." Day's treatment of Zelmane is an extended inversion of the disguised heroine motif found in a number of New Romantic Comedies of the 1590s. As Zelmane's beloved, Violetta, puts it, *"Zelmane's* humor would afford project for a pretty Court comedy; my father courts her for a woman, and as I fear she is; my mother dotes upon her for a man, and as I wish he were . . ." (sig. D3ᵛ).

As this quotation suggests, Day underscores the conventionality of his material. The Prologue readily admits that "the argument . . . [is] a little string or Rivulet, drawn from the full strain of the right worthy Gentleman, Sir *Philip Sidney's* well-known Arcadia." Day borrows Sidney's characters without even changing their names, although he coarsens their personalities considerably, and he lifts a few other characters from Shakespeare's *A Midsummer Night's Dream* and Daniel's court pastoral, *The Queen's Arcadia* (Christ Church, Oxford, 1605), again without rechristening them. If *The Isle of Gulls* is a vulgar travesty of Arcadian pastoralism, as has been suggested,[10] then Day clearly wished his spectators to know what they were condescending to.

Writing for private-theater audiences in the early years of James's reign was not easy. Day dramatizes the problem—as he perceived it—in the Induction to *The Isle of Gulls,* where three "spectators" demand three different things—bawdry, topical satire, and rich poetry, and while the Prologue assures them they cannot all be satisfied by the same play, Day manages to supply them with generous amounts of the first two categories. Sometimes he does so in the traditional manner of Edwardes and Lyly, by introducing a witty page who furnishes the usual assortment of bawdy riddles, puns, and chop-logic, as in the following passage:

> *Demetrius:* Boy, how dost like me in this attire?
> *Page:* As the audience do a bad play, scurvily.
> *Demetrius:* Is it not strange a prince should be thus metamorphosed?
> *Page:* Not so strange as the metamorphosis of *Ajax* and like your grace.
>
> (sig. B4ᵛ)

But Day makes relatively little use of the page, and all of Day's characters make ribald jests, even—or especially—his "innocent" heroines:

> *Hippolita:* I warrant you, sister, an old lady in Lacedemon taught me a preservative against that.
> *Violetta:* For the love of cherries what.
> *Hippolita:* Marry this it was, still said she, betwixt every cherry said she, be sure to crack a stone, said she.

Violetta: Then let me alone, I'll crack a couple of stones betwixt every cherry, rather than surfeit on 'em.

(sig. D2^v)

Like the bawdry, the satire spills out over the subplot, where Lyly, Shakespeare, and Greene would have confined it, and seeps through the entire play. As we have already noted, Day's satire of James and his favorites was audacious enough to cause a minor scandal. Dametas, the chief favorite, is a gentleman "of the best and last edition, of the Duke's own making" (sig. B2). He and his minions are doubly corrupt, taking bribes and then betraying their clients, while the Duke occupies himself, like James, with hunting. The following exchange exposes the irresponsibility and obsequiousness behind the pecking order at court:

Duke: Dametas, reward their travails with 200 Crowns. . . .
Dametas: Manasses, see the fellows entertained; I must attend of the Duke.
Manasses: Boy, see the fellows entertained. I must wait of my lord.
Boy: Fellows, be as merry as you may, I must follow my M[aster].

(sig. E3)

The ridicule of these comic villains comes to a head at the end of the play, where Dametas and Manasses, along with their wives, are thoroughly discomfited. The satiric pulse is further quickened by a host of incidental anachronistic or indecorous references that creep into the dialogue as metaphors:

Now doth my Master long more to finger that gold, then a young girl married to an old man, doth to run her husband ashore at Cuckhold's Haven.

(sig. C2)

Well-trained from his prentice days in Henslowe's workshop to give an audience what it wanted, Day took an old form and adapted it along lines calculated to flatter (and abuse) the real or would-be aristocrats at Blackfriars. He did so by handling the conventions of Arcadian pastoralism with pedestrian ingenuity and by stuffing it with bawdry and topical satire, frequently reminding his audience of the theatrical artifice with words like "scene," "comedian," "plot," and "stage." Although we cannot be sure if his intention was to parody New Romantic Comedy, he clearly lacked confidence in the imaginative power of the traditional form and in his own ability to handle or to enliven it. Whether parody or inept imitation, the work of writers like Day indicates that the form established by Greene and Shakespeare had run its course. By this time, even Shakespeare had stopped writing New Romantic Comedies after ambitious but flawed attempts in *All's Well* (1602–3) and *Measure for Measure* (c.1604) to incorporate complex moral and psychological problems into the form.

"Comical Satire" and Humors Satire

Other writers for the children's troupes shortly after the turn of the century adapted New Romantic Comedy without subverting it as thoroughly as Day had done. Their strategy was to combine a conventional romantic action with a fully developed satiric plot, not merely with a series of loosely connected satiric episodes. The satiric plot is usually an elaborate intrigue designed to discomfit one or more "humors" characters, whom Northrop Frye describes as "people in some kind of mental bondage, who are helplessly driven by ruling passions, neurotic compulsions, social rituals, and selfishness . . . [,] people who do not know fully what they are doing, who are slaves to a predictable self-imposed pattern of behavior."[11] In the children's plays, a "humor" can be anything from foolish role-playing to deceitful imposture, from harmless idiosyncrasy to menacing psychosis. To choose a late example, in *The Woman Hater* (Paul's, 1605–7), Beaumont combines the love story of the Duke of Milan and the slandered virgin, Oriana, with relentless attacks on a misogynist, a gluttonous parasite, and a lecher. In some of the children's plays closer to the turn of the century, such as Marston's *Antonio and Mellida* (1599–1600), Chapman's *Sir Giles Goosecap* (c.1603), Middleton's *The Family of Love* (1602–3), and possibly Jonson's *The Case Is Altered* (1600–8), we find servant episodes and satiric "humors" plot either fused or side by side. But these Lylyesque servant scenes are clearly the vestiges of an archaic convention and eventually disappear, while the satiric "humors" plot burgeons until it counterbalances and even dwarfs the complementary romantic action.

The importance of satiric victims to the success of children's plays is nicely illustrated by a passage in Chapman's *Monsieur D'Olive*. The main action of this comedy includes two parallel romantic actions of symbolic death-and-rebirth in high-flown blank verse. In one, the Count St. Anne forsakes his pathological devotion to his wife's corpse, while in the other, the Countess Marcellina forsakes her morbid vow never to leave her chamber or see daylight. Yet the satiric "humors" plot of the discomfiting of the title character—a self-styled courtier who is deluded into preparing for an imaginary ambassadorship—is apparently what the audience came to see. When D'Olive's bubble finally bursts, Chapman keeps the spectators from leaving by promising additional mirth at the expense of the satiric butt: "Here we may strike the *Plaudite* to our Play, my Lord fool's gone: all our audience will forsake us . . . if need be, our Muse is not so barren, but she is able to devise one trick or other to retire *D'Olive* to Court again" (IV.iv.151–61). The play ends with D'Olive humiliated once more, though patted on the head for his desire to please the Duke.

Marston, too, frequently combines conventional New Romantic Comedy with "humors" satire. *Jack Drum's Entertainment* is subtitled "The Comedy of Pasquil and Katherine" and its romantic action follows the "labyrinth of these strange crosses" that precede the final union of the lovers. Anticipating Middleton's city comedy, Marston makes his hero, Pasquil, a "low-ebbed gallant" (III, 198), while the rival suitor, Mammon, a wealthy usurer, is representative of the impotent older generation with his "dead rheumy chops" and "shrunk bloodless arm" (III, 201). On two occasions, Katherine rejects Mammon's suit, and when the usurer witnesses her warm reception of Pasquil, he hires Monsieur John fo de King to assassinate his rival. The Frenchman, however, reveals the plot to Pasquil, who pretends to be dead but then arises to beat the gloating usurer. Katherine, who believes that Pasquil is really dead, wanders off "tearing her hair" (III, 205), laments his death, and tries to kill herself, but is stopped by Pasquil himself. The happiness of the reunited lovers is shattered by a motif borrowed from the *Arcadia* when Mammon disfigures Katherine's face with a deadly "oil of Toads" (III, 217), and the heroine runs off again while Pasquil goes mad. When Katherine's beauty is miraculously restored by "a skillful Beldam with the Juice of herbs" (III, 235) and Pasquil is cured of his madness, the lovers are permanently reunited.

Marston's attitude toward his romantic lovers oscillates between reverence and ridicule. Sometimes, he has them exchange Lylyesque balanced speeches, rhymed couplets, or rhymed stichomythia, while their symmetrical vows in the final scene end in unison to suggest blissful concord:

Pasquil:. . . Dear *Katherine,* the life of *Pasquil's* hopes.
Katherine: Dear *Pasquil,* the life of *Katherine's* hopes.
Pasquil: Once more let me embrace the constant'st one
    That e're was termed her Sex['s] perfection.
Katherine: Once more let me be valued worth his love,
    In decking of whose soul, the graces strove.
Pasquil: Spite hath outspent itself, and thus at last,
Both speak: We clip with joyful arm each other's waist.
                               (III, 236)

There is a playfulness in the extravagant rhetoric of Marston's lovers which usually stops just short of parody or burlesque. But not always. During one of his searches for Katherine, Pasquil is so desperate to hear news of her that he virtually invites the page to torment him, Marston employing a device of verbal slapstick which he used at least twice in *Antonio and Mellida:*

Pasquil: Now my kind Page, canst thou nor hear, nor see,
    Which way my *Katherine* hath bent her steps?
Page: Sir, I can.
Pasquil: What canst thou, my sweet Page?
    What canst thou, Boy?
    Oh, how my soul doth burn in longing hope,
    And hangs upon thy lips for pleasing news.
Page: Sir, I can tell ye.
Pasquil: What? o, how my heart doth quake & throb with
    fear.
Page: Sir, I can tell you nothing of her in good faith.
                              (III, 213–14)

Had Marston used more banter of this sort, he could easily have turned all of the scenes of romantic comedy into burlesque. But as in the Antonio plays, Marston evidently wanted to jolt his audience with violent contrasts in tone. After the passage just quoted, for example, Pasquil dismisses the boy, prays to the "omnipotent infinity" to spare him "racking torment" and "sharp affliction," and disavows any "lustful or profane intent" toward Katherine. This speech provides a transition from the humorous exchange with the page to the melodramatic scene in which he saves Katherine from killing herself.

While Pasquil is a standard romantic-comedy hero with touches of irony, Mammon, like Piero in *Antonio and Mellida,* is the stock "heavy" of low comedy who invites his own discomfiting. Thus, the usurer's gloating over his rival's supposed death is swiftly terminated by the thrashing which Pasquil gives him. Furthermore, after Mammon has disfigured Katherine's face and escaped, Marston makes him reenter on the flimsiest of pretexts: he is looking for his lost spectacles. Pasquil, in his madness, mistakes the usurer for an astrologer and vents his rage at *"dira fata"* by ripping up what he thinks are "prognostications" but which are actually the usurer's indentures, or bonds (III, 217-18); Mammon is further discomfited by the news, delivered by his page with obvious glee, that his house and property have gone up in flames. So jolted is Mammon by these reverses that he loses his mind, and at the end of the play is reportedly being whipped in Bedlam. Thus, as he did in the two-part Antonio play, Marston inserts a farcical villain and verbal slapstick into a New Romantic Comedy, producing the violent juxtapositions we noticed in those "seriously fantastical" works.

Romantic elements in *Jack Drum's Entertainment* are not only complicated by tonal contrasts but overwhelmed by "humors" satire. Indeed, there are three separate satiric and low-comic actions: (1) the courting of Camelia by Ellis, Puff, and Brabant Junior—respectively, an affected malcontent, a tobacco-smoking euphuist and a dejected inamorato, (2) the wooing of Camelia's maid Winifred which leads to the beating and humiliation of Jack Drum and John fo de King, and (3) the cuckolding of Brabant Senior. Whatever artistic unity emerges from this medley of satiric and low-comic action is due to the presence of Ned Planet, who, like Quadratus in *What You Will,* coolly directs the audience's ridicule toward the usual collection of "humors" types, as well as toward Brabant Senior, a conventional satirist. Planet's style as a satirist is more detached, less bilious than Brabant Senior's. In addition to exposing Camelia's inconstancy and Winifred's duplicity, Planet has been working for the discomfiting of Brabant Senior since Act I:

> I will eat his meat, and spend's money, that's all the
> spite I can do him: but if I can get a Patent for concealed
> Sots, that Daw shall troop among my Idiots.
>
> (III, 194)

When Brabant Senior offers to take John fo de King to "a loose, lascivious Courtesan," intending to introduce the lecherous fool to his (Brabant's) wife, Planet prays that the scheme will boomerang—"The wicked Jest be turned on his own head, / Pray God he may be kindly Cuckolded" (III, 222)—and finds his prayer answered in the last act.

Marston's *What You Will* (Paul's, 1601) is a similar blend of romantic and satiric actions, but when we compare Marston's romantic action with its source, Sforza D'Oddi's *I Morti Vivi* (pub. 1576), we can see that Marston deliberately avoided the type of high romance which formed the main plots of *Antonio* and *Jack Drum's Entertainment.* Marston ignored the main plot of D'Oddi's play, a tragicomic story of a heroine who is separated from her lover by disguise and rumored death, and who nearly sacrifices her claim to him because she believes, mistakenly, that he will be happier with another woman. He turned instead to the more comical subplot, which he made still livelier and more farcical.[12] Whereas D'Oddi's "widow" was a noble heroine made sympathetic by slander, by her own misgivings about a second marriage, and by an unrequited passion, Celia, who doesn't appear until the fourth act, is besieged by suitors and has no qualms about remarrying. Marston's other alterations lighten the atmosphere by compounding confusion. First, unlike D'Oddi he withholds the knowledge of Albano's return from all but Albano's servant and the audience; secondly, he introduces the idea of yet another "false" Albano—Laverdure's fiddler, which leads to a second scene in which Albano vainly tries to establish his identity, where D'Oddi had only one; thirdly, Marston adopts the Plautine device of bringing Albano face to face with his alter ego, as D'Oddi did not. Thus, Marston omitted the tragicomic main plot of D'Oddi's play in favor of the comical subplot, which he made even more comical while preserving its romantic outlines. The result is a comic action which can accommodate both the pathos and the farcicality of lost identity and fuse them with a conventional romantic comedy of a husband returning from the dead to reclaim his faithful wife.

To the romantic material borrowed from D'Oddi, Marston added a number of discrete satiric actions involving cheeky "cracks," a witty young woman, and a raisonneur. The pages, led by Bidet and Holofernes Pippo, figure in three distinctly saturnalian episodes: (1) after the usual Lylyesque remarks about dicing, cheating their masters, and servants' life, the pages set up a mock-court and crown Bidet as *"Emperor of Cracks, Prince of Pages, Marquis of Mumchance, and sole regent over a bale of false dice"* (II, 270); (2) a doltish pedant is outwitted by his pupils, who, like Lyly's pages, subvert the forms and jargon of academic discourse; and (3) Simplicius

Faber is gulled into a liaison with a page disguised as a merchant's wife, and is fleeced in the bargain by another page disguised as the lady's fool. Meletza, Celia's sister, resembles Rossaline in *Antonio and Mellida*, Beatrice in *Much Ado*, and other witty female companions who enjoy mocking their wooers. Act IV opens with Meletza's scornful appraisal of her and Celia's suitors, some of whom do not appear in the play and are simply the familiar targets of formal satire:

> *Dupatzo* the elder brother, the fool, he that bought the half-penny ribbon, wearing it in his ear, swearing 'twas the Duchess of *Milan's* favor, he into whose head a man may travel 10 leagues before he can meet with his eyes; . . . then there's the cap-cloaked Courtier *Baltazar:* he wears a double treble quadruple ruff, aye in the summer time.
>
> (II, 276)

The chief agent of satiric ridicule is not Meletza nor any of the pages, but Quadratus, the authorial spokesman who directs the audience's derision toward such conventional targets as the love-sick amorist, the effiminate courtier, and the fashion-hound. But Quadratus reserves his heaviest artillery for Lampatho Doria, the ex-scholar and conventional satirist, as Marston turns satiric ridicule back upon the railing persona of verse satire and "comical satire." Early in the play, Quadratus complains that satiric railing has become commonplace and inhibits the development of colorful idiosyncrasies, or "fantasticness":

> . . . 'tis now grown fashion,
> What's out of railing's out of fashion:
> A man can scarce put on a tucked-up cap,
> A buttoned frizado suit, scarce eat good meat,
> *Anchovies, caviar,* but he's *Satired*

And termed *Fantastical* by the muddy spawn
Of slimy Newts.

(II, 250)

In *The Dutch Courtesan* (Queen's Revels, 1603–5) Marston
moved further away from "humors" satire by transforming his
raisonneur into the mad prankster, Cocledemoy, who tor-
ments a single victim, the Puritan vintner Mulligrub, "for wit's
sake" (V.iii.135), but in *What You Will,* an earlier play, Marston shows a characteristic ambivalence toward the "humors"
satire tradition.

"Comical satire," the term Jonson applied to his brand of
"humors" satire, is a dramatic adaptation of nondramatic satire of the 1590s. It preserves the basic structural principle of
formal satire, whereby a blunt, plain-speaking adherent to
old-fashioned virtues encounters a series of fools, and describes and denounces them. The pattern of action in formal
satire generally included three stages: the fools "had to be introduced with much identifying detail, exhibited in characteristic action, and finally deflated and discomfited." [13] Using
Every Man Out of His Humor (Lord Chamberlain's Men, 1599)
as a model, Campbell finds this pattern in several satiric comedies by Jonson and Marston. Whereas Marston combines
satire with romantic comedy, Jonson's *Every Man Out,
Cynthia's Revels,* and *Poetaster* are essentially dramatic adaptations of contemporary verse satire, sometimes adding a final
phase in which the chastened fools are readmitted to society. The various types of fools that appeared in verse satire,
such as the prodigal gallant, the puritan usurer, and the
lecherous citizen's wife—were easily transferred to the stage,
sometimes as "humors" characters, while the formal satirist's
persona, as Alvin Kernan has argued, appeared in dramatized
satire as a quasiauthorial spokesman. Such spokesmen

frequently forsake their self-proclaimed stoic patience for violent indignation, following their Juvenalian models and the belief that "satire," falsely derived from "satyr," signified a harsh and biting form of literature. The function of these satyr-like commentators in dramatic satire, as in formal satire, is to kindle the audience's indignation and "to keep alive in the spectators a hostile spirit of mockery toward practically all of the other figures in the comedy." [14] But in dramatic satire, at least those performed by the children's troupes, they also fulfilled two other vital functions: they embodied the spirit of festal abuse and deflected the spectators' mockery toward victims provided by the playwright.

Nearly all of the plays Campbell classifies as "comical satires" were performed by children's troupes, and the exceptions—*Every Man Out, Histriomastix,* and *Troilus and Cressida*—may have been written for similar audiences at court or at one of the inns of court.[15] We can easily understand why private-theater spectators and similar audiences were attracted to "comical satire." First of all, as John Wilcox has argued, satiric epigrams and formal satire based on classical models had come to be regarded as literary forms appropriate to young courtiers.[16] Following the pattern established by Sir John Harington when he came to court in the early 1580s, men like Davies, Donne, Hall, and Marston—young men of good family and university background, often connected with inns of court—used these forms to advertise their wittiness. Wilcox suggests that these satires and epigrams generally circulated among the courtiers in manuscript and were not intended for publication, Marston being the first to write his satires with publication in mind, just as in the roles of playwright and investor he helped bring courtly plays to a slightly wider audience.

A second reason for the cordiality of private-theater audiences to formal satire and subsequently to "comical satire" was the satirists' espousal of conservative, aristocratic values. When dealing with economic and social matters, the satirists or their personae tend to sound like landed aristocrats feeling the pinch of economic change or like scholar-courtiers resentful of ill-bred parvenus. Thus, the satires protest the enrichment of merchants, puritans, and usurers, the importation of "luxury" goods, the rise of the *nouveaux riches* and other upstarts, and the decay of "housekeeping." As Hallet Smith has written, the satirist of the 1590s usually supported the traditional ideal of " 'honesty,' meaning a kind of rugged simplicity and practicality" against the more recent ideal of " 'bravery,' meaning refinement, bravado, the flourish of superiority," the latter having a decidedly Italianate cast.[17] In the private theaters after 1599, "comical satire" allowed courtiers and upstarts alike to flatter themselves by accepting the satirists' conservative aristocratic values, at least for the duration of the play.

"Comical satire" flourished in the private theaters in many forms: in its pure state in *Poetaster,* more often combined or juxtaposed with other elements, with Lylyesque comedy in *Cynthia's Revels,* with New Romantic Comedy in early plays by Chapman and Marston, and with duke (or gallant)-in-disguise plots in plays like Middleton's *Your Five Gallants,* Marston's *The Fawn,* and later Sharpham's *The Fleer.* But in the opening years of the seventeenth century, the children's troupes were parodying conventions of "comical satire," especially its central device of the encounter between a satiric persona and a series of stock fools, just as in the late 1590s the children's troupes had parodied the conventions of Lyly's comedy, the staple of their repertories in the 1580s and early 1590s. Such parody, or self-parody, was in keeping with the festal abuse underlying children's plays and with the drama-turgical strategies designed to channel the audience's deri-sion toward appropriate targets. Such targets include not only the standard kinds of fools—the "others," the deviants from the aristocratic ethos, but "other" playwrights, acting compa-nies, and audiences unfashionable enough to accept the out-worn conventions of an antiquated form like "comical satire."

Campbell has traced the influence of Jonson's "comical sat-ire" on the structure of Marston's satiric "humor" plots. In plays like *The Malcontent* (Queen's Revels, c.1603) and *The Fawn*, a duke disguises himself as a conventional satirist and then encounters, ridicules, and exposes a procession of stock satiric fools. But, as we already noted, Marston frequently sat-irized the conventional satirist. In both Antonio plays, Feliche's constant railing clashes oddly with his proclamations of con-tentment, and in *Antonio's Revenge*, the hero prefers a fool's disguise to "some habit of a spitting critic," which he calls "the very flesh of solid folly" (IV.i.4–8). In *Jack Drum's Enter-tainment*, the real raisonneur, Ned Planet, criticizes the sa-tirist Brabant Senior for surveying his friends "with an eye / Only create[d] to censure from above" (III, 229). Planet calls Brabant Senior one of the "bombast wits, / That are puffed up with arrogant conceit / Of their own worth" (III, 229), and likens the conventional satirist to "a pair of Bal-ance, / . . .[which] weighest all saving thyself" (III, 221). In Marston's *What You Will*, Quadratus encourages the audience to mock the fledgling satirist, Lampatho Doria, and forces him to admit that his railing is merely a popular sort of posturing:

This is the strain that chokes the theaters,
That makes them crack with full-stuffed audience,
This is your humor only in request,
Forsooth, to rail, this brings your ears to bed,

This people gape for, for this some do stare,
This some would hear, to crack the Author's neck,
This admiration and applause pursues.

(II, 266)

Having exposed the conventional satirist's true motives, Quadratus dismisses him as an "envy-starved Cur," "a scrubbing railer," and a "Don Kinsayder" (II, 248–49), the name of Marston's own satiric persona in *The Scourge of Villainy.* Although some scholars have tried to extend the *poetomachia*—the "flyting" between Jonson and Marston—to include *What You Will* and *Jack Drum's Entertainment,* neither Brabant Senior nor Lampatho Doria have any specifically Jonsonian traits.[18] Rather than singling out Jonson for special lampooning, Marston is probably declaring his independence from conventional satiric techniques which he and other writers for the children's troupes had used and continued to use.

Satiromastix (Lord Chamberlain's Men and Paul's, 1601), however, which Marston wrote in collaboration with Dekker, attacks Jonson the satirist in pointed particular. The main action, the discomfiting of Horace, the satirist, is indicated by the title, translated loosely in the subtitle as "the untrussing of the humorous poet." Borrowing characters from *Poetaster,* the authors of *Satiromastix* make Captain Tucca collaborate with Demetrius and Crispinus (the Dekker and Marston figures mocked in Jonson's play) in directing the audience's ridicule toward Horace, Jonson's alter ego. A professional satirist, theoretically committed to attacking the vice and not the individual, Horace accepts two shillings from Sir Vaughan to write a general satire on baldness, but, taking his cue from his patron, he actually composes a personal attack on Sir Adam Prickshaft. Like Lampatho Doria, he also composes satiric epigrams against his own patrons, such as the one he circulates against Tucca, and then tries to ingratiate himself with his benefactor-victims. As Tucca charges, " 'Tis thy fashion to flirt Ink in every man's face; and then to crawl into his bosom, and damn thyself to wipe't off again" (IV.ii.77–79). In his plays, Horace mocks his enemies, assaults "a company of honorable and worshipful Fathers of the Law," and maligns "worshipful Citizens" (IV.iii.185–86,194–95).

With pointed reference to Jonson, Tucca seconds Quadratus' attack on satire for inhibiting the cultivation of idiosyncrasy:

> A Gentleman, or an honest Citizen, shall not Sit in your penny-bench Theaters, with his Squirrel by his side cracking nuts; nor sneak into a Tavern with his Mermaid; but he shall be Satyred, and Epigrammed upon, and his humor must run upo'th' Stage: you'll ha' *Every Gentleman in's humor,* and *Every Gentleman out on's humor.*
> (IV.ii.52–57) [19]

Horace, then, clearly represents Jonson in his role of professional satirist, and the play, acted at Paul's and the Globe, provides revenge for gallants and citizens who felt themselves victimized by such railers.

In the last scene, Horace is brought onstage to be punished in the costume of a satyr, a literal representation of the satirist's biting, snarling persona. Asked why he played the satyrlike railer, Horace's stock rationalization is interrupted by Tucca, who exposes its conventionality:

> *Horace:* I did it to retire me from the world;
>   And turn my *Muse* into a *Timonist,*
>   Loathing the general Leprosy of Sin,
>   Which like a plague runs through the souls of men:
>   I did it but to—
> *Tucca:* But to bite every Motley-head vice by th' nose, you
>   did it

> Ningle to play the Bugbear Satire, and make a Camp
> royal of fashion-mongers quake at your paper
> Bullets.
>
> (V.ii.194–201)

Although *Satiromastix* singles out Jonson as its chief victim, the satirizing of the satirist is found throughout Marston's plays and is itself a convention. Stung by the attack nonetheless, Jonson decided to forsake the field of "comical satire," as he declared in the Apologetical Dialogue appended to *Poetaster*, for the loftier realms of tragedy, thereby also shifting to the adult troupes.

Chapman, like Marston, also kindled his audience's resentment of conventional satire. In *All Fools*, a courtly gallant protests, "Faith, that same vein of railing / Became now most applausive; your best Poet, / Is he that rails grossest" (II.i.336–38), while the foolish title character of Monsieur D'Olive thinks he has arrived in fashionable society when he invites a pair of gallants to his chamber, "where we may take free use of ourselves, that is, drink sack, and talk *Satire* (I.ii.107–08).

In this manner Chapman and Marston led or exploited a reaction against the very type of satiric comedy that had flourished in the private theaters for which they wrote, another illustration of the theatrical self-consciousness and distrust of convention shared by writers and spectators of the children's troupes. Within a few years, "comical satire" had become the butt of other dramatists. In *Northward Ho!* (Paul's, 1605), Dekker and Webster savagely mock Bellamont, possibly a caricature of Chapman.[20] This playwright-poet, whom one character bribes to "bring my wife upon the stage" (I.iii.32–33), is taken for a lunatic while visiting a madhouse, and is then bound, beaten, and kicked. Always quick to follow the trends set by the other two children's troupes, the

Children of the King's Revels also dissociated itself from conventional modes of satire. The Prologue to Barry's *Ram Alley* offers "home-bred mirth" rather than "the Satire's tooth and Waspish sting," while a character in Day's *Humor out of Breath* complains that "humors are picked so near the bone, a man can scarce get humor enough to give a flea his breakfast" (p. 286).

City Comedy

Until "comical satire" itself became the object of satire, it had served the children's troupes and their playwrights very well. Around 1603 or 1604, the more innovative dramatists devised a more flexible mode of satiric drama that dispensed with the rigid structure and explicit moralizing of "comical satire." The form they devised was city comedy, which I have already discussed as an outgrowth of the festal tradition underlying the work of the children's troupes. The most obvious characteristics of city comedy are its many references to well-known places in and around London, and the use of recognizable character types, familiar social tensions, and colloquial diction. But the "realism" of these plays is superficial. Given the age and size of the actors, city comedies performed by children's troupes were refractions rather than reflections of social reality, not photographs but miniaturized caricatures strongly tinged with satiric mimicry. Although the dramatists writing satiric city comedy for the children's troupes found some of their material through first-hand observation, the bulk of it derives from traditional literary sources and contemporary rogue literature—jest books and conny-catching pamphlets, reshaped in ways that would appeal to the private-theater audiences and given a "patina of realism." The city comedies of adult troupes are also distortions of social reality,

idealizing bourgeois values, celebrating innocence over experience, and tending toward romance rather than satire. Made-
leine Doran has succinctly described the difference between
the two types of plays:

> The esstential difference . . . is not so much one of real-
> ism . . . as it is one of attitude and tone. The emphasis is
> on a different set of human motives—on the one hand,
> on poetic longings for love and adventure; on the other,
> on the grosser appetites for women, money, or power.
> The defining difference of tone is the difference between
> lyrical sentiment sympathetically expressed and critical
> satire.[21]

One way to gauge the satiric distortion involved in the children's city comedies is to notice the particular motifs these
plays develop. Indeed, of all the possible motifs to abstract
from the life and literature around them, the writers of these
plays return again and again to a mere three: (1) the triumph
of a prodigal son over an avaricious authority-figure, (2) the
courtship of a rich heiress or widow, and (3) a liaison between
a young gallant and the wife of a jealous old citizen.

The parable of the prodigal son, as we noticed in the last
chapter, provided the material for many of the moralities and
"Christian Terence" plays acted in the latter half of the sixteenth century by children's troupes, probably by troupes of
provincial schoolboys. In the first decade of the seventeenth
century, adult troupes also performed didactic versions of the
parable, like *How a Man May Choose a Good Wife from a Bad*
and *The Wise Woman of Hogsden,* which graphically illustrate
the dangers of the sin of prodigality. At the same time, the
London children's troupes took the opposite tack, developing
the parable satirically, by evoking sympathy for the prodigal,
mocking the adult world through miniaturization and mim-

icry, and supplementing the Biblical narrative with episodes taken from conny-catching pamphlets and jest books. Most of these sympathetic prodigals are attractive young gallants cheated of their patrimony by unscrupulous father-figures. This tendency is clear even before the rise of city comedy, as in a play like Marston's *Jack Drum's Entertainment* (1600), where the romantic hero, Pasquil, is an impoverished gallant and his adversary, Mammon, a lecherous old usurer. In the children's city comedies, the prodigal heroes command even more sympathy than the bizarre Pasquil. We easily forgive them their follies as the peccadilloes of hot-blooded youth, applaud the intrigues by which they regain their wealth, and approve their acquisition of worldly experience. Middleton seems to have been the first to develop this theme, and did so in a brilliantly varied series of plays for the Children of Paul's—*Michaelmas Term, A Mad World, My Masters,* and *A Trick to Catch the Old One,* all three generally dated between 1604 and 1606.[22] The last of these plays was somehow acquired by the Children of the Queen's Revels, probably in 1607 after the Paul's boys disbanded. Other Queen's Revels plays like Jonson's *Epicoene* and Fletcher's *The Scornful Lady* [23] are later modifications of the prodigal-son parable for the same troupe, while two of their plays—*Eastward Ho!* and *The Knight of the Burning Pestle*—parody the public-theater variety of prodigal-son play. The third boy company, the short-lived Children of the King's Revels which flourished in 1607 and 1608, found their own prodigal-son play in Barry's *Ram Alley,* the first half of which is a close imitation of *A Trick to Catch the Old One.*

The prodigal-son motif often blends with another—the courting of wealthy heiresses and widows—for a good match helps the prodigal-heroes to recoup their losses. There is usually a fortune-hunter hiding inside every romantic hero,

but public-theater dramatists, like Shakespeare in his treatment of Bassanio, do all they can to make the heroine's
wealth seem incidental or the just deserts of a fairy-tale hero.
The children's playwrights, on the other hand, strip away the
romantic veil and expose the commercial nature of such relationships, and for that reason prefer widows to young heiresses. Here too the tendency precedes city comedy. In *Satiromastix*, by Marston and Dekker, several rivals compete for
the hand of a rich widow, Mistress Miniver, while both actions of Chapman's *Sir Giles Goosecap* revolve around the
wooing of the wealthy widow Eugenia. Here too the Children
of Paul's was the first boy company to develop the motif into
a full city comedy: Chapman's lost *The Old Joiner of Aldgate*,
produced just before March 19, 1603, when the theaters
closed because of Elizabeth's illness. They remained closed
for about a year because of her death and the plague that followed. Shortly after they reopened, the Children of the
Queen's Revels performed their own "fortune-hunter" city
comedies, such as *Eastward Ho!*, where the impoverished Sir
Petronel Flash lures a goldsmith's social-climbing daughter
into marriage. Though not a city comedy because of its Cyprian setting, half of Chapman's *The Widow's Tears* is devoted
to the pursuit of the widow Eudora by Tharsalio, a typical
Jacobean younger-brother. The Children of Paul's responded
with Middleton's *The Puritan* (1606), in which an impoverished but nobly born scholar and an ex-captain stalk a wealthy
widow and her daughter.[24] The Children of the King's Revels
once again wasted no time producing its own "fortune-hunter" play: the second half of Barry's *Ram Alley* dramatizes Will
Smallshanks' audacious conquest of the rich widow, Mistress
Taffeta.

The third theme of the children's city comedies is the liaison between a lecherous gallant, sometimes a prodigal-son,

and the wife of a jealous old citizen. The contemporaneous public-theater plays using this theme emphasize the suffering of a chaste heroine, who is assaulted, slandered, or wrongly suspected, and they always end with the preservation of her innocence and the restoration of her good name, as in pathetic-heroine plays performed much earlier by children's troupes—*Virtuous and Godly Susanna, Patient Grissel, Godly Queen Hester.* Shakespeare, Heywood, and Dekker are particularly fond of the abused heroine, and some even wander into Dekker's private-theater plays, although we shall find that their significance there is curtailed.

As we saw in an earlier chapter, the subplot of Middleton's *A Mad World, My Masters* parodies the public-theater handling of this motif: afflicted by guilt, the lecherous Penitent Brothel forswears his adulterous passion—after it has been gratified; as he and his mistress pledge their allegiance to chastity, the jealous husband applauds, unaware that he has already been cuckolded. Whether or not such affairs are consummated in private-theater plays often depends more on circumstance than on resolute virtue, as the women are often witty and flirtatious even when they are honest, unlike the humorless exemplars of female purity we find in the public-theater plays of Heywood and Dekker. The husbands too are handled differently. Public-theater plays present them as sober and responsible, private-theater plays as impotent and jealous, and generally ridicule the folly of jealous "humors." Again the presence of the gallant-city wife motif in children's plays antedates city comedy. In Jonson's *Poetaster* (1601), Chloe, the wife of the citizen Albius, entertains a crowd of gallants at supper and later plays Venus to Tucca's Mars. The first children's city comedy to develop this motif is once more a Paul's play—Dekker's and Webster's *Westward Ho!* (1604), with its lecherous earl, innocent wife, jealous husband, and three more such triangles. Even before the Children of Paul's could follow up its own success by producing Dekker's and Webster's *Northward Ho!* (1605), the Children of the Queen's Revels echoed the title in *Eastward Ho!*, which includes Sir Petronel Flash's affair with Winifred, wife of the old usurer, Security. The Prologue to the play suggests how eager the Children of the Queen's Revels was to cash in on the success of its rivals at Paul's:

> Not out of Envy, for there's no effect
> Where there's no cause; nor out of Imitation,
> For we have evermore been imitated;
> Nor out of our contention to do better
> Then that which is opposed to ours in Title,
> For that was good; and better cannot be.

The polite bow to the competition clashes with the specious insistence that "*we* have ever more been imitated" (my italics) and fails to conceal a raid on their rivals' clientele. Baring their rampant commercial rivalry would be unseemly for purveyors of dramatic entertainment to the court and nobility. Whoever was first in the field, we can agree, I think, with Chapman, Jonson, and Marston that "Eastward . . . westwards still exceeds," as it does northwards, too. In fact, *Eastward Ho!* surpasses both of Dekker's and Webster's collaborations not only in quality, but also by developing all three of the motifs of satiric city comedy—the prodigal son (which it parodies), the fortune hunter, and the class conflict played out as sexual rivalry. This last motif was particularly favored by the writers for the Children of the King's Revels. In nearly all their plays—whether or not they are set in London—gallants like Sir Petronel try to seduce citizens' wives, and several of these works, like Day's *Law Tricks* and Machin's *The Dumb*

Knight, ridicule the husband's jealous "humor." With *Cupid's Whirligig,* a true city comedy by Sharpham, the King's Revels had already reached the limit of such ridicule, for in this play the jealous husband has himself gelded to prove that any children his wife bears are the fruit of adultery, and while the play ends with the couple remarried after a divorce, Sharpham has failed to include a miraculous reversal of the husband's condition.

Several patterns emerge from a close study of the three most prevalent motifs in children's city comedies. First of all, they occur in other kinds of children's plays written between 1600 and 1603, so that a list of literary sources for satiric city comedy should include earlier children's plays as well as Roman comedy and rogue literature. Secondly, while these motifs occur peripherally in the plays acted before 1603, they are central thereafter. Thirdly, the Children of Paul's were the first to develop each of the three motifs into a full-fledged city comedy; they were followed soon after (and sometimes outdone) by the Children of the Queen's Revels, and somewhat later by the Children of the King's Revels, who generally cheapened and coarsened as they imitated.

One can also notice how differently the adult troupes handled the same motifs. Eventually, adult troupes produced satiric city comedies, like Jonson's *The Alchemist* (King's Men, c.1610), which have the satiric qualities of the children's city comedies and none of the usual distancing devices of earlier adult city comedies. However, these two plays were performed several years after the choristers had established the mode of satiric city comedy. Most of the city comedies performed by the adult companies in the first decade of the seventeenth century are predominantly romantic rather than satiric comedies, including the city comedies which Dekker and

Middleton wrote for adult companies. On the other hand, all
of the city comedies acted by the children's troupes are satiric.

Writing City Comedy for Boy Companies and Adult Troupes: Dekker and Middleton

Dekker seems to have been naturally inclined toward romantic and sentimental comedy. His favorite central character is
not the prodigal son, who can be handled either satirically or
romantically, but the "abused wife," who demands to be
treated as a romantic heroine. Nearly all of his plays contain a
radiant and stainless heroine of this type, who undergoes
some form of "death and rebirth," demonstrates her innocence in some striking way, and utters or inspires lyrical
expressions of tender feelings. These elements are present
even in Dekker's Paul's plays, but they are the heart and soul
of the city comedies he wrote for adult troupes. *The Shoe-
makers' Holiday* (Lord Admiral's Men, 1599), for instance, has
not one but two pure-hearted heroines, Rose and Jane, both
of humble birth, and a tender-hearted comic villain, Ham-
mon.

Possibly written in collaboration with Middleton, Dekker's
1 Honest Whore (Prince's Men, 1604) is not strictly speaking a
city comedy.[25] The action is set in Milan, but it is a Milan
which includes Bedlam and other features of Jacobean London and the play is therefore distanced in the same fashion as
are other adult-troupe comedies that deal with contemporary
London. Moreover, the play combines two romantic actions
with a farcical subplot. The double main action opens with
the funeral procession of Infelice, daughter of the Duke of
Milan and beloved of Count Hippolito. Infelice is not really

dead, however, but has been given a sleeping potion by her father to prevent her from marrying the son of his enemy.

Interwoven with this conventional romantic comedy is the sentimentalized story of a repentant prostitute. Bellafront, a courtesan, falls in love with the grief-stricken Hippolito, is moved to contrition by his extended attack on prostitution, resolves to become chaste in order to merit his love, and disguises herself as a page. For "comic relief," Dekker includes the farcical tale of Candido, or "the Humors of the Patient Man, and the Longing Wife" (as the play is subtitled), but this action is subordinated to the romantic actions of the play, as it is in all of Dekker's public-theater comedies.

Dekker deemphasizes the romantic actions in his private-theater comedies. In *Westward Ho!* and *Northward Ho!*, both written with Webster as junior collaborator, he offers a satiric main action broken up by brief episodes of "romantic relief." [26] The ostensible hero of *Westward Ho!* is Justiniano, an Italian merchant living in London, who dons a disguise to conceal his intrigue and becomes a middle-class version of Marston's disguised Italian dukes or Middleton's Phoenix. The romantic plot deals with Justiniano's excessive jealousy, the Earl's vain attempt to seduce the merchant's wife through the bawd Birdlime, and Mistress Justiniano's mock-death, which, like Caelestine's in *Satiromastix*, dazzles her would-be seducer into reformation. Most of this episode is written in appropriately stylized verse, often rhymed, which is typified by the Earl's speech of repentance:

> Mirror of dames, I look upon thee now,
> As men long blind, (having recovered sight)
> Amazed: scarce able are to endure the light:
> Mine own shame strikes me dumb: henceforth the book
> I'll read shall be thy mind, and not thy look.
>   (IV.ii.162–66)

The entire action of Justiniano, his slandered wife, and the Earl takes place in three scenes and a few lines (I.i, II.ii, IV.ii, and III.iii.102–8), leaving the rest of the play, largely written in prose, to the adulterous intrigues of the gallants and the citizens' wives, and the counterintrigues of their husbands.

Justiniano's central role in these intrigues links the satiric main action with the romantic action involving his wife and the Earl. In fact the satiric intrigues arise out of the romantic action, when Justiniano, disguised as a writing master, leads the three city wives to the brink of adulterous affairs in order to console himself for what he thinks is his wife's infidelity. Justiniano eventually helps reconcile the citizens with their wives; when it is revealed that the men had visited Birdlime's brothel, they have no choice but to forgive their wives' near-adultery, and the comic resolution of the play is achieved on this note of mutual forgiveness ("amnesty" may be a more accurate term).

Northward Ho!, Dekker's and Webster's second collaborative effort, borrows its romantic action from an "abused-wife" novella by Malespini, but confines this material to two scenes—I.i. and iii. Just as Justiniano suspected his wife's fidelity because of a philandering Earl and his bawd, the mischievous slander of Greenshield and Featherstone causes Mayberry to think himself a cuckold. However, *Northward Ho!* lacks the usual trial of the woman's innocence by mock-death, for Mrs. Mayberry establishes her chastity through sheer eloquence, using the stylized blank verse of Dekker's abused wives:

If ever I had thought unclean,
In detestation of your nuptial pillow:
Let *Sulphur* drop from Heaven, and nail my body
Dead to this earth.

(I.iii.100–3)

After this brief flowering of the romantic mode establishes Mrs. Mayberry's innocence, the play moves on to a number of satiric intrigues: the gulling of the self-righteous Bellamont by his prodigal son, Philip, and the courtesan, Doll; Bellamont's revenge upon Doll; and the discomfiting of Bellamont in the madhouse scene. Mayberry achieves revenge upon his wife's slanderers, Greenshield and Featherstone, by tricking the former into making himself a cuckold and the latter into marriage with Doll. As in *Westward Ho!*, a romantic situation is the mainspring for a satiric action, but while *Westward Ho!* attempts to integrate the two actions, *Northward Ho!* abandons the romantic material after the first act, and is predominantly satiric.

A comparison of Dekker's public- and private-theater plays indicates that he and his collaborators used rather similar romantic and satiric motifs in both kinds of plays, deliberately allowed the latter to predominate in plays for the children's troupes, but reversed the proportion in plays for adult troupes. Just how deliberate this procedure was can be seen in *The Roaring Girl* (Prince's Men, 1610). Here one would suspect that collaboration with Middleton, the writer of a number of satiric city comedies, would result in a satiric play, but the influence of the adult troupe and the public-theater audience was stronger. *The Roaring Girl* is essentially a romantic comedy sprinkled with satiric echoes from Dekker's and Webster's *Ho!* plays for the Children of Paul's. The central and controlling action of the play is the triumph of young love—the story of how Sebastian Wengrave overcomes his father's opposition and marries Mary Fitz-Allard. The romantic treatment of this action is obvious from the first scene, where Mary appears on stage disguised as a seamstress in order to enter the Wengrave house without arousing the old man's suspicion, just as she later assumes the Fletcherian disguise of a page for the same reason. Unlike the heroines of most satiric city comedies, Mary Fitz-Allard is not stolen away from a father, father-surrogate, or doltish rival(s), and even though Sebastian intrigues against his father, the old man is in no way discomfited. To force his father to accept Mary Fitz-Allard as a daughter-in-law, Sebastian pretends to dote on an even less acceptable girl—Moll Cutpurse, the Roaring Girl, an Amazon with a heart of gold. The subplot is a satiric episode of near-adultery between gallants and citizens' wives, and the similarity to *Westward Ho!* is acknowledged:

> *Master Openwork:* . . . pray tell me why
>   Your two flags were advanced; the Comedy,
>   Come what's the Comedy?
> *Mistress Gallipot:*   Westward ho.
> *Master Openwork:*   How?
> *Mistress Openwork:* 'Tis Westward ho she says.
>   (IV.ii.121–26)

But unlike *Westward Ho!*, *The Roaring Girl* confines the intrigue between the gallants and the citizens' wives to three long scenes in the middle of the play (II.i, III.ii, and IV.ii) and the reconciliation scene heavily stresses the women's innocence and the gallants' discomfiture.

If Dekker was returning to his own predilection for romance in *The Roaring Girl,* his collaborator Middleton was working against his own inclinations. Despite this difference, a comparison of Middleton's private- and public-theater plays yields the same pattern found in the study of Dekker's work, although the results must be more tentative in Middleton's case because he wrote most of his plays for the adult troupes after the children's troupes had dissolved.

Middleton, far more than any other dramatists for the children's troupes, is identified with satiric city comedy. Even *The*

Phoenix, nominally set in Ferrara, abounds in local allusions, analyzes the social tensions of Jacobean London, and satirizes familiar English character types. His other duke-in-disguise plays—*The Family of Love* and *Your Five Gallants*—are even more thoroughly domesticated. Their action takes place in London, the protagonists are not princes but English gentlemen who disguise themselves as a doctor and a scholar. Despite their surface "realism," these three plays are essentially "comical satires," with a brief romantic action thrown in for contrast or to add a sexual dimension to the hero's triumph over his adversaries. Like Jonson's and Marston's satiric raisonneurs, the heroes of these three plays observe, expose, and correct or punish a conventional assortment of fools and knaves of the various "estates" of English life—cheating lawyers, corrupt courtiers, grasping merchants, lecherous citizens' wives, hypocritical puritans, and upstart gallants.

Far more original are the three satiric city comedies which Middleton cast in the form of the prodigal-son parable between 1604 and 1606. *Michaelmas Term,* probably the earliest one, is unique in that half of the action is devoted to the swindling of the hero, Easy, "a fair, free-breasted gentleman, somewhat too open" (I.i.5), by the merchant Quomodo and his two "spirits," Shortyard and Falselight. By means of "gullgroping" and loans upon commodity—techniques described in Greene's *Notable Discovery of Cozenage* (1591) and other works of rogue literature—they soon fleece Easy of his family estate in Essex.[27] Quomodo is extremely successful in gulling Easy, though the hero's early defeats function as Tharsalio's do in *The Widow's Tears* to quicken our appetite for his eventual triumph. When Quomodo overreaches himself by feigning death, like Volpone, Easy frees himself from the merchant's trap, having learned the ways of the city by painful experience.

In the brief romantic intrigue of the main plot of *Michaelmas Term*, Thomasine, Quomodo's wife, watches from above as her husband cheats the young gallant. She declares her love for the victim in a six-line soliloquy at the end of one such gulling scene (III.iv.242–47), proposes to him in a brief encounter after Quomodo's supposed death (IV.iv.75–78), and denies that Mistress Quomodo is her "right name" in spite of her husband's reappearance (V.iii.140–42). Even less attention is devoted to the romantic intrigue of Easy's friend, Rearage, to win Susan, Quomodo's daughter, from Sir Andrew Lethe, a new knight who chooses to forget that his father was a Scottish tooth-drawer. Middleton's swift handling of both romances depends on the audience feeling that the women rightfully belong to the young gallants rather than to an old merchant and an upstart Scots knight. With Thomasine, Middleton creates this impression by isolating her both physically and morally from Quomodo's villainy, and by stressing her youth through the presence of her mother and Quomodo's grown son by a previous wife. If Easy lacks the ingenuity and wit of Middleton's other prodigal rogues, he is their equal in sexual vitality. His winning of Thomasine's love, even though the merchant ultimately repossesses her, leads to the restoration of his patrimony, and thus underscores the satiric triumph of innocent virtue over villainous guile, youth over age, sons over fathers.

Unlike *Michaelmas Term, A Trick to Catch the Old One* does not show us the prodigal hero being gulled by the father-figure, but begins with his counterintrigue to recoup his patrimony, and his scheme is spectacularly successful. As we noted in the discussion of the play in chapter 2, there *is* a romantic heroine, whom the hero loves and marries, but she appears very briefly and is usually confined to a balcony, while the hero has been more intimately involved with his courtesan, and even at the end of the play, when they have both married others, he indicates that their relations will continue. Once again, the abbreviated romantic action merely heightens the satiric thrust of the play.

In *A Mad World, My Masters*, Middleton deviates slightly from the typical children's prodigal-son plays but handles the material no less satirically. *A Mad World* is less biting than the last two plays we have discussed, because Middleton transforms the conventional avaricious and conniving father-figure into a genial spendthrift, Sir Bounteous Progress, the hero's grandfather, who is guilty only of squandering his estate before he dies and neglecting his poor young relative, Follywit. Whereas Lucre preys on his kin, Sir Bounteous merely ignores his: "We'll feast our lechery though we starve our kin" (IV.iii.90). For such a minor sin, and one readily atoned for with Follywit's help, Sir Bounteous need not be discomfited as severely as Quomodo or Lucre. Indeed, the prodigal's triumph is momentarily deflated when he finds his wife is really Frank Gullman, his grandfather's ex-mistress, though Sir Bounteous' generosity (not to mention his impotence) lessens the disgrace. The satiric thrust of the typical children's prodigal-son play is further blunted by the failure of Follywit's last intrigue, though here again his grandfather's magnanimity prevents total disaster from overtaking the young rogue. However good-natured the satire in this play, the romantic element is nonexistent, or perhaps parodied in Gullman's pretending to be a bashful virgin, and in the subplot, where Penitent Brothel and Mrs. Harebrain miraculously regain their pristine innocence.

Compared with Middleton's Paul's plays, his comedies for adult troupes contain less satire and more romance. Middleton's last satiric city comedy, *A Chaste Maid in Cheapside* (Lady Elizabeth's Men, 1613) appears to complicate this pattern until one realizes that by the time of this production the adult troupe listed on the title page of the 1630 quarto had absorbed the Children of the Queen's Revels. The most recent editor of the play argues that the use of child actors is indicated by the presence of eighteen female characters with little possibility of doubling.[28] The romantic heroine of the play, the virginal daughter of a greedy goldsmith, is as shadowy a character as Joyce or Thomasine, and she and her pure-hearted lover—the younger son of a noble house—stand out in a world where family life is conducted like a business venture. The goldsmith and his wife hope to match their children with aristocrats, even after they discover that their prospective son-in-law has been renting Allwit's wife and is the real father of Allwit's brood. Allwit boasts about this arrangement, Touchwood Senior and his wife separate because they breed more children than they can support, and the barren Kixes long for children to qualify for a large inheritance. Amidst all this and more peddling of human flesh, the heroine of the play is clearly the *only* chaste maid in Cheapside.

But with the complete disappearance of the children's troupes—through disbanding and amalgamation—Middleton began to write for adult companies. It is significant that he never returned to satiric city comedy after *A Chaste Maid in Cheapside*. *No Wit Like a Woman* (Lady Elizabeth's Men?, c.1615) combines a romantic Terentian tale of daughters exchanged, lost, and rediscovered with a slightly sentimentalized version of the prodigal-son story. *A Fair Quarrel* (Prince Charles' Men, c.1616), written with Rowley, joins a romantic story of a secretly married young couple with an equally romantic plot in which two noble friends fight over questions of honor, the mother of one combatant slandering herself to keep her son from dueling. *Anything for a Quiet Life* (King's Men, c.1621) is closer to satiric comedy than the two plays just mentioned but even here the prodigal-son story is treated sentimentally, while the Fletcheresque device of a woman disguised as a page preserves one of the heroines from adultery and pushes the play in the direction of romantic comedy.

The Widow (King's Men, c.1616) is nominally set in Capo D'Istria but uses much detail of the London scene to give a slight satiric coloration to the love-intrigues of two prodigal gallants. The first, Ricardo, has decided to woo Valeria, a rich widow, but his claim that he loves her "not for her wealth, but for her person too" (I.ii.160) is validated by his persisting in his suit even after she gives all her wealth to her brother. The second gallant, Francisco, an "Inns-a'-court man" (I.i.216), is pursuing the wife of Justice Brandino, but his adulterous intentions are frustrated by Martia, a pure-hearted Fletcheresque heroine disguised as a page, whose love inspires him to repent. Starting with potentially satiric material (the prodigal-son and widow-hunting motifs), Middleton turned *The Widow* in the direction of romantic comedy, as he did with nearly all of the city comedies he wrote for adult troupes. Although these works for the adult companies are later than the plays he wrote for the children—and were probably the result of collaboration, it would appear that Middleton, like Dekker, felt that children's plays should highlight satiric elements, while adults' plays should stress romance.

Conclusion

A survey of the repertories of the children's troupes from 1596 to 1613 forces one to refine Harbage's categorization of the vast majority of these plays as "satirical comedies." The children's troupes did not begin to specialize in satire until the early 1600s, gradually introduced more and more satire into their plays, and also experimented with different varieties of satire. Although difficulty in dating so many of the children's plays of this phase prevents us from plotting the chronological development of their repertories, we can perhaps discern the rough outline of a series of overlapping movements. That is, the children's troupes resumed their theatrical activities with plays either by Lyly or in his manner, tried to adapt the New Romantic Comedy developed by Greene and Shakespeare, experimented with "comical satire" alone or in various combinations, and finally devised satiric city comedy. Even if we could accurately date all of the children's plays, the overall pattern would be blurred because innovators and imitators alike were writing at any given time. Within each movement, moreover, we find imitation and parody following hard upon the innovation that launched the movement. The frequent repetition of this process in so short a time suggests that the audiences of the children's troupes were very much aware of theatrical convention and were determined to be in the forefront of theatrical fashion, although the boy companies apparently tried on occasion to offer as novelties extremely old plays (like *The Contention between Liberality and Prodigality*) or to make forays into an obsolete mode (like Marston's *Sophonisba,* a pathetic-heroine play). In the boy companies' desperation to satisfy their audience's craving for novelty, their more imaginative dramatists accelerated the normal artistic impulse toward experimentation, while their less talented dramatists shamelessly plundered successful innovations. Yet all of their playwrights advertised whatever innovative quality their work possessed, if not explicitly then by encouraging spectators to mock what had only yesterday been in vogue in the public theaters, in the other private theater(s), and even in the very playhouse they now attended.

The children's emphasis on the novelty of their offerings

must be qualified by our knowledge of certain practical considerations of theatrical life in the period. In point of fact, the adult companies probably produced greater numbers of new plays than the children's troupes did. In his study of Shakespeare's company at the Globe, Bernard Beckerman estimates that its average play lived for a season on the stage, though some were kept longer or later revived, and that it produced about 17 new plays each year, or a new one every 14 or 15 days, plus a few carry-overs or revivals.[29] Performing fewer times a week and over a shorter season, the children's troupes could not exceed this rate of new offerings, but claimed instead to offer new *types* of plays and pressed this claim by ridiculing almost everything else as old-fashioned.

While scholars have always known of, and have often exaggerated, the children's tendency to parody plays acted by adults, few have noticed how they frequently parodied their own work as well. In this chapter we have noticed how the boy companies ridicule conventions of their own Lylyesque comedies and "comical satire." Sometimes one children's troupe seems to ridicule another, but some of this ridicule is self-mockery: In *Jack Drum's Entertainment,* a Paul's play, Marston characterizes other Paul's plays as "musty fopperies of antiquity," while in the Induction to *Cynthia's Revels,* a Blackfriars play, Jonson complains that the house is haunted by "the *umbrae,* or ghosts of some three or four plays departed a dozen years since." We tend today to regard these statements as evidence of rivalry between authors, of the same kind that erupted in the *poetomachia.* In part it *was* a sort of "flyting"—playful, vicious, or promotional, but I think we overemphasize the authorial aspect and fail to see that kinds of plays are ridiculed more often than particular playwrights. It is questionable, moreover, whether the average playgoer of the period even knew who wrote the play he was watching. We hear much of the circulation and posting of bills, or advertisements, for plays, though none are extant, but authors' names evidently did not appear on them until well after the Restoration.[30] Perhaps some of the cognoscenti would know whose play they were watching and perhaps authors revealed their identity at performances, but the average spectator—even at a private playhouse—probably associated the play primarily with the acting troupe, whose property in fact it was, rather than with the dramatist who wrote it. When a Paul's or Blackfriars play parodied another Paul's or Blackfriars play, the audience would perceive such parody as self-mockery, an elaborate if desperate form of *sprezzatura*.

Such a posture was traditional for the children's troupes and their writers. Lyly's prologues gracefully discount the value of the play, especially when compared to the magnanimity and splendor of the audience, and plays like *Summer's Last Will and Testament* and *The Maid's Metamorphosis* invite the audience to ridicule a part of the work as a defense against mockery of the whole. In the same fashion, a troupe parodying its own plays achieves an aristocratic nonchalance and shares in its audience's illusion of its own modishness and critical sophistication. Self-parody, like satire, is a defense against ridicule, directing it inward, whereas satire directs it outward. One or both of these two strategies appears in nearly every play acted by the children's troupes after the late 1590s, except for the odd tragedies by Chapman, Daniel, and Marston. Inasmuch as such tactics are ultimately self-destructive, their heavy use may explain the early demise of the children's troupes.

Satire must escalate in virulence to remain interesting. What was audacious or scandalous yesterday is routine or boring today. If satire continues to strive for shock, either audiences recoil in disgust or the authorities, who are prime targets, are provoked to interfere. The Blackfriars troupe, its writers, and its operators frequently ran afoul of the government for satirizing Scots knights, foreign dignitaries, and the King himself, and suffered various forms of reprisal and harassment, changed managers, theaters, and finally dissolved.

Although self-parody accounts for a smaller part of the children's repertories, it too contributed to their demise by forcing the playwrights to sacrifice progressively larger parts of their work to the audiences' determination to ridicule, until there was no standpoint left within the work from which the ridicule could be directed. It was as if one were to achieve mastery over lightning by converting his entire house into a gigantic lightning rod, or to keep from starving by eating his own flesh. The last plays of the children's troupes, especially those written for the Children of the King's Revels by hacks like Day, Sharpham, Barry, and Field, seem to have carried self-parody to this suicidal extreme.

In surveying the several dozen plays which the children's troupes acted between 1596 and 1613, I have sketched patterns of development in the repertories at the expense of individual plays. Nevertheless, I hope this chapter, like the preceding ones, will provide helpful background for critical interpretation of these works and will illuminate the role of the boy companies in theatrical and literary history.

The children's troupes are an essential link in the development of English theater in that they established the indoor playhouse as the normal place for commercial production of plays. Beginning in 1609, when the King's Men took over Blackfriars, the professional adult companies supplanted or imitated the children's troupes in using their own indoor playhouses, gradually moving away from the larger, open-roofed theaters like the Globe where they had been performing for several decades. New indoor playhouses were built under James I and Charles I, and as England became progressively polarized as the Civil War approached, the private theater—with its built-in aristocratic ethos—became dominant. In 1660, when London theatrical life revived, the only theaters reopened or built—except for, very briefly, the Red Bull—were indoor playhouses. Studies of the late Jacobean, Caroline, and Restoration theater show that the indoor playhouses were the conduits through which the English commercial theater received innovations in theater architecture and conventions of staging from the court masque and various continental influences. We can credit the children's troupes with the first step in this movement—the distribution of traditional courtly and aristocratic theatrical entertainment to a wider audience.

The contribution of the children's troupes from the literary point of view is harder to assess. Their sophisticated audiences, whose critical attitude and awareness of technique encouraged dramatists to experiment, exerted an influence on all plays written in the period, which scholars like Kirsch and Reibetanz have begun to investigate.[31] But the intrinsic importance of the children's troupes derives from their having performed several dozen extant plays—many of them by such dramatists as Jonson, Chapman, Marston, Middleton, Dekker, Beaumont, and Fletcher. Moreover, the best of these plays become even richer and more exciting when we understand the milieu in which they were created, presented, and received, and they can regain something of their original vitality in the informed imaginatcon of the modern reader.

# APPENDIX A

Songs and Music in Children's Plays

THE study of songs and music in English Renaissance drama is fraught with problems. To begin with, many printed dramatic texts merely have stage directions like *"cantat"* or *"music sounds"* to indicate the place for vocal or instrumental selections in performance, and occasionally one even has to infer this information from the dialogue alone. Some texts provide lyrics, which may or may not be the ones chosen by the playwright. Indeed, the absence of lyrics in so many texts suggests that the choice of songs was often made by those responsible for production. But even when lyrics are printed with the play, a modern reader trying to reconstruct the original performance in his mind would like to know what the setting sounded like.[1]

Here the difficulties mount. In the simplest cases, playwrights or producers chose popular songs of the period, often known to modern scholars, as in *Summer's Last Will and Testament,* where Bacchus and his men sing "Monsieur Mingo." [2] In *Patient Grissel,* we have fresh lyrics to be sung to old tunes, familiar to Elizabethan if not modern readers, like "Damon and Pythias," "Malkin," and "The Latter Almain," but it is far more common to have only the lyrics, with no indication of the setting used in performance. By studying printed and manuscript collections of music of the period, scholars have discovered settings for lyrics found in plays, but such discoveries do not assure us that a particular setting was the one actually used in production. For some lyrics, we have more than one setting, or a setting that seems later than the play, or a setting that doesn't seem to fit the lyrics printed in the text of the play. For example, the words to "Slow, slow, fresh fount," Echo's song in I.ii of *Cynthia's Revels,* appear in Henry Youll's *Canzonets to Three Voices* (1608), but A. J. Sabol rejects Youll's three-part polyphonic setting as inappropriate for what the play clearly introduces as a solo, while other scholars argue that Youll's published setting is a rearrangement of a solo song, which simply substitutes two vocal for instrumental parts and provides additional words.[3] Finally, we have a number of songs that seem to belong to plays but which cannot be linked to any extant dramatic texts.

In spite of these difficulties, some scholars have been able to do valuable work on songs in Elizabethan drama, though much remains to be done. Scholars have until recently concentrated on Shakespeare's use of songs and music, creating the misleading impression that his or his company's practices are typical for public and private theaters, adult and boy companies. A growing body of recent scholarship suggests that after 1608, when the first major adult troupe acquired its own private theater, adult troupes began to use songs and music as children's companies had done, although a full-scale comparative study of this topic is beyond the scope of this appendix.

As we have seen in chapter 1, many of the first children's troupes were choristers, while the two leading boy companies of London were closely associated with the Chapel Royal and the choir of St. Paul's Cathedral. Choirboys naturally received extensive musical training. They learned to read music, to sing polyphonic compositions, and to play instruments, such as organs, viols, cornets, virginals, and recorders. Most of the boy choristers became adult choristers when they reached maturity, and some, like the composer Thomas Ravenscroft, a boy chorister at Paul's from about 1598 to 1604, went on to make significant contributions to English musical life. It is difficult to say whether the members of the acting companies were more than nominally choirboys after the late 1590s. The members of a children's troupe like the Children of the King's Revels, which acted at Whitefriars, were not choristers. The children's troupe that acted at Blackfriars, once called the Children of the Chapel Royal, probably lost direct connection with the Chapel Royal shortly after the Accession of James in 1603, but the Children of Paul's probably consisted of choristers and was directed by the Cathedral choirmaster until the company's dissolution in 1607. In any event, the quality of music presented by the two principal children's troupes was probably high. When the Duke of Stettin-Pomerania and his party attended Blackfriars in 1602, his diary records that they heard a boy sing more beautifully than anything they had heard on their travels, except perhaps the singing of the nuns of Milan.[4]

In view of the origin and history of the boy companies, it should be no surprise that their plays contain more songs and music than contemporaneous plays acted by adult companies, although it is an exaggeration to describe the children's plays as resembling "the musical (or operetta) of today."[5] Statistics are illuminating. Of the 32 extant children's plays acted before 1591, 29 (91%) have a total of 128 songs, or an average of 4.4 each. Garter's *Virtuous and Godly Susanna*, one of the 3 plays that have no songs, apologizes in the Epilogue for this lack. After the late 1590s, 16 of the 21 plays (76%) acted by the Children of Paul's contain a total of 80 songs, or an average of

5 each, while 72% of the plays acted by the Chapel Children contain an average of 2.4 songs per play. By comparison, only 49% of the plays acted by Shakespeare's troupe during a corresponding period contain songs; the average of 1.4 songs per play is considerably lower than that for the plays acted by children's troupes, and plays acted by other adult troupes contain even fewer songs.[6]

These quantitative differences are due not only to the superior musical training of the choirboy actors, but also to the circumstances of production: the boy companies performed for more sophisticated spectators than adult troupes did and could achieve more subtle musical effects in their small, enclosed private theaters than adult actors could in large, open-roofed public theaters.

Qualitative differences are harder to establish, although in general the children's troupes relied less on popular and folk songs and more on art songs. Nevertheless, Mary Chan has suggested that the sophistication of the children's songs was rather superficial:

> The songs texts are simple, and although many of the songs are part-songs they are not really contrapuntal: the melody is usually in the treble and the other parts simply support this harmonically. The songs in all the Ravenscroft collections are mostly canons, rounds, and simple imitative polyphonic songs. Many are related in style to the canzonet and use obviously "fashionable" musical devices, particularly affective devices. Others are in the style of the ballet and use "fa-la" or nonsense refrains. The songs are essentially light, spontaneous, and fashionable and while avoiding any serious musical statement would have a charm when sung by children. The songs are "popular" but unlike ballads they are also self-consciously sophisticated.[7]

Unfortunately, Mrs. Chan relies too heavily on Ravenscroft's compositions, only a few of which can be linked with extant plays, and overlooks the fact that complex polyphonic settings would render lyrics unintelligible, making them unsuitable for most dramatic productions.

Moving from the standard of musical quality to that of dramatic effectiveness, Mrs. Chan is just as harsh. The typical song in a children's play, she contends, has "little or no real relationship with the play itself." [8] It is difficult to measure the dramaturgical relevance of songs and music without detailed discussion of each example in its context. Instead, I propose to outline first the major types of songs in children's plays from a functional viewpoint, and second the most common ways in which instrumental music is used. As we shall see, the vocal songs in children's plays are generally complaints, servant songs, pastoral or supernatural songs, or religious songs; and the instrumental music usually separates acts and accompanies dancing. These conventions are more prevalent in plays acted before 1591 (when the children's troupes entered a period of enforced dormancy), but also occur in plays acted after their resuscitation in the late 1590s. In the plays of the later period, however, one notices a growing independence from these conventions, and in the work of Marston and others, an ability to use songs and music to create ingenious and powerful dramatic effects. [9]

Complaints

One type of song which is virtually unique to the plays acted by children's troupes before 1591 is the complaint, usually a solo song by a female character. Bowden describes such characters as temporarily frustrated lovers, forsaken lovers, or bereaved lovers, [10] but the complaint tradition originated earlier and is broader than Bowden suspects, and includes laments of friends, children, and parents, as well as lovers. The complaint is almost always a personal expression of the character's emotions and, as such, usually has some relevance to the dramatic action. The complaint thus differs from sad but impersonal songs, like the one sung to viol accompaniment in *Wit and Science* or the "doleful ditty" that laments Summer's approaching death in *Summer's Last Will and Testament*.

The lyrics of a typical complaint are like a set speech. They are heavily alliterative, contain repeated exclamations and stock phrases ("I die," "grievous groans," "weep and wail"), begin with an invocation to the Gods or the elements, and end with a plea for death. The complaint was usually accompanied by a quartet of viols, though sometimes a lute or keyboard instrument was used, and the overall effect of such songs was more striking than one would suspect from the heavy-handed lyrics alone. Philip Brett describes the typical setting of a complaint:

> The accompaniment fluctuates between a simple chordal, and a freely contrapuntal, style; it derives and develops some material from the slower-moving voice part but rarely stages a regular set of contrapuntal entries upon one theme. The solo part is not always the top voice of the quintet; sometimes it is the second or even the third, but it can always be sung by a boy, either a high treble or an alto. There is no attempt at word-painting in the madrigalian sense and the text is treated syllabically, although the penultimate syllable of a phrase is sometimes briefly extended. Strophic settings are the rule rather than the exception, and the final couplet of a stanza is usually repeated to the same music.[11]

One of the earliest of these dramatic complaints is "Awake ye woeful wights," the lament of Pythias for Damon in Edwardes' *Damon and Pythias* (Chapel, 1564–65). The stage direction (l. 691) stipulates that Pythias be accompanied by regals, but the song also survives in settings for lute accompaniment. Long has printed the tune which was probably used in the play.[12] Like most dramatic and nondramatic complaints of the period, "Awake ye woeful wights" is highly alliterative, intoning Pythias' sorrow in such lines as: "Gripe me, you greedy griefs, / and present pangs of death" (ll. 716–17). Similar complaints occur in *Patient Grissel*, *The Arraignment of Paris*, and *Sapho and Phao*. At the beginning of this century, G.E.P. Arkwright discovered a number of extant complaints, which seem to belong to plays, in manuscript collections of music.[13] The most famous of these is "Alas, ye salt sea gods," a lament for treble voice and four strings probably by Richard Ferrant, which may come from an extant play entitled *The Wars of Cyrus*.[14] It is one of several complaints sung by noble women who are threatened with captivity, sexual violation, the death of or separation from a lover, or some equally heart-rending fate, and it is therefore quite possible that the type of dramatic complaint under discussion was a standard feature of the "pathetic-heroine" play, which was popular with the children's companies in the 1570s and early 1580s. Complaints even occur in a few plays acted by children's troupes after the late 1590s. In the anonymous *The Maid's Metamorphosis*, the pathetic heroine sings "Ye sacred fires, and powers above" and "Since hope of help my froward stars deny," while Marston and Daniel seem to have had their heroines sing complaints of this type in *Sophonisba* and *Philotas*, respectively.

Servant Songs

A second type of song in children's plays is the servant song, usually a sprightly, comic piece for two to four singers. Sabol has pointed out the use of servant songs by Edwardes and

Lyly,[15] but songs of this type also occur in *Tom Tyler, Respublica, Ralph Roister Doister, Nice Wanton,* and *The Bugbears.* The pages and maidservants of children's plays are descended from the slaves of Roman comedy and the vices of morality plays, and are the agents of mischief, merriment, and mockery. Their songs usually celebrate festive revelry, proclaim the singers' animal appetites, and ridicule figures of authority. Frequently, the songs are miniature dramatic actions in themselves, and suggest accompanying business, as in *Damon and Pythias,* where the pages Will and Jack shave their victim Grim, who joins them in singing a song about the shaving of Grim the Collier (ll. 1663 ff.). Nearly every one of Lyly's plays includes a song of this type; a good example is "O for a bowl of fat canary," sung by three pages in *Campaspe:*

> *Granichus:* O For a Bowl of fat Canary,
>   Rich Palermo, sparkling Sherry,
>   Some Nectar else, from Juno's Dairy,
>   O these draughts would make us merry.
> *Psyllus:* O for a wench, (I deal in faces,
>   And in other daintier things,)
>   Tickled am I with her Embraces,
>   Fine dancing in such Fairy Rings.
> *Manes:* O for a plump fat leg of Mutton,
>   Veal, Lamb, Capon, Pig, & Conny,
>   None is happy but a Glutton,
>   None an Ass but who wants money.
> *Chorus:* Wines (indeed,) & Girls are good,
>   But brave victuals feast the blood,
>   For wenches, wine, and Lusty cheer,
>   *Jove* would leap down to surfeit here.
>   (I.ii.88–103)

In some plays acted after the late 1590s, small groups of servants sing very much as they did in the plays of Edwardes and

Lyly, that is at the end of short scenes of pert, audacious dialogue. As in the pre-1591 plays, such scenes rarely further the dramatic action but they supply contrasting attitudes, parody theme and action of the main plot, create an atmosphere of levity and bawdry, and usually culminate in song. Such scenes, with this type of song, occur in a few plays acted by the Chapel Children at Blackfriars, but more often in plays acted by the Children of Paul's, as well as in plays by William Percy, intended for Paul's but probably never performed there.

In Act II of Marston's *Antonio and Mellida,* two pages and a maid sing "the descant on our names," the lyrics to which are lost but must have been extremely bawdy because the pages' names—Dildo and Catzo—are Italian terms for penis. Marston's *What You Will* requires three page songs, the lyrics of all three unfortunately lost, although Sabol has suggested possible songs from Ravenscroft's *Melismata.*[16] In *Blurt, Master Constable,* two maidservants sing a bawdy question-and-answer duet, "In a fair woman what thing is best?" This song is sung in response to a request for a "light" song, of the kind that "go nimbly and quick, and are full of changes, and carry sweet division" (II.ii.47–49). The lyrics are ostensibly a sonnet written by another character, which the maids read before singing, perhaps because a polyphonic setting rendered the words unintelligible.[17] Earlier in the play, a trio of pages sings "What meat eats the Spaniard?" As a typical servant song, the piece caps a passage of pert, witty dialogue, and laments the meager rations of dried fish which the page Pilcher receives in the employ of the Spaniard Lazarillo de Tormes, the play's principal comic butt:

Doit: What meat eats the Spaniard?
Pilcher: Dried pilchers and poor-john.

Dandyprat: Alas, thou art almost marred!
Pilcher: My cheeks are fall'n and gone.
Doit: Wouldst thou not leap at a piece of meat?
Pilcher: O, how my teeth do water! I could eat:
      'Fore the heavens, my flesh is almost gone
      With eating of pilcher and poor-john.

                                              (I.ii.209–16)

From manuscript part-books, where this song is set for a single voice, Sabol has reconstructed the setting probably used in production. In this version, Pilcher, an alto, sings the bulk of the vocal part, with Doit and Dandyprat, both sopranos, dividing the remaining few lines. All three vocal parts, Sabol observes, are demanding and require "a trained voice and considerable understanding of music," while the viol accompaniment is "rich and brilliant in its five-part texture, [and] is conceived for the most part homophonically, although individual voice parts move linearly with considerable independence." [18]

This type of song belongs exclusively to the plays acted by children's companies, for adult troupes rarely if ever had more than two or three boys capable of taking anything beyond a walk-on role and those boys usually played female roles. When adult companies did use groups of children, as in *A Midsummer Night's Dream* and *The Merry Wives of Windsor,* the children are given roles which require a good deal of singing and dancing but little or no speaking. Many of the plays of the children's troupes, however, count heavily on the pages to fulfill their traditional functions both in speech and song until the mid-1600s, when the convention of servant scenes began to seem antiquated, and finally disappeared from children's plays altogether.

Pastoral and Supernatural Songs

A third type of song in children's plays is the song for pastoral or supernatural characters, usually a choral song, such as the nymphs' and shepherds' songs in Peele's *The Arraignment of Paris*. When choral groups were assigned a collective role, they were usually cast as muses, nymphs, shepherds, or fairies, probably because of the traditional association of music with such groups. Muses sing in Edwardes' *Damon and Pythias*, while Cupid sings with a group of nymphs in II.ii of Lyly's *Gallathea*, and troupes of fairies dance in II.iii of *Gallathea* and sing and dance in IV.iii of Lyly's *Endimion*. Such songs occur in a few plays acted after the late 1590s. There is a fairy chorus in Act III of *The Wisdom of Doctor Dodypoll*, and *The Maid's Metamorphosis* calls for rival singing choruses of shepherds and woodsmen in Act I and a chorus of fairies in Act II, who sing and dance first alone and then with pages.[19] Songs of this type were naturally used rarely by adult companies, although they do occur in *A Midsummer Night's Dream* and *The Merry Wives of Windsor*. Even the children's troupes abandoned this type of song in the early 1600s as they began to perform "comical satires" and satiric city comedies instead of the Ovidian romantic comedies made popular by Lyly.

Religious Songs

A fourth type of song in plays acted by children's troupes was the religious song—a hymn or prayer, usually sung by a chorus. As most of the children's companies were groups of boy choristers, they were accustomed to singing hymns or prayers in choral settings during religious services, and may therefore have used the same or similar pieces in their dramatic productions. A number of plays contain such hymns or prayers, usually at the end. For example, the "Hymnus" at the end of Act III of *Sapientia Solomonis* is a Latin verse rendering of Psalm 72. In other plays, where the lyrics are not given, almost any religious selection would fit the context, as in *Godly Queen Hester,* where Hester asks her chapel to "Sing some holy hymn to speed us this day" (l. 861). Many of these religious songs come at the ends of plays, invoking blessings for the Queen, the court, and sometimes the commons. This type of song has little relevance to the dramatic action but is highly relevant to the theatrical occasion of a court play, the function of which was to praise or flatter the sovereign and, by extension, the members of the court and the country as a whole.

None of the children's plays written after the late 1590s concludes with a prayer for the health and well-being of the sovereign and nobility, with the possible exception of Marston's *Antonio's Revenge,* which ends with a request for "a solemn hymn . . . / To close the last act of my vengeance." The request and the hymn which must have followed it underscore the revengers' desire for purification, a context which probably precluded the conventional prayer for the sovereign. Other plays use final songs, not necessarily religious, for dramatic effects, and such songs are usually integrated with the theme and action. Thus, *The Maid's Metamorphosis* concludes with a "roundelay" of general rejoicing, and *Westward Ho!* closes with a rowing song for the trip back to London, which turns into a *plaudite.* Plays like *The Maid's Metamorphosis* and *Sophonisba,* which are set in classical antiquity, use hymns to Phoebus and Hymen, just as Shakespeare uses a song to Bacchus in II.vii of *Antony and Cleopatra.* It would be interesting to know whether these pagan hymns and prayers were set to or modelled after Christian religious music. Some scholars have suggested that Shake-speare's song to Bacchus, for example, may be a parody or imitation of the Pentecostal hymn "Veni Creator." [20]

In the first few years after their revival in the late 1590s, the children's troupes continued to employ the same basic types of song that they used before 1591, albeit with greater flexibil-ity and dramatic relevance. Even the few new types of song, which they probably borrowed from adult companies, were used in more interesting ways. The serenade, for example, is generally sung by a suitor's servants or hired musicians to a lady who usually appears "above" at a window or balcony. Because nearly all the sponsors of serenades are rejected as lovers, modern scholars regard the serenade as a conven-tional means of representing unsuccessful courtship. The convention of the vicarious serenade was evidently based on contemporaneous notions of social and dramatic decorum. No one of noble rank, either on or off stage, would sing or play an instrument except on very rare occasions and then only after great protestation. In plays, the production of music is generally left to servants, professional musicians, ef-feminate courtiers, lower-class characters, or characters as-sociated with loose sexual behavior. The vicarious serenade is used in the conventional way in plays acted by adult troupes, such as Shakespeare's *Two Gentlemen of Verona,* as well as in *Blurt, Master Constable,* where a soon-to-be rejected suitor instructs his musicians to "speak movingly" beneath his love's casement. But other plays acted by the children's troupes use the convention in a freer and more playful manner. In *Jack Drum's Entertainment* three rival suitors appear in succession under the lady's casement. One directs his page to sing "Deli-cious beauty that doth lie," the second, Mammon the miser, has his page sing a song of money, "Chunck, chunck, chunck," while the third, the successful lover, makes music out of his apology for not bringing any music:

> Unequaled *Katherine*
> I bring no Music to prepare thy thoughts
> To entertain an amorous discourse:
> More Music's in thy name, and sweet dispose,
> Than in *Apollo's* Lyre, or *Orpheus'* close.
> I'll chant thy name, and so enchant each ear,
> That *Katherina's* happy name shall hear.
> My *Katherine,* my life, my *Katherine.*
>
> (III, 198)

Similarly, the lover in *What You Will* directs his page to sing a lute song under the lady's window, but Marston then undercuts the convention of the vicarious serenade by having the lover lament the professional singer's inability to express authentic emotion:

> Fie, peace, peace, peace, it hath no passion in't.
> O melt thy breath in fluent softer tunes
> That every note may seem to trickle down
> Like sad distilling tears and make—O God!
> That I were but a Poet now t-express my thoughts,
> Or a Musician but to sing my thoughts,
> Or any thing but what I am, sing't o'er one more:
> My grief's a boundless sea that hath no shore.
>
> (II, 240)

The most unconventional use of the serenade occurs in Marston's *Dutch Courtesan,* in which a young gallant twice sings to his lady without protest or fear of debasing his rank.

The Dutch Courtesan also contains another type of serenade—the song of a lascivious woman to a man, a type which first occurs in children's plays and later in adult plays.

David O'Neill notes that songs sung by women to men in
plays usually express lust, whereas those sung by men to
women are generally meant to express a purer sort of love.[21]
In this play, the title character Franceschina sings "The dark is
my delight" to her own lute accompaniment:

> The dark is my delight,
>   So 'tis the nightingale's.
> My music's in the night,
>   So is the nightingale's.
> My body is but little,
>   So is the nightingale's.
> I love to sleep 'gainst the prickle,
>   So doth the nightingale.
> , (I.ii.111–18)

Sabol, who discovered the setting probably used in production, comments on "its gaily lilting vocal line, tinged with an
appealing wistfulness." [22] Singing is associated with brothels
in other children's plays. In *Blurt, Master Constable*, for example, the courtesan Imperia sings "Love for such a cherry
lip" to the offstage accompaniment of a group of viols, according to a setting which Sabol recently discovered, while in
Westward Ho! the bawd Birdlime entertains a party of gallants
by singing to her own viol accompaniment.[23] Whether the
female singer is a courtesan or bawd, for whom singing could
be considered a professional requirement, or a lascivious amateur like Camelia in *Jack Drum's Entertainment*, a serenade
by a woman suggests unnatural sexual aggressiveness and in-
timates danger or even death for the men who listen. One of
the most unusual of these Syrens is the Succubus in Middleton's *A Mad World, My Masters*, who comes to Penitent
Brothel in the shape of his mistress and sings a "fa, le, la"
song as she dances around him enticingly. Such imaginative

use of the serenade is typical of the way the children's troupes revitalized conventional types of songs after their theaters reopened in the late 1590s.

Two more examples will show how far the boy companies advanced beyond these conventional categories of songs. The first is from *Cynthia's Revels,* one of the first plays performed when Blackfriars reopened in late 1599. Spectators were surely aware from the first act, when Echo sang "Slow, slow, fresh fount," that the songs in the play would not be mere variations of familiar types. Whether or not Youll's setting was used in production, Echo seems to be singing a highly sophisticated art song, quite distinct from the conventional types of songs used in earlier children's plays. This musical sophistication was even more important in IV.iii, where Hedon sings "The Kiss" to a gathering of decadent courtiers. Jonson's satiric intent is obvious not only from the context but also from the triteness of the lyrics:

> O, That joy so soon should waste!
>   or so sweet a bliss
>   as a kiss,
> Might not for ever last!
> So sugared, so melting, so soft, so delicious,
>   The dew that lies on roses,
>   When the morn herself discloses,
>   is not so precious.
> O, rather then I would it smother,
> Were I to taste such another;
>   It should be my wishing
>   That I might die, kissing.
>   (IV.iii.242–53)

The setting—probably the one Sabol discovered—also invites the audience to mock the singer's lack of originality. Sabol writes:

Just as the poet provides a saccharine lyric to ridicule the courtier's effete passion, so does the composer supply a setting which in its preciosity admirably complements the lyric. This effect in the music is accomplished largely by means of the emphasis accorded the words and phrases which lend themselves to a cloying treatment, occasionally through sustained notes high in the vocal range, but more frequently through repetition of key phrases. . . . The vocal phrases, frequently disjunct and occasionally syncopated, invite the singer to display, in a self-conscious way, the breathless rapture of his ardor.[24]

If this setting or one like it was used, it had a complex effect, for despite its superficial appeal, it elicited the ridicule of the more discriminating auditors. While the songs in children's plays written after the late 1590s were rarely this subtle in their effects, they nevertheless achieve more complex effects than do the songs in plays acted before 1591.

A second example from the later period, from Middleton's *A Trick to Catch the Old One,* is Audrey's song to her loathed master, Harry Dampit, which she sings while the demonic usurer lies drunk upon his deathbed:

Let the usurer cram him, in interest that excel,
There's pits enow to damn him, before he comes to hell;
In Holborn some, in Fleet Street some,
Where'er he come, there's some, there's some.

(IV.v.1–4)

Sabol has discovered a setting by Thomas Ravenscroft for alto voice and four viols, which was probably used in production: "The lively instrumental accompaniment and the forthright simplicity of the vocal line would permit the actor playing Audrey to express her sardonic views with some vigor."[25] This increasing subtlety and flexibility in the use of song is paralleled in the use of music.

Instrumental Music

The children's troupes apparently entertained their patrons
with generous amounts of instrumental music, both extradramatic and incidental. When the Duke of Stettin-
Pomerania visited Blackfriars in 1602, he heard—if we can
trust the journal kept by his secretary—an hour-long offering
by a broken consort. When the King's Men performed *The
Malcontent,* after having stolen it from the Chapel Children of
Blackfriars, their Induction informed the audience that certain
"additions" had been made to the text "to abridge the not-
received custom of music in our theater." Scholars disagree
as to whether this customary music came before the performance, as the Duke's diary suggests, or between acts, as was
more common.[26] An early children's play, *Sapientia Solomonis,* follows humanist school productions on the continent
in using choral songs to separate acts, perhaps in imitation of
Seneca's use of a chorus.[27] Most entr'acte selections in the
children's plays after the late 1590s were instrumental pieces,
except for a few servant songs. *Antonio's Revenge* illustrates
the phenomenon. Act IV ends with the stage direction *"The
cornets sound for the Act,"* while Act V begins with a dumb
show, presumably to this cornet music. Act III begins similarly: *"A dumb show. The cornets sounding for the Act, enter
Castilio. . . ."* Entr'acte music is sometimes woven into the
fabric of the action, as at the end of Act I, when Pandulpho
gives the musicians their cue:

> Sound louder music; let my breath exact
> You strike sad tones unto this dismal act.

Some of the plays of William Percy indicate the prevalence of
entr'acte music, as every act but the last is followed by the
stage direction: *"Here they knocked up the consort."*

Related to entr'acte music is the convention of ending a play with song or instrumental music, a sort of grand finale. Most of the pre-1591 children's plays conclude with a vocal selection—frequently a choral prayer—but after the late 1590's the boy companies rarely ended with songs of any type, though they did occasionally use an instrumental selection for that purpose. At the close of *Antonio and Mellida*, for example, Piero orders his "Lydian wires" to sound. In some children's plays, the closing instrumental music is actually accompaniment for a dance, as in *Blurt, Master Constable*, where in the final speech the Duke ordains that "this bright morning merrily be crowned / With dances, banquets, and choice music's sound."

Dancing to instrumental accompaniment is less common at the end of children's plays than in the middle, where it can dramatize court revelry or festive mirth. A few playwrights skillfully integrate dances with action and dialogue, as in the opening scene of *Blurt, Master Constable*, where a love-triangle develops during the measures. One gallant, Hippolito, breaks off the conversation with a peremptory invitation to dance: "Enough of this; come, wenches, shake your heels." Camillo, another gallant, signals the musicians— "music, advance thee on thy golden wing, / And dance division from sweet string to string"—and evidently begins dancing with his beloved, Violetta. While *"they dance a strain,"* Camillo's prisoner, Fontinelle, watches them and falls in love with Violetta. But Violetta, noticing Fontinelle abruptly stops dancing before the "measure" is over, and asks Camillo to make Fontinelle dance too. The dramatic pattern now repeats itself, Violetta falling in love with Fontinelle as she watches him dance with someone else. Dances are not always so well-integrated with the action of children's plays. The most contrived or decorative dances would have been the two entr'acte dances in *The Knight of the Burning Pestle* had not Beaumont made Nell, the Citizen's wife, show a maternal interest in the "little boy" by awarding him "two-pence to buy you points withall" (I,63), even though he can not tumble or eat fire. Apparently enough of the boy actors were sufficiently talented dancers to justify the inclusion of dancing in a great many of the children's plays.

Although entr'acte music and accompaniment for dancing are the most common functions of instrumental music in children's plays, a few works demonstrate greater sophistication. Marston's plays in particular not only require elaborate use of specific instruments for the sennets and flourishes that announce and accompany ceremonial entrances and exits, but also display some concern for the psychological effects of music on the spectators. After the Induction of *The Malcontent,* a stage direction calls for *"The vilest out-of-tune music,"* which continues for several lines of dialogue, reflecting the tragicomic discord of the Genoese court and the bizarre eccentricity of the title character. Similarly, in *Sophonisba,* a play unusually rich in incidental music and in specifications for the instruments to produce it, Marston requires "Infernal Music" to create the proper atmosphere for the conjuring of the witch Erictho out of Hell near the end of Act IV.

Two of the technical problems connected with instrumental music in children's plays require special consideration: Who were the musicians, and what instruments did they play?

Some of the instrumental music in children's plays acted before 1591 seems to have been played offstage, like the mourning song played by the regals in *Damon and Pythias.* Offstage regals also produced the unusual effect called for in I.iii of *The Arraignment of Paris*—"an artificial charm of birds being heard within." In *Sylva Sylvarum* Bacon explains how the effect is produced: "in regals, (where they have a pipe they call the nightingale-pipe, which containeth water) the sound hath a continual trembling." [28] The same effect was later called for in *The Dutch Courtesan* and *Blurt, Master Constable*. We have no way of knowing who produced such offstage music.

The instrumental music which was produced onstage in children's plays before 1591 was clearly played by the choirboy-actors, who were often trained instrumentalists. Only occasionally are there groups of supernumeraries who may have been professional musicians, such as the "noise of Musicians" in *Summer's Last Will and Testament*. Four of the performers of *Wit and Science* were skilled violists and relatively competent actors, for they each assumed several roles in order to accompany the hero's dancing and their own singing. Characters in plays by Udall, Lyly, and Peele also play pipes, fiddles, and lutes.

Instrumental music was used even more frequently in children's plays acted after the late 1590s than in those acted before 1591. For accompanying songs, the lute or lyra viol was commonly used, as it was in the public theaters, although the harp is called for in *The Maid's Metamorphosis* and *Antonio and Mellida,* and the tabor and pipe and a viol consort in *Jack Drum's Entertainment*. But for purely instrumental music, the children's plays after the late 1590s require a wide variety of instruments. Probably for acoustical reasons, the indoor private theaters used different instruments from those used in the larger, open-roofed public theaters. Thus, cornets rather than trumpets are used for sennets and flourishes, and may have been played offstage by professional musicians.[29] Stage directions in some plays acted by children's troupes call for "still flutes," or recorders, while those in *Sophonisba* or *A Mad World, My Masters* call for organs.

For instrumental ensembles, the Children of Paul's seems to

have employed whole consorts, usually of viols and sometimes of cornets, whereas the Chapel Children, like the adult
troupes, was by 1602 employing a broken consort of organ,
lute, mandolin, bandora, viol, and pipe, according to the
diary of Duke Philip Julius of Stettin-Pomerania. Some Blackfriars plays, however, mention viol consorts. The music following Act II of *The Knight of the Burning Pestle,* for example, was
supplied by a group of fiddlers, although there is some confusion about their identity:

> *Wife:* The Fiddlers go again, husband.
> *Citizen:* Aye, *Nell,* but this is scurvy music: I gave the
>   whoreson gallows money, and I think he has not
>   got me the waits of Southwark. . . . You Musi-
>   cians, play *Baloo.*
> *Wife:* No, good *George,* let's ha' *Lachrimae.*
> *Citizen:* Why, this is it, conny.

If Nell cannot recognize "Lachrimae" when she hears it, then
George may not know the waits of Southwark when they play
before him. In general it is difficult for us to tell whether the
members of the whole consorts used at Paul's and Blackfriars
were professional musicians or whether they were specially
trained choirboys, like the viol players in *Wit and Science.*
Unlike the musicians in earlier plays, like *Wit and Science,* the
consorts rarely play onstage after the late 1590s. In *Westward
Ho!,* where they do appear onstage, they are described as
"the Town consort" and a "noise of Fiddlers," and we are
told that the offstage music in Mulligrub's tavern in *The Dutch
Courtesan* is provided by "Master Creak's noise." Even
when a consort does appear on stage after the late 1590s, it is
rare for any of its members to have a speaking part. It is
therefore possible that the children's troupes hired professional musicians, or waits, for their plays, as was apparently

done for college plays at Cambridge and for plays the King's
Men produced at Blackfriars after 1609,[30] but it is also possible
that the musicians at the private theaters after the late 1590s
were choirboys, as they had been before 1591.

From this survey of the songs and music used in children's
plays, it appears that the rather rigid conventions established
before 1591 continued after the late 1590s, but that the later
plays are generally characterized by freer and more inventive
uses of songs and music. One hopes that as musicologists like
Mary Joiner Chan and Philip Brett and literary scholars like
Andrew Sabol continue to discover more about the songs and
music in children's plays, we will be better able to imagine
the effects created by these works when the boy companies
produced them.

APPENDIX B

Recorded Court Performances by Children's Troupes, 1559-1613[1]

Year	Date	Troupe	Play
1559–60	Aug. 7	Paul's	
	Dec. 31	Chapel (?)	
1560–61	Christmas	Paul's	
1561–62	Christmas	Paul's	
	Feb. 2–10	Paul's	
1562–63	Christmas	Paul's	
1564–65	Christmas	Chapel	*Damon and Pythias* (?)
	Christmas	Paul's	
	January	Westminster Grammar School	*Miles Gloriosus* and *Heautontimorumenus* (?)
	Feb. 2	Paul's	
1565–66	before Jan. 3	Paul's (3 performances)	
	Jan. 17	Westminster Grammar School	*Sapientia Solomonis*
1566–67	Dec. 25–Jan. 11	Paul's (2 performances)	
	Feb. 9–11	Westminster Choristers	
	Feb. 11	Windsor	
1567–68	Christmas	Westminster Choristers	
	Christmas	Paul's (2 performances)	*Wit and Will* (?) and *Prodigality* (?)
	Feb. 29–Mar. 2	Chapel	*King of Scots* (?)
	Feb. 29–Mar. 2	Windsor	

1568–69	Jan. 1	Paul's	
	Feb. 22	Windsor	
1569–70	Dec. 27	Windsor	
	Jan. 6	Chapel	
1570–71	Dec. 28	Paul's	
	Feb. 25–27	Chapel	
	Feb. 25–27	Windsor	
	Feb. 25–27	Paul's	
1571–72	Dec. 28	Paul's	*Iphigenia*
	Jan. 1	Windsor	*Ajax and Ulysses*
	Jan. 6	Chapel	*Narcissus*
	Feb. 19	Westminster Choristers	*Paris and Vienne*
1572–73	Christmas	Paul's	
	Jan. 1	Windsor	
	Jan. 6	Eton	
	Feb. 3	Merchant Taylors'	
1573–74	Dec. 27	Paul's	*Alcmeon*
	Jan. 1	Westminster Choristers	*Truth, Faithfulness and Mercy*
	Jan. 6	Windsor	*Quintus Fabius*
	Feb. 2	Merchant Taylors'	*Timoclea at the Siege of Thebes*
	Feb. 23	Merchant Taylors'	*Perseus and Andromeda*
1574–75	Jan. 6	Windsor	*Xerxes* (?)
	Feb. 2	Paul's	*Prodigality* (?)
	Feb. 13	Chapel	
	Feb. 15	Merchant Taylors'	
1575–76	Dec. 27	Windsor	
	Jan. 6	Paul's	
	Mar. 6	Merchant Taylors'	
1576–77	Jan. 1	Paul's	*The History of Error*
	Jan. 6	Chapel & Windsor	*Mutius Scaevola*
	Feb. 19	Paul's	*Titus and Gisippus*
1577–78	Dec. 27	Chapel	
	Dec. 29	Paul's	
1578–79	Dec. 27	Chapel	
	Jan. 1	Paul's	*The Marriage of Mind and Measure*
	Mar. 2	Chapel	*Loyalty and Beauty*

1579–80	Dec. 27	Chapel	*Alucius*
	Jan. 3	Paul's	*Scipio Africanus*
1580–81	Jan. 6	Paul's	*Pompey*
	Feb. 5	Chapel	
1581–82	Dec. 26	Paul's	
	Dec. 31	Chapel	
	Feb. 27	Chapel	
1582–83	Dec. 26	Chapel	*A Game of Cards*
	Feb. 12	Merchant Taylors'	*Ariodante and Genevora*
1583–84	Jan. 1	Oxford's Boys	*Campaspe* (?)
	Jan. 6	Chapel	
	Feb. 2	Chapel	
	Mar. 3	Oxford's Boys	*Sapho and Phao* (?)
1584–85	Dec. 27	Oxford's Boys	*Agamemnon and Ulysses*
	Jan. 1	Oxford's Boys	
1585–86	Jan. 9	Stanley's Boys	
1586–87	Feb. 26	Paul's	
1587–88	Jan. 1	Paul's	*Gallathea* (?)
	Feb. 2	Paul's	*Endimion* (?)
1588–89	Dec. 27	Paul's	
	Jan. 1	Paul's	
	Jan. 12	Paul's	
1589–90	Dec. 28	Paul's	
	Jan. 1	Paul's	
	Jan. 6	Paul's	*Midas* (?)
1600–1	Jan. 1	Paul's	
	Jan. 6	Chapel	*Cynthia's Revels* (?)
	Feb. 22	Chapel	*The Contention between Liberality and Prodigality* (?)
1601–2	Jan. 6	Chapel	
	Jan. 10	Chapel	
	Feb. 14	Chapel	
1602–3	Jan. 1	Paul's	
1603–4	Feb. 20	Paul's	*The Phoenix* (?)
	Feb. 21	Queen's Revels	

1604–5	Jan. 1	Queen's Revels	*All Fools* (?)
	Jan. 3	Queen's Revels	
1606	July 30	Paul's	*Abuses*
1608–9	Christmas	Children of Blackfriars (3 performances)	
	Jan. 1	Children of Blackfriars	*A Trick to Catch the Old One* (?) [2]
	Jan. 4	Children of Blackfriars	
1609–10	Christmas	Children of Whitefriars (5 performances)	
1611–12	Jan. 5	Children of Whitefriars	*Cupid's Revenge*
1612–13	Nov. 2 or 3	Queen's Revels	*The Coxcomb* (?)
	Jan. 1	Queen's Revels	*Cupid's Revenge*
	Jan. 9	Queen's Revels	*Cupid's Revenge*
	Feb. 27	Queen's Revels	*The Widow's Tears*

 APPENDIX C

Repertories of the Children's Troupes[1]

IN most cases, I have relied on the title page of the first printed edition for the name of the company that produced the play. For lost or unprinted plays, or when there is some question about the auspices and date of performance, I accept what I consider to be the most plausible conjectures. Lost plays are indicated by (L); highly speculative dates and attributions to troupes and dramatists by (?). All dates refer to the time of initial performance by the troupe in question, not to the year of composition, the year the copy was entered in the *Stationers' Register,* or the year given on the title page of the first printed edition. Bracketed titles are those assigned by later scholars.

The Children of Paul's

The Play of the Weather	Heywood	1525–33
Wit and Science	Redford	1531–47
[D, G, and Tom] [2]	Redford	1531–47
[Courage, Kindness, and Cleanness]	Redford	1531–47
Patient Grissel (?)	Phillip	1558–61
The Marriage of Wit and Science (?)		1567–68

The Contention between Liberality and Prodigality (? see Chapel)		1567–68
Iphigenia (L)		1571–72
The History of Error (L)		1576–77
Titus and Gisippus (L)		1576–77
The Marriage of Mind and Measure (L)		1578–79
Scipio Africanus (L)		1579–80
Pompey (L)		1580–81
Cupid and Psyche (L)		c.1580–82
Campaspe (see Chapel)	Lyly	1580–84
Sapho and Phao (see Chapel)	Lyly	1582–84
Agamemnon and Ulysses (L see Chapel)		1584–85
Gallathea	Lyly	1585–88
Endimion	Lyly	c.1587–88
Mother Bombie	Lyly	1587–90
Midas	Lyly	1589–90
The Woman in the Moon (?)	Lyly	1590–95
Love's Metamorphosis (see Chapel)	Lyly	1597 (?)
The Maid's Metamorphosis		1597(?)–1600
The Wisdom of Doctor Dodypoll		1597(?)–1600
Antonio and Mellida	Marston	1599–1600
Antonio's Revenge	Marston	1599–1600
Jack Drum's Entertainment	Marston	1600
Satiromastix	Marston and Dekker	1601
What You Will (?)	Marston	c.1601

Blurt, Master Constable	Dekker (?)	1601–2
The Family of Love (? see King's Revels)	Middleton and Barry (?)	1602–3 (?)
The Old Joiner of Aldgate (L)	Chapman	1603
The Phoenix	Middleton	1603–4
The Fawn (see Chapel) [3]	Marston	c.1604
Bussy D'Ambois	Chapman	1604
Westward Ho!	Dekker and Webster	1604
A Trick to Catch the Old One (see Chapel) [4]	Middleton	1604–6
Michaelmas Term	Middleton	1604–6
A Mad World, My Masters	Middleton	1604–6
Northward Ho!	Dekker and Webster	1605
The Woman Hater	Beaumont	1605–7
The Puritan	Middleton	1606
Abuses (L)		1606

The Children of the Chapel Royal (also called the Children of the Queen's Revels and the Children of Blackfriars)

Troilus and Pandor (L)	Cornish	1516
Summer and Lust (L)	Cornish (?)	1519
[*Friendship, Prudence and Might*] (L)	Cornish	1522
Love and Riches (L)	Rastell (?)	1527
Genus Humanum (L)		1553–54
Damon and Pythias	Edwardes	1564–65

Appius and Virginia (?)	R. B[ower (?)]	1559–67
The King of Scots (L)		1567–68
Narcissus (L)		1571–72
Mutius Scaevola (L see Windsor)		1576–77
The Wars of Cyrus	Ferrant (?)	1576–80 (?)
Loyalty and Beauty (L)		1578–79
Alucius (L)		1579–80
Campaspe (see Paul's)	Lyly	1580–84
The Arraignment of Paris	Peele	c.1581–84
Sapho and Phao (see Paul's)	Lyly	1582–84
A Game of Cards (L)		1582–83
Agamemnon and Ulysses (L see Paul's)		1584–85
Dido, Queen of Carthage	Nashe and Marlowe	1585–88 (?)
Hieronimo		1600–4
Love's Metamorphosis (see Paul's)	Lyly	1600
Cynthia's Revels	Jonson	1600
The Contention between Liberality and Prodigality (? see Paul's)		1600–1
The Case Is Altered	Jonson	1600–8
Poetaster	Jonson	1601
May Day	Chapman	1601–2
Sir Giles Goosecap	Chapman (?)	1601–3
[*A Royal Widow of England*] (L) [5]		1602
The Gentleman Usher (?)	Chapman	1602–3
The Malcontent	Marston	c.1603
The Dutch Courtesan	Marston	1603–5

The Fawn (see Paul's)	Marston	c.1604
All Fool's	Chapman	1604
Philotas	Daniel	1604
Monsieur D'Olive	Chapman	1604–5
A Trick to Catch the Old One (see Paul's)	Middleton	1604–6
Your Five Gallants	Middleton	1604–7
Law Tricks (? see King's Revels)	Day	1604–7 (?)
Eastward Ho!	Chapman, Marston and Jonson	1605
The Widow's Tears	Chapman	c.1605
Sophonisba	Marston	1605–6
The Isle of Gulls	Day	1606
The Fleer	Sharpham	1606
The Viper and Her Brood (L)	Middleton	1606
The Knight of the Burning Pestle	Beaumont	1607
Cupid's Revenge	Beaumont and Fletcher	1607–8
The Contention and Tragedy of Byron	Chapman	1608
[*The Silver Mine*] (L)		1608
The Faithful Shepherdess	Fletcher	1608
The Coxcomb	Beaumont and Fletcher	1609
A Woman is a Weathercock	Field	1609–10
Epicoene	Jonson	1609–10
The Insatiable Countess	Marston and Barkstead	1609–11

The Revenge of Bussy D'Ambois	Chapman	1610
Amends for Ladies	Field	1610–11
The Scornful Lady (?)	Beaumont and Fletcher	c.1610

The Children of the King's Revels

Law Tricks (? see Chapel)	Day	1607
The Family of Love (see Paul's)	Middleton	1607
Everywoman in Her Humor (?)	Machin (?)	1607
The Turk	Mason	1607
Cupid's Whirligig	Sharpham	1607
The Two Maids of Moreclack (?)	Armin	1607–8
Ram Alley	Barry	1607–8
The Dumb Knight	Markham and Machin (?)	1607–8
Torrismount (L) [6]		1607–8
Humor out of Breath	Day	1608

The Merchant Taylors' Boys

Perseus and Andromeda (L)	1573–74
Timoclea at the Siege of Troy (L)	1573–74
Ariodante and Genevora (L)	1582—83

The Children of the Windsor Chapel

Ajax and Ulysses (L)	1571–72
Quintus Fabius (L)	1573–74

Xerxes (L)		1574–75
Mutius Scaevola (L see Chapel)		1576–77

St. Paul's Grammar School

Dido (L)	Rightwise	1522–32
Heretic Luther (L)	Rightwise	1527
Menaechmi	Plautus	1527
Phormio	Terence	1528
[*Religion, Peace, and Justice*] (?)		1528
[*Philomathes' Dream*] [7]	John Harrison	1583–84
[*Philomathes' Second Dream*]	John Harrison	1585–86

Westminster Grammar School
(College of St. Peter)

Ralph Roister Doister (?)	Udall	1553–56 (?)
Miles Gloriosus	Plautus	1564–65
Heautontimorumenus	Terence	1564–65
Sapientia Solomonis	Birck	1565–66

Westminster Choirboys [8]

Paris and Vienne (L)	1571–72
Truth, Faithfulness, and Mercy (L)	1573–74

Grammar School at Hitchen

The Condemnation of John Huss (L)		
The Afflictions of Job (L)		
The Revolt of Jonah (L)		
The Courage of Judith (L)		
Lazarus and Dives (L)		
The Burning of Sodom and Gomorrah (L)	Radcliffe	1548(?)–56
The Deliverance of Susanna (L)		
Chaucer's Melibeus (L)		
Titus and Gisippus (L)		
Patient Griseldis (L)		

Unknown Children's Troupes

Godly Queen Hester		c.1525–29
Thersites	Udall (?)	1537
Ezekias (L)	Udall	1537–56
Nice Wanton		c.1535–53
Jacob and Esau		1550–57
Respublica	Udall (?)	1553
Jack Juggler		c.1553–58
Tom Tyler and His Wife		1558–63
The Disobediant Child	Ingelond	c.1558–69
The Bugbears	Jeffere	c.1563–65
Virtuous and Godly Susanna	Garter	1563–69
The Glass of Government	Gascoigne	1575
Summer's Last Will and Testament	Nashe	1592

Editions of Plays

Barry, Lording. *Ram Alley.* Ed. Claude E. Jones. *Materialien.* Louvain: Uystpruyst, 1952.

Beaumont, Francis. *The Dramatic Works in the Beaumont and Fletcher Canon.* Ed. Fredson Bowers. Vols. I and II. Cambridge: Cambridge University Press, 1966 and 1970.

Blurt, Master Constable. See Middleton, ed. Bullen.

Chapman, George. *The Plays of George Chapman: The Comedies.* Ed. Allan Holaday. Urbana: University of Illinois Press, 1970.

—— *Bussy D'Ambois.* Ed. N. Brooke. *Revels.* London: Methuen, 1964.

—— *The Conspiracy and Tragedy of Charles, Duke of Byron.* In *The Plays and Poems of George Chapman.* Ed. T.M. Parrott. Vol. I, *Tragedies.* London: Routledge, 1910.

—— *Eastward Ho!* (with Marston and Jonson). See Jonson.

[——] *Sir Giles Goosecap.* In *The Plays and Poems of George Chapman.* Ed. T.M. Parrott. Vol. II, *Comedies.* London: Routledge, 1914.

The Contention between Liberality and Prodigality. Ed. W.W. Greg. *MSR.* London: Oxford University Press, 1913.

Daniel, Samuel. *Philotas.* Ed. L. Michel. New Haven: Yale University Press, 1949.

Day, John. *The Isle of Gulls.* Ed. G.B. Harrison. *Shakespeare Association Facsimiles No. 12.* London: Oxford University Press, 1936.

—— *Humor Out of Breath.* In *Nero and Other Plays.* Ed. Arthur Symons. London: Vizetelly, 1888.

Dekker, Thomas. *The Dramatic Works of Thomas Dekker.* Ed. Fredson T. Bowers. 4 Vols. Cambridge: Cambridge University Press, 1953.

Edwardes, Richard. *Damon and Pythias.* Ed. C. Batey. *MSR.* Oxford: Oxford University Press, 1957.

The Fair Maid of the Exchange. Ed. P.A. Davison and A. Brown. *MSR.* Oxford: Oxford University Press, 1962.

Field, Nathan. *A Woman is a Weathercock.* In *The Plays of Nathan Field.* Ed. William Peery. Austin: University of Texas Press, 1950.

The First Part of Hieronimo. Ed. A.S. Cairncross. *RRD.* Lincoln: University of Nebraska Press, 1967.

Godly Queen Hester. Ed. W.W. Greg. *Materialien.* Louvain: A. Uystpruyst, 1904.

Ingelond, Thomas. *The Disobedient Child. Tudor Facsimile Texts.* Ed. J.S. Farmer. London: 1908.

Jonson, Ben. *Ben Jonson.* Ed. C.H. Herford and P. and E. Simpson. 11 Vols. Oxford: Clarendon Press, 1925–52.

Lyly, John. *The Complete Works of John Lyly.* Ed. R.W. Bond. 3 Vols. Oxford: Clarendon Press, 1902.

The Maid's Metamorphosis. See Lyly.

Marlowe, Christopher. *Dido, Queen of Carthage.* Ed. H.J. Oliver. *Revels.* London: Methuen, 1968.

Marston, John. *The Plays of John Marston.* Ed. H.H. Wood. 3 Vols. Edinburgh: Oliver and Boyd, 1934–39.

—— *Antonio and Mellida.* Ed. G.K. Hunter. *RRD.* Lincoln: University of Nebraska Press, 1965.

—— *Antonio's Revenge.* Ed. G.K. Hunter. *RRD.* Lincoln: University of Nebraska Press, 1965.

—— *The Dutch Courtesan.* Ed. M.L. Wine. *RRD.* Lincoln: University of Nebraska Press, 1965.

—— *The Fawn.* Ed. Gerald Smith. *RRD.* Lincoln: University of Nebraska Press, 1965.

—— *The Malcontent.* Ed. G.K. Hunter. *Revels.* London: Methuen, 1975.

—— *Eastward Ho!* (with Chapman and Jonson). See Jonson.

Middleton, Thomas. *The Works of Thomas Middleton.* Ed. A.H. Bullen. 8 Vols. London: Nimmo, 1885–86.

—— *A Mad World, My Masters.* Ed. S. Henning. *RRD.* Lincoln: University of Nebraska Press, 1965.

—— *Michaelmas Term.* Ed. R. Levin. *RRD.* Lincoln: University of Nebraska Press, 1966.

—— *A Trick to Catch the Old One.* Ed. G.J. Watson. *The New Mermaids.* London: Benn, 1968.

Mucedorus. In *The Shakespeare Apocrypha.* Ed. C.F.T. Brooke. London: Clarendon Press, 1918.

Nashe, Thomas. *The Works of Thomas Nashe.* Ed. R.B. McKerrow. 5 Vols. London: Bullen, 1904–10.

—— *Dido, Queen of Carthage* (with Marlowe). See Marlowe.

Peele, George. *The Arraignment of Paris.* Ed. H.H. Child. *MSR.* Oxford: Oxford University Press, 1910.

Percy, William. *Cuck-Queans and Cuckolds Errant* and *The Fairy Pastoral.* Ed. J. Haslewood. London: Roxburghe Club, 1824.

Sapientia Solomonis. Ed. E.R. Payne. New Haven: Yale University Press, 1938.

Sharpham, Edward. *Cupid's Whirligig.* Ed. A. Nicoll. *The Berkshire Series,* I. Waltham St. Lawrence: Cockerel, 1926.

Shakespeare, William. *The Riverside Shakespeare.* Ed. G.B. Evans. Boston: Houghton Mifflin, 1974.

Tomkis, Thomas. *Lingua.* London: Waterson, 1607.

Udall, Nicholas. *Ralph Roister Doister.* In *Chief Pre-Shakespearean Dramas.* Ed. J.Q. Adams. Boston: Houghton Mifflin, 1924.

The Wars of Cyrus. Ed. J. P. Brawner. *Illinois Studies in Language and Literature,* 28. Urbana: University of Illinois Press, 1942.

The Wisdom of Doctor Dodypoll. Ed. M.N. Matson. *MSR.* Oxford: Oxford University Press, 1965.

Notes

Chapter One: The Companies

1. *ES,* II, 1–76; and *CA.*

2. *The Scholemaster,* in *The English Works of Roger Ascham,* ed. W. A. Wright (Cambridge: Cambridge University Press, 1904), pp. 286–88. See also T. H. Vail Motter, *The School Drama in England* (London: Longmans, Green and Company, 1929; T. W. Baldwin, *William Shakespere's Small Latine and Lesse Greeke* (Urbana: University of Illinois Press, 1944), I, passim) and W. Nelson, ed., *A Fifteenth Century School Book* (Oxford: Clarendon Press, 1956), pp. xxiv–xxix and 26–27.

3. Charles Hoole, *A New Discovery of the Old Art of Teaching School,* ed. T. Mark (Syracuse: C. W. Bardeen, 1912), pp. 180–81.

4. Bale, *Scriptores,* I, 700, as quoted in *CA,* pp. 18–19; James Whitelocke, *Liber Famelicus* (Camden Society), p. 12, as quoted in *ES,* II, 76.

5. C. H. Herford, *Studies in the Literary Relations between England and Germany in the Sixteenth Century* (Cambridge: Cambridge University Press, 1886), pp. 79–98; M. T. Herrick, *Tragicomedy* (Urbana: University of Illinois Press, 1962), pp. 29–45; R. W. Bond, ed., *Early Plays from the Italian* (Oxford: Oxford University Press, 1911), pp. xciii ff.; and H. H. Adams, *English Domestic or, Homiletic Tragedy, 1575 to 1642* (New York: Columbia University Press, 1943), pp. 67–74.

6. Herrick, *Tragicomedy,* pp. 46–51.

7. David Bevington, *From "Mankind" to Marlowe* (Cambridge, Mass.: Harvard University Press, 1962), pp. 63–64. Bevington argues that plays requiring more than eight or ten actors were probably acted by children's troupes (p. 29 ff.) and offers a list of children's plays acted at court between 1530 and 1570 (p. 65). Some of the plays in this list were probably performed outside of London by troupes of provincial schoolboys rather than at court; see chapter 5, pp. 151–53.

8. G. K. Hunter, *John Lyly: The Humanist as Courtier* (London: Routledge and Kegan Paul, 1962), pp. 17–18.

9. *Athenae Oxoniensis*, I, 35, as quoted in *MS*, II, 215.

10. Order of Mary to the Master and Yeoman of the Revels, Kempe's *Loseley MSS*, p. 63, as quoted in *CA*, p. 69n.

11. K. M. Lea, *Italian Popular Comedy* (Oxford: Clarendon Press, 1934), I, 5–11; and Gustave Reese, *Music in the Renaissance*, revised edition (New York: W. W. Norton, 1959), pp. 690–91. The English court revels are described in *MS*, I, 390–419; Glynne Wickham, *Early English Stages: 1300 to 1660* (London: Routledge and Kegan Paul, 1959–72), I, 179–253; John Stevens, *Music and Poetry in the Early Tudor Court* (Lincoln: University of Nebraska Press, 1961), pp. 233–64; and Sydney Anglo, *Spectacle, Pageantry, and Early Tudor Policy* (Oxford: Oxford University Press, 1969), and G. K. Hunter, *John Lyly*, pp. 89–158.

12. Revels Books of Richard Gibson, as quoted in *CA*, p. 324. For an excellent description of the organization and activities of the Chapel Royal, see W. L. Woodfill, *Musicians in English Society from Elizabeth to Charles I* (Princeton: Princeton University Press, 1953), pp. 161–76. Cf. C. C. Stopes, *William Hunnis and the Revels of the Chapel Royal* (Louvain: A. Uystpruyst, 1910); and M. Bradbrook, *The Rise of the Common Player* (London: Chatto and Windus, 1962), pp. 211–40.

13. Order of Alexander Nowell, Dean of St. Paul's, as quoted in *CA*, p. 107. For background information on choristers of ecclesiastical institutions, see Woodfill, *Musicians in English Society*, pp. 135–58; and F. L. Harrison, *Music in Medieval Britain* (London: Routledge and Kegan Paul, 1958) pp. 9–14 and passim. Cf. William R. Davies, *Shakespeare's Boy Actors* (London: J. M. Dent and Sons, 1939), pp. 35–36; and A. Smith, "The Cultivation of Music in English Cathedrals in the Reign of Elizabeth I," *PRMA*, 94 (1967–68), 40–42.

14. For a full account of the Boy Bishop, see *MS*, I, 336–71. The Feast of Fools is described in *MS*, I, 274–335. Descriptions of similar saturnalian festivals and traditions in other cultures can be found in James Fraser, *The Golden Bough*, 3rd edition (New York: Macmillan, 1935), VIII, 66–67, and IX, 136–37, 306 ff.; and Robert C. Elliott, *The Power of Satire* (Princeton: Princeton University Press, 1960), pp. 78–84.

15. Robert Dodsley, *A Select Collection of Old Plays* (1744), I, xii,

as quoted in *MS*, II, 380. For a general discussion of mystery plays, see *MS*, II, 68–148. For particular information on the participation of choirboys, see F. Collins, "Music in the Craft Cycles," *PMLA*, 47 (1932), 613–21; R. W. Ingram, "The Use of Music in English Miracle Plays," *Anglia*, 75 (1957), 55–76; J. Stevens, "Music in Mediaeval Drama," *PRMA*, 84 (1957–58), 81–95; *Records of Plays and Players in Kent*, ed. Giles Dawson; *MSC*, 7 (1965), 192–201; and A. J. Mill, "The Hull Noah Play," *MLR*, 33 (1938), 495–96. Cf. Grace Frank, *The Medieval French Drama* (Oxford: Clarendon Press, 1954), pp. 168 and 172; and Howard M. Brown, *Music in the French Secular Theater: 1400–1550* (Cambridge, Mass.: Harvard University Press, 1963), pp. 24–26, 42–46 and 51–53.

16. *MS*, II, 121.

17. Trevor Lennam, "The Children of Paul's, 1551–1582," in *Elizabethan Theatre, II*, ed. David Galloway (Waterloo: Archon Books, 1970), pp. 20–36, summarizes and amplifies recent scholarship on Redford and Westcote. This and other valuable material can be found in his book, *Sebastian Westcott, the Children of Paul's, and the Marriage of Wit and Science* (Toronto: University of Toronto Press, 1975). See my review, *MLR*, 71 (1976). Heywood's role in the company is discussed in A. W. Reed, *Early Tudor Drama* (London: Methuen and Company, 1926), pp. 54–61.

18. *Catholic Record Society*, I, 21, as translated in W. H. G. Flood, "Master Sebastian of Paul's," *The Musical Antiquary*, 3 (1912), 152.

19. *Privy Council Registers, Elizabeth, II*, 408, as quoted in *CA*, p. 124n.

20. *A Calendar of Dramatic Records in the Books of the Livery Companies of London: 1485–1640*, ed. J. Robertson et al., *MSC*, 3 (1954), 138–39.

21. *Repertories of the Court of Common Council*, December 8, anno 18 Elizabeth, as quoted in *CA*, p. 123. For the location of the playhouse at Paul's, see Lennam, *Elizabethan Theatre, II*, 28–32, and *Sebastian Westcott . . .* , pp. 43–50; and my note in "Three Notes on the Theatre at Paul's," *TN*, 24 (1970), 147–48.

22. As quoted in *CA*, p. 330.

23. *Masters' Accounts*, as quoted in *ES*, II, 75. Cf. R. L. De Molen, "Richard Mulcaster and the Elizabethan Theatre," *ThS*, 13 (1972), 28–31; and *TN* 25 (1971), 109.

24. Both statements are quoted in C. W. Wallace, *The Evolution of*

English Drama up to Shakespeare (Berlin: George Reimer, 1912), pp. 175 and 154n. All relevant documents are printed in *Blackfriars Records, MSC,* 2, Part 1 (1913).

25. Alfred Harbage, *Shakespeare and the Rival Traditions* (New York: Macmillan, 1952), p. 33.

26. I quote from the label of my plaid wool cap, purchased from Herbert Johnson, 38 New Bond Street, London. Beneath the royal insignia and the passage quoted is Johnson's coat of arms, complete with his motto, *"Nunquam non paratus."*

27. As quoted in *CA,* p. 330.

28. John T. Murray, *English Dramatic Companies: 1558–1642* (Boston: Houghton Mifflin Company, 1910), II, 292, 366, 305.

29. Both Harvey's statement and Roberts' letter are quoted in Hunter, *John Lyly,* pp. 75–76.

30. *Le Prince d'Amour* (London: W. Leake, 1660), p. 56. A fuller discussion of this evidence appears in my note, " 'Le Prince d'Amour' and the Resumption of Playing at Paul's," *N & Q,* 216 (1971), 14–16.

31. White's letter appears in the De L'Isle and Dudley papers and is quoted in C. H. Herford and P. and E. Simpson, eds., *Ben Jonson* (Oxford: Clarendon Press, 1925–52), IX, 186. Fanner's letter appears in *State Papers Dom. Eliz.,* cclxxi, 34, 35, and is quoted in *ES,* II, 127. Cf. W. R. Gair, "La Compagnie des Enfants de St. Paul," in *D&S,* II, 655–74; exaggerating Derby's role in the resumption of playing at Paul's, Gair sees the troupe purely as an expression of aristocratic vanity until it was taken over by commercial interests around 1602.

32. *ES,* II, 556n. Cf. *ES,* II, 21, and my note, *TN,* 24 (1970), 151–54.

33. As quoted in C. J. Sisson, *Lost Plays of Shakespeare's Age* (Cambridge: Cambridge University Press, 1936), p. 61. The full discussion is on pp. 12–79.

34. *The Defendant's Rejoinder,* Keysar-Burbage suit of 1610, as quoted in *CA,* pp. 215–16.

35. As quoted in Sisson, *Lost Plays,* p. 70.

36. As quoted in Sisson, *Lost Plays,* p. 61. See also pp. 64–65.

37. See *CA,* pp. 213, 230. Writing before Sisson published his work, Hillebrand had no idea of Woodford's investment in the Children of Paul's.

38. *Declared Accounts,* as quoted in *CA,* p. 211n.

39. *The King of Denmark's Welcome* (1606), as quoted in *ES*, II, 22*n*.

40. C. W. Wallace, *The Children of the Chapel at the Blackfriars, 1597–1603* (New York: AMS Press, 1970 [first edition Lincoln: University of Nebraska Studies, 1908]), p. 75.

41. Mark Eccles, "Martin Peerson ànd the Blackfriars," *ShS*, 11 (1958), 104.

42. See my note, *TN*, 24 (1970), 151–54.

43. Diary of the Duke of Stettin-Pomerania. The relevant passage is printed, with useful commentary, in CA, p. 165 and *ES*, II, 46–47, and translated in Wallace, *The Children of the Chapel,* pp. 106–7. Wallace's theory that the Queen subsidized theatrical activities at Blackfriars is based largely on a dubious statement in this diary.

44. William Shakespeare, *Hamlet, the First Quarto,* 1603, ed. A. B. Weiner (Great Neck: Barron's Educational Series, 1962), pp. 111–12.

45. As quoted in *CA,* 196–97, and *ES,* II, 52.

46. The indenture governing the apprenticeship of Abel Cooke to Thomas Kendall, a member of the Blackfriars syndicate, is printed in *CA,* pp. 197–99.

47. Letter from Sir Thomas Lake to Lord Salisbury, March 11, 1608, as quoted in *ES,* II, 53–54.

Chapter Two: The Occasion

1. *ES,* II, 72. G. Wickham, *Early English Stages,* II, part 2, 148–65, argues the primacy of court performance for all acting companies, but perhaps overstates the case for adult professional troupes.

2. *ES,* II, 15; and G. E. Bentley, *The Jacobean and Caroline Stage* (Oxford: Clarendon Press, 1968), VI, 256. For an excellent discussion of theatrical performances in Tudor great halls, see Richard Southern, *The Staging of Plays Before Shakespeare* (New York: Theatre Arts Books, 1973), pp. 45–55. Cf. M. Paterson, *The Stagecraft of the Revels Office During the Reign of Elizabeth,* in *Studies in the Elizabethan Theatre,* ed. C. Prouty (Hamden, Connecticut: The Shoe String Press, 1961), passim; and R. Hosley, "Three Renaissance Indoor Playhouses," *ELR,* 3 (1973), 166–76.

3. *ES,* II, 554. See L. Hotson, *Shakespeare's Wooden O* (London: Rupert Hart-Davis, 1960), pp. 155–92. The title page of the first edi-

tion assigns the play to the King's Revels, but some scholars believe it was first acted earlier by another troupe, probably the Children of Paul's. See *CA*, pp. 234–35. D. J. Lake, *The Canon of Thomas Middleton's Plays* (Cambridge: Cambridge University Press, 1975), pp. 91–107, argues for 1602–3 as the date of initial composition, but finds evidence of revision, possibly by Barry.

4. See my note, *TN*, 24 (1970), 150–51; and T. Lennam, *Sebastian Westcott . . .* , pp. 43–48.

5. *ES*, II, 516, and G. Wickham, *Early English Stages*, II, part 2, 123. Wickham's succinct remarks on both Blackfriars theaters are useful: see pp. 125–38.

6. I. Smith, *Shakespeare's Blackfriars Playhouse* (New York: New York University Press, 1964), pp. 130–54. Cf. R. K. Sarlos, *Development and Operation of the First Blackfriars Theatre*, in *Studies in the Elizabethan Theatre*, ed. C. Prouty, p. 157; A. Harbage, *Shakespeare and the Rival Traditions*, p. 43; and R. Hosley, "Elizabethan Theatres and Audiences," *RORD*, 10 (1967), 12. Estimates of seating capacity vary with the amount of space allotted for the stage and for each spectator, the latter figure depending on whether one assumes that Elizabethan fashions required a larger space for each spectator than is allotted in a modern theater, or whether Elizabethans would tolerate more crowding than present-day spectators.

7. The legal document is quoted in *CA*, p. 176. Smith, *Shakespeare's Blackfriars Playhouse*, pp. 164–73, 297, and 304*n*10. Cf. R. Hosley, "A Reconstruction Playhouse, pp. 164–73, 297, and 304*n*10. Cf. R. Hosley, "A Reconstruction of the Second Blackfriars," in *The Elizabethan Theatre I*, ed. D. Galloway (Toronto: Archon Books, 1969), pp. 74–88; and G. T. Forrest [and J. H. Farrar], "Blackfriars Theatre: Conjectural Reconstruction," *The Times*, November 21, 1921. Farrar's drawing is reprinted in W. A. Armstrong, *The Elizabethan Private Theatres: Facts and Problems* (The Society for Theatre Research, Pamphlet Series No. 6, 1957–58). See also D. F. Rowan, "The Tiring-house Wall and the Galleries in the Second Blackfriars," *TN*, 26 (1972), 101–4.

8. G. E. Bentley, *The Jacobean and Caroline Stage*, VI, 12 and 291–309. G. Wickham, *Early English Stages*, II, part 2, 138–65. James Wright, *Historia Histrionica* (1699), quoted in Bentley, VI, 53–54, recalled that "the *Blackfriars*, *Cockpit*, and *Salisbury court* . . . were all three built almost exactly alike, for Form and Bigness."

9. E. R. Payne, ed., *Sapientia Solomonis* (New Haven: Yale University Press, 1938) pp. 4–8 and 41–45; and *ES*, IV, 378. See also M. C. Bradbrook, *The Rise of the Common Player*, Chapters XI ("Drama as Offering") and XII ("The Private Audience").

10. J. Huisinga, *The Waning of the Middle Ages* (New York: Longmans, Green, 1949), p. 229.

11. C. L. Barber, *Shakespeare's Festive Comedy* (Princeton: Princeton University Press, 1959), p. 7. F. M. Cornford, *The Origin of Attic Comedy*, ed. T. H. Gaster (Garden City, New York: Doubleday, 1961), pp. 101 ff., follows Aristotle's statement in Chapter 4 of the *Poetics* that poetry originated in praise and abuse of real men.

12. N. Frye, *A Natural Perspective* (New York: Columbia University Press, 1965), p. 102.

13. O. B. Hardison, *The Enduring Monument* (Chapel Hill: University of North Carolina Press, 1962), traces the theory and practice of literature of praise from classical antiquity through the Renaissance.

14. J. Barish, *Ben Jonson and the Language of Prose Comedy* (Cambridge, Mass.: Harvard University Press, 1960), p. 244.

15. M. P. Tilley, *A Dictionary of the Proverbs in England in the Sixteenth and Seventeenth Centuries* (Ann Arbor: University of Michigan Press, 1950), C-328. Cf. Lyly's *Endimion* (IV.ii.101–2), Marston's *Jack Drum's Entertainment* (III, 221) and Sharpham's *Cupid's Whirligig* (p. 32, ll. 32–33). R. Ascham, *The Scholemaster*, in *The English Works*, p. 210.

16. The film is Stanley Kramer's *It's a Mad, Mad, Mad, Mad World* (1963); the play is Peter Handke's *Offending the Audience*, in *Kaspar and Other Plays* (New York: Farrar, Straus, and Giroux, 1969).

17. *Biographia Dramatica*, ed. David Baker et al. (London: Longman et al., 1812), II, 55.

18. V. W. Turner, *The Ritual Process* (Chicago: Aldine, 1969), p. 176.

19. G. K. Hunter, *John Lyly*, p. 135.

20. Even if *All Fool's* is the same play mentioned by Henslowe in 1599, or a revision of that play, a new Prologue and Epilogue would probably have been written for the Queen's Revels production.

21. See H. G. Lesnick, "The Structual Significance of Myth and Flattery in Peele's *Arraignment of Paris*," *SP*, 65 (1968), 163–70; G. K. Hunter, *John Lyly*; P. Saccio, *The Court Comedies of John Lyly* (Princeton: Princeton University Press, 1969); Marion Jones, "The

Court and the Dramatist," in *Elizabethan Theatre,* ed. J. R. Brown and B. Harris (New York: St. Martin's Press, 1967), p. 177–81; and the criticism of *The Phoenix* cited in note 30, below.

22. As quoted in *CA,* p. 99.

23. M. Doran, *Endeavors of Art* (Madison: University of Wisconsin Press, 1954), pp. 169–70; and Herford and Simpson, eds., *Ben Jonson,* IX, 396–99.

24. Evidence of adult actors playing with children's troupes is discussed in chapter 4. The title page of the first edition of *What You Will* mentions no acting company, but most scholars think Marston wrote the play before he joined the Blackfriars directorate in 1602 or 1603, or while he was writing for the Children of Paul's; cf. *CA,* p. 296. Recent scholarship suggests that Dekker rather than Middleton wrote *Blurt, Master Constable;* see S. Schoenbaum," 'Blurt, Master Constable': A Possible Authorship Clue," *RN,* 13 (1960), 7–9; J. Gowan, "*Edward Pudsey's Booke* and the Authorship of *Blurt Master Constable,*" *RORD,* 8 (1965), 46–48; and D. J. Lake, *The Canon of Thomas Middleton's Plays,* pp. 66–90. The title page of the first edition of *Sir Giles Goosecap* mentions no author, but most scholars believe Chapman wrote the play; see *ES,* IV, 15–16; and T. M. Parrott, "The Authorship of 'Sir Gyles Goosecap,' " *MP,* 4 (1906–7), 25–37, and notes to his edition of the play, pp. 890 ff.

25. O. J. Campbell, *Comicall Satyre and Shakespeare's Troilus and Cressida* (San Marino: Huntington Library Publications, 1938).

26. The title page of the first edition mentions no acting troupe, but most scholars follow Parrott in assigning the play to the Chapel Children and accept his dating of 1602–3. See J. H. Smith, ed., *The Gentleman Usher* (Lincoln: University of Nebraska Press, 1970), pp. xiii–xvi.

27. As quoted in *ES,* IV, 253. *Pro forma* denials of deliberate application occur in the Prologues to Jonson's *Epicoene,* Chapman's *All Fools,* Marston's *The Fawn,* and Beaumont's *The Woman Hater*—all acted by children's troupes in private theaters. For similar denials in other plays, see D. Klein, *The Elizabethan Dramatists as Critics* (New York: Philosophical Library, 1963), pp. 111–21, but the evidence suggests that "application" was more common in plays acted by children. In the Epilogue to the 1610 edition of *Mucedorus* (King's Men), added for court performance, Comedy scoffs when Envy

threatens to accuse her of personal satire: "This is a trap for Boys, not Men." N. C. H. Wijngaards, "The Function of the Audience in Satiric Drama," *Die Nieuwe Taalgids*, 64 (1971), 185–92, argues that the audience as much as or more than the author is often responsible for "application." A. Harbage, *Shakespeare and the Rival Traditions*, pp. 79–80, lists instances of "application" in plays acted by children's troupes; for other instances, see M. A. Taylor, "Lady Arabella Stuart and Beaumont and Fletcher," *PLL*, 8 (1972), 252–60, for a personal allusion in *The Knight of the Burning Pestle;* and P. Finkelpearl, *John Marston of the Middle Temple* (Cambridge, Mass.: Harvard University Press, 1969), pp. 127 ff. W. R. Gair, "La Compagnie des Enfants de St. Paul," in *D&S*, ed. J. Jacquot, II, 657–68, relates "application" to the tradition of "flying" and to inns-of-court entertainment. David Bevington, *Tudor Drama and Politics* (Cambridge, Mass.: Harvard University Press, 1968), generally finds references to political issues more significant than those to personalities, and denounces "lock-picking" scholars for trying to decode obscure personal allusions (pp. 1–26), but admits that plays like *Godly Queen Hester* fuse issues and "application" (pp. 86–95).

28. See C. J. Sisson, *Lost Plays*.

29. W. A. Armstrong, "The Audience of the Private Theatres," *RES*, n.s., 10 (1959), 237 ff. See also P. J. Finkelpearl, *John Marston of the Middle Temple*, p. 27; Lawrence Stone, *The Crisis of the Aristocracy, 1558–1641* (Oxford: Clarendon Press, 1965), pp. 386–89 and 690–91; A. Bry, "Middleton et le Public des 'City Comedies,' " in *D&S*, ed. J. Jacquot, II, 715–16; and B. Johansson, *Law and lawyers in Elizabethan England as evidenced in the plays of Ben Jonson and Thomas Middleton, Stockholm Studies in English*, 18 (1967). D. Bevington, *Tudor Drama and Politics*, pp. 271–88. On the date and company for *Law Tricks*, see *ES*, III, 285–86; and *CA*, pp. 235, 316.

30. For evidence of performance in 1603 or 1604, see B. Maxwell, "Middleton's *The Phoenix*," in *Joseph Quincy Adams Memorial Studies*, ed. J. G. McManaway et al. (Washington: Folger Library, 1948), pp. 745–51. For the parallel with James, see N. W. Bawcutt, "Middleton's 'The Phoenix' as a Royal Play," *N & Q*, 201 (1956), 287–88; W. Power, "Thomas Middleton vs. King James I," *N & Q*, 202 (1957), 526–34, and " 'The Phoenix,' Raleigh, and King James," *N & Q*, 203 (1958), 57–61; D. B. Dodson, "King James and 'The Phoenix'—

Again," *N & Q*, 203 (1958), 434–37; and M. Williamson, "The *Phoenix:* Middleton's Comedy *de Regimine Principum,*" *RN*, 10 (1957), 183–87.

31. A. Kernan, *The Cankered Muse* (New Haven: Yale University Press, 1959), p. 10.

32. R. Levin, *The Multiple Plot in English Renaissance Drama* (Chicago: University of Chicago Press, 1971), pp. 127–37. Levin also makes some useful comments on the Oedipal rivalries in city comedy (pp. 182–83).

33. G. J. Watson, ed., *A Trick to Catch the Old One*, pp. xxii, xxxii–xxxiii. R. B. Parker, "Middleton's Experiments with Comedy and Judgment," in *Jacobean Theatre*, ed. J. R. Brown and B. Harris (New York: St. Martin's Press, 1960), p. 187.

Chapter Three: The Audience

1. M. Paterson, *The Stagecraft of the Revels Office*, p. 48.

2. Harbage, *Shakespeare and the Rival Traditions*, p. 49. Cf. A. J. Cook, *The London Theater Audience, 1576–1642*, unpublished dissertation (Vanderbilt, 1972), who argues that both public and private theater audiences were dominated by elite spectators. Unfortunately, I did not become aware of this study in time to consider its implications for my own work.

3. Armstrong, *RES*, pp. 236 ff. See above, chapter 2, p. 51. L. G. Salingar's description of the gallants in *Epicoene* might also fit the spectators at the private theaters: "men like Donne and others in Jonson's circle of friends, enjoying a sophisticated idleness somewhere between the court and the city while they wait for the property that will establish them or the patronage that will direct their abilities or scholarship into a purposeful career"—"Farce and Fashion in *The Silent Woman*," *E & S*, n.s., 20 (1967), 38.

4. Lawrence Stone, *The Crisis of the Aristocracy, 1558–1641*, p. 547 and passim. Stone's work is indispensable for understanding the economic and social forces affecting the children's troupes and their plays. See also L. C. Knights, *Drama and Society in the Age of Jonson* (London: Chatto and Windus, 1937), pp. 1–168; and Patricia Thomson, "The Old Way and the New Way in Dekker and Massinger," *MLR*, 51 (1956), 168–72. For a discussion of the importance of public esteem to the Renaissance aristocrat, see C. B. Watson, *Shakespeare*

and the Renaissance Concept of Honor (Princeton: Princeton University Press, 1960), pp. 11–13 and 136–62. For a case study of self-dramatization, see S. J. Greenblatt, Sir Walter Raleigh (New Haven: Yale University Press, 1973).

5. This chapter is printed in ES, IV, 365–69. See also the descriptions of audience behavior in Beaumont's The Woman Hater, I, 165–66, and Jonson's Induction to Cynthia's Revels. As Arthur Kirsch, Jacobean Dramatic Perspectives (Charlottesville: The University Press of Virginia, 1972), p. 31, writes: "Judging by the testimony of the dramatist who wrote for them, coterie audiences had to be continually flattered into watching the plays they had presumably come to watch and assured that they would not have to suspend their sophistication. This kind of detachment, like many other circumstances of the theater, could be a creative challenge for a dramatist. . . ."

6. G. E. Bentley, The Jacobean and Caroline Stage, VI, 7.

7. Erving Goffman has invented the term "role distance" for this kind of sprezzatura, which affirms the richness of one's identity. See Encounters (Indianapolis: Bobbs-Merrill, 1961). I am also indebted to his book, The Presentation of Self in Everyday Life (New York: Doubleday, 1959).

8. Scholars have speculated that Shakespeare wrote both of these plays with courtly or aristocratic audiences in mind; see E. K. Chambers, William Shakespeare (Oxford: Clarendon Press, 1930), I, 338 and 358–60. A. Harbage, "Love's Labor's Lost and the Early Shakespeare," PQ, 41 (1962), 18–36, argues unconvincingly that this play was written for the Children of Paul's. For other references to similar behavior by private-theater audiences, see Lyly's Prologue to Midas and Marston's Epilogue to The Fawn. In 1 Honest Whore (Prince Henry's Men, 1604), Dekker seems to be alluding to the same phenomenon:

> If you'll needs play the madman, choose a stage
> Of lesser compass, where few eyes may note
> Your actions error; but if still you miss,
> As here you do, for one clap, ten will hiss.
>
> (III.i.60–63)

9. The argument of Hillebrand, CA, p. 148n, that the Croydon performance was given by the Children of Paul's, seems stronger than

the objections to a London troupe raised by R. B. McKerrow, ed., *The Works of Thomas Nashe* (London: A. H. Bullen, 1904–10), IV, 416–19. M. R. Best, "Nashe, Lyly, and *Summer's Last Will and Testament,*" *PQ*, 48 (1969), 1–11, contends that the play is Nashe's expansion of an earlier entertainment by Lyly, but he overlooks the simpler possibility that Nashe is merely satirizing an old-fashioned theatrical form. For useful criticism of the play, see C. L. Barber, *Shakespeare's Festive Comedy* (Princeton: Princeton University Press, 1959), pp. 58–86; and G. R. Hibbard, *Thomas Nashe: A Critical Introduction* (Cambridge, Mass.: Harvard University Press, 1962), pp. 85–105.

10. E. M. Waith, "The Voice of Mr. Bayes," *SEL*, 3 (1963), 341. Cf. Waith, "Spectacles of State," *SEL*, 13 (1973), 317–30.

11. O. J. Campbell, *Comicall Satyre and Shakespeare's Troilus and Cressida*, pp. 166–81.

12. See the note in Ethel Smeak's edition of the play (Lincoln: University of Nebraska Press, 1966), p. 48. For a convenient summary of attacks on the new Scots knights in children's plays by Barry, Chapman, Day, Marston, and Middleton, see *ES*, III, 215, 252–55, 286, 432, and 439–40. Significantly, such attacks are virtually unknown in plays acted by adult troupes in public theaters. Nicholas Brooke, ed., *Bussy D'Ambois* (London: Methuen, 1964), p. 23*n*, points out that "in the first two months of his reign, James I created as many knights as Elizabeth in the previous ten years," and quotes a telling phrase—"this almost prostituted title of knighthood"—from Bacon's letter to Cecil (July 3, 1603).

13. Millar Maclure, *George Chapman: A Critical Study* (Toronto: University of Toronto Press, 1966), p. 103; and Thelma Herring, "Chapman and an Aspect of Modern Criticism," *RenD*, 8 (1965), 158*n*16.

14. E. M. Waith, *Ideas of Greatness* (London: Routledge and Kegan Paul, 1971), p. 131. I am indebted to Mr. Robert Funk for pointing out the relationship to the Cyprian setting of the allusions to Venus.

15. Henry Weidner, "Homer and the Fallen World," *JEGP*, 62 (1963), 518–32, regards Tharsalio as the play's "chief object of satire," a nihilistic lord of misrule who "stands for everything Chapman denounces" (p. 519); Samuel Schoenbaum, "*The Widow's Tears* and the Other Chapman," *HLQ*, 23 (1959–60), 321–38, considers Tharsalio

"the play's only realist" and "the dramatist's spokesman" (p. 334), but stresses the sinister side of his realism. For an excellent sympathetic study of Tharsalio, see Herring, *RenD,* pp. 155–67. She also finds a number of parallels between Tharsalio and Chapman himself; and suggests that the playwright may have created a wishful fantasy out of his own unsuccessful pursuit of a wealthy widow. See also M. L. Williamson, "Matter of More Mirth," *RenP,* 1956, pp. 34–41.

16. Ian Donaldson, *The World Upside-Down* (Oxford: Clarendon Press, 1970), p. 43; and A. Leggatt's unpublished paper read at the Ben Jonson Conference, Toronto, October 1972.

17. Jonas Barish, "Ovid, Juvenal, and *The Silent Woman,*" *PMLA,* 71 (1956), 214. In his later study of the play, *Ben Jonson and the Language of Prose Comedy* (Cambridge, Mass.: Harvard University Press, 1960), pp. 142–86, Barish still finds "a suspension of strong conviction on the part of Jonson himself" (p. 177). I am nevertheless deeply indebted to Barish's astute commentary, as well as to the following studies: Edward B. Partridge, *The Broken Compass* (New York: Columbia University Press, 1958), pp. 161–77; Ray L. Heffner, "Unifying Symbols in the Comedy of Ben Jonson," in *English Stage Comedy,* ed., W. K. Wimsatt, *English Institute Essays, 1954* (New York: Columbia University Press, 1955), pp. 74–97. A number of recent critics have challenged Barish's contention, arguing that *Epicoene* embodies a moral vision too complex to be pigeon-holed under the rubrics "Ovidian" and "Juvenalian." See Salingar, *E & S,* pp. 35–38; John Ferns, "Ovid, Juvenal and 'The Silent Woman': A Reconsideration," *MLR,* 65 (1970), 248–53. W. David Kay, "Jonson's Urbane Gallants: Humanistic Contexts for *Epicoene,*" *HLQ,* 39 (1975–76), 251–66, finds the play illustrative of the tension between humanistic and courtly values felt throughout the Renaissance.

18. G. K. Hunter, *John Lyly,* pp. 291–97.

19. T. M. Greene, "Ben Jonson and the Centered Self," *SEL,* 10 (1970), 325–48. For a concise statement of Jonson's notion of "the centered self," see the last eight lines of "To the World" (VIII, 101–2).

20. G. B. Jackson, *Vision and Judgment in Ben Jonson's Drama* (New Haven: Yale University Press, 1968), pp. 60–61, suggests that "Dauphine" connotes French "courtliness, delicacy, and polish," while "Eugenie" means either well-born or good spirit: "His courtliness is substantiated by his given name, which suggests not only

princely deportment but also his position as Morose's rightful heir";
cf. Edward B. Partridge, ed., *Epicoene* (New Haven: Yale University
Press, 1971), pp. 173–74. Sir Toby Belch expresses aristocratic respect
for bonds of kinship in *Twelfth Night* (c.1600–1), when he challenges
Malvolio's authority as steward: "Am not I consanguineous? Am I
not of her blood?" (II.iii.82–83). Disregard for consanguinity is
harshly critized in plays acted by children's troupes; see, for example, the discussion of Middleton's *A Trick to Catch the Old One*,
chapter 2, pp. 59–66. To my knowledge, *Epicoene* has never been
studied in relation to other city comedies; Knights, *Drama and Society*, has a few fleeting references to the play, while Brian Gibbons,
Jacobean City Comedy (Cambridge, Mass.: Harvard University Press,
1968), ignores *Epicoene* completely.

21. Herford and Simpson, *Ben Jonson*, X, 20; and Barish, *Ben Jonson and the Language of Prose Comedy*, pp. 162–63, comment on the
infantile quality of the construction "it knighthood," which Morose
uses nine times in this speech. Cf. Jonson's Epigram 115, "On the
Town's Honest Man."

22. L. A. Beaurline, ed., *Epicoene* (Lincoln: University of Nebraska
Press, 1966), points out the "phallic insinuations in the play" (p. 27*n*)
and "the ritual castration" (p. 117*n*) of Daw and La Foole; cf. Mark
Anderson, "The Successful Unity of *Epicoene*," *SEL*, 10 (1970), 360.
Like Morose, both Daw and La Foole oscillate between extremes of
passivity and assertiveness, submitting to symbolic castration in Act
Four when they surrender their weapons, and boasting of their sexual conquests of Epicoene in Act Five. By contrast, Dauphine's wish
to have all the collegiate ladies suggests a virility second only to
Tharsalio's. One suspects that this emphasis on male potency in the
heroes of children's plays is in part intended to compensate the audience for its social and economic weakness.

23. Barish, *Ben Jonson and the Language of Prose Comedy*, p. 177.
Ferns, *MLR*, refuses to take Truewit seriously at all and dismisses him
as a "zany" and a "chameleon clown" (p. 252). Partridge, ed., *Epicoene*, p. 190, comes closer to my view: "He is . . . always a cool
observer of a life he plays with, while rejecting its values. Jonson's
handling of Truewit is far from irresolute; rather, it constitutes a
triumph of artistic control."

24. S. F. J[ohnson], "enemies of the stage," in *The Reader's En-*

cyclopedia of Shakespeare, ed. O. J. Campbell (New York: Thomas Y. Crowell Company, 1966), p. 210.

25. Anderson, *SEL,* p. 366; and L. A. Beaurline, "Ben Jonson and the Illusion of Completeness," *PMLA,* 84 (1969), 58.

26. W. Slights, "*Epicoene* and the Prose Paradox," *PQ,* 49 (1970), 178–82; and E. G. Fogel, review of Jonas Barish's, *Ben Jonson and the Language of Prose Comedy, RN,* 15 (1962), 44.

27. A number of recent studies of Chapman's tragedies emphasize ambivalent responses to the protagonists. See Charles Barber, "The Ambivalence of Bussy D'Ambois," *Review of English Literature,* 2 (1961), 38–44; S. R. Homan, "Chapman and Marlowe: The Paradoxical Hero and the Divided Response," *JEGP,* 68 (1969), 391–406; E. M. Waith, *The Herculean Hero in Marlowe, Chapman, Shakespeare, and Dryden* (New York: Columbia University Press, 1962), pp. 88–111; and *Ideas of Greatness,* pp. 124–38; J. Jacquot, " 'Bussy D'Ambois' and Chapman's Conception of Tragedy," *English Studies Today,* 2 (1961), 129–41; G. R. Hibbard, "Goodness and Greatness: An Essay on the Tragedies of Ben Jonson and George Chapman," *RMS,* 9 (1967), 32–49; M. Maclure, *George Chapman,* pp. 108–44; and Peter Ure, *Elizabethan and Jacobean Drama,* ed. J. C. Maxwell (New York: Barnes and Noble, 1974), pp. 123–44, 166–86.

28. Stone, *Crisis of the Aristocracy,* p. 582.

29. On the question of Essex as a model for Philotas, see L. Michel, ed., *Philotas* (New Haven: Yale University Press, 1949), pp. 36–66; and B. Stirling, "Daniel's *Philotas* and the Essex Case," *MLQ,* 3 (1942), 583–94. For opposing arguments, see G. A. Wilkes, "Daniel's *Philotas* and the Essex Case: A Reconsideration," *MLQ,* 23 (1962), 233–42. See also M. Maclure, *George Chapman,* pp. 133–34, and "Shakespeare and the Lonely Dragon," *UTQ,* 24 (1954–55), 109–20.

30. E. Jenkins, *Elizabeth the Great* (New York: Coward-McCann, 1959), p. 319. If the extant text of *Byron* is a revision of an earlier play, Chapman probably added this passage to the later version. For evidence of an earlier version, see M. Jones and G. Wickham, "The Stage Furnishings of George Chapman's The Tragedy of Charles, Duke of *Biron,*" *TN,* 16 (1962), 113–17.

31. E. Schwartz, "Chapman's Renaissance Man: Byron Reconsidered," *JEGP,* 58 (1959), 620, describes Byron's death scene as fol-

lows: "The action of the scene builds gradually to a powerful crescendo of terror, as Byron tries first to avoid, then to face, and finally to transcend Death. Striving to maintain the dignity of his self hood in the face of imminent extinction, Byron achieves a dignity and grandeur only suggested earlier."

Chapter Four: The Style

1. Samuel Johnson, "Preface to Shakespeare" (1765), in *Johnson on Shakespeare*, ed. A. Sherbo, in *Works* (New Haven: Yale University Press, 1968), VII, 77.

2. "Shakespeare's Actors," *RES*, n.s., I (1950), 203. A fuller discussion of this matter can be found in Bethell's book, *Shakespeare and the Popular Dramatic Tradition* (Durham: Duke University Press, 1944), pp. 28–42. See also Anne Righter, *Shakespeare and the Idea of the Play* (London: Chatto and Windus, 1962), passim. Whereas Bethel and Righter both link "dual consciousness" with popular drama, A. Kirsch, *Jacobean Dramatic Perspectives*, connects it with the children's troupes in the private theaters: "the spectacle of children playing adults . . . helped give all writers for the children's companies a built-in emphasis upon the artificiality of the play world and an intrinsic means of manipulating the audience's sense of distance from the stage" (p. 18).

3. *ES*, II, 316 and 332. Field, who was baptized on Oct. 17, 1587, was twelve or thirteen when the Blackfriars syndicate impressed him into their troupe in late 1600. From then until 1613, he continued to act with the same company in its various forms, long after he had ceased to be a child actor. Field's case was probably atypical. Of all the child actors listed in the Folio for *Cynthia's Revels* (1600) and *Poetaster* (1601), Field is the only one also listed for *Epicoene* (1609–10). Apparently, Field alone remained with the troupe after other boys who had started when he did dropped out and were replaced by newly impressed recruits. After 1606, when Giles lost the power to "take up" boys, such replacements were evidently apprentices. Cf. L. Le Cocq, "Le Théatre de Blackfriars de 1596 à 1606," in *D & S*, II, 687–88.

4. *CA*, pp. 62n77 and 324. The passage from Hollyband is quoted in *The Elizabethan Home*, ed. M. St. Clare Byrne, new and revised ed. (London: Methuen, 1949), p. 33. Cf. T. W. Craik, *The Tudor In-*

terlude (Leicester: Leicester University Press, 1958), pp. 28–29 and 43.

5. Lennam, *Sebastian Westcott*, p. 39.

6. *John Lyly*, p. 237. Cf. Bond, ed., *Lyly*, I, 27.

7. Anne C. Lancashire, "Lyly and Shakespeare on the Ropes," *JEGP*, 68 (1969), 237–41. For other examples of bawdry used to highlight the immaturity of the child actors, see Marston's *What You Will* II, 265, Middleton's *Blurt, Master Constable* II.ii.107–110, Field's *A Woman is a Weathercock* II.ii.38–50, and Barry's *Ram Alley*, II. 327.

8. See P. Ariès, *Centuries of Childhood*, trans. R. Baldick (New York: Knopf, 1962), pp. 101–27.

9. These passages were probably added sometime after 1616, when the King's Men acquired the text, or perhaps in 1610–11, when the Children of the Queen's Revels may have revived the play. N. Brooke, ed., *Bussy D'Ambois* (London: Methuen, 1964) provides a brief discussion of the play's early stage history (pp. liv–lv) and a fuller treatment of textual problems connected with the two quartos (pp. lx–lxxiv). Cf. M. Maclure, *George Chapman*, pp. 118–19; B. Sturman, "The 1641 Edition of Chapman's *Bussy D'Ambois*," *HLQ*, 14 (1950–51), 171–201; R. P. Adams, "Critical Myths and Chapman's Original *Bussy D'Ambois*," *RD*, 9 (1966), 143–44, and A. H. Tricomi, "The Revised Version of Chapman's *Bussy D'Ambois*: A Shift in Point of View," *SP*, 70(1973), 288–305.

10. T. N. Greenfield, *The Induction in Elizabethan Drama* (Eugene: University of Oregon Books, 1969), pp. 147–48.

11. For a useful survey of the problem, see B. Beckerman, *Shakespeare at the Globe* (New York: Macmillan, 1962), pp. 109 ff.

12. E. Auerbach, *Mimesis* (Princeton: Princeton University Press, 1953); and E. Gombrich, *Art and Illusion* (New York: Pantheon Books, 1960).

13. E. J. Jensen, "The Style of the Boy Actors," *CompD*, 2 (1968), 100–14, ignores the effect of the audience's dual consciousness in his effort to show that Marston's plays were "serious" works rather than parodies or burlesques. G. D. Kiremidjian, "The Aesthetics of Parody," *JAAC*, 28 (1969), 231–42, points out that the categories of "serious" and "parodic" are not mutually exclusive.

14. J. Barish, "Feasting and Judging in Jonsonian Comedy," *RD*, n.s., 5 (1972), 24.

15. A. Harbage, "Elizabethan Acting," *PMLA*, 54 (1939), 685–708, who contends that all acting of the period was declamatory, argues

that the children's troupes were even more inclined than the adults toward such a style because they could not "succeed in the imaginative interpretation of adult roles" (p. 702). The case for the parodic style is made by A. Caputi, *John Marston, Satirist* (Ithaca: Cornell University Press, 1962), pp. 101–16; and R. A. Foakes, "John Marston's Fantastical Plays: *Antonio and Mellida* and *Antonio's Revenge*," *PQ*, 41 (1962), 229–39. Foakes has broadened his conception of parody in his more recent work on Marston, "Tragedy at the Children's Theatres after 1600: A Challenge to the Adult Stage," in *Elizabethan Theatre* II, pp. 37–59; a condensed version of this essay appears in his recent book, *Shakespeare: the Dark Comedies to the Last Plays* (Charlottesville: University of Virginia Press, 1971), pp. 63–74.

16. J. Reibetanz, "Hieronimo in Decimosexto: A Private-Theater Burlesque," *RenD*, n.s., 5 (1972), 90.

17. R. Levin, "The New *New Inn* and the Proliferation of Good Bad Drama," *EC*, 22 (1972), 41–47, chastises critics who redeem bad plays by labeling them parodies or burlesques. Levin accepts these labels only when "we can point to clear evidence provided by the author in the play to indicate his purposes" (p. 46). What constitutes such "clear evidence," however, is the heart of the problem, as R. A. Foakes points out in his rejoinder to Levin, pp. 327–29.

18. A. H. Quin, ed., *The Faire Maide of Bristowe* (Philadelphia: University of Pennsylvania Publications in Philology and Literature, 1902), p. 27. Cf. R. G. Hunter, *Shakespeare and the Comedy of Forgiveness* (New York: Columbia University Press, 1965). A. Leggatt, *Citizen Comedy in the Age of Shakespeare* (Toronto: University of Toronto Press, 1973), pp. 33–46, shows how some of the lesser-known public-theater playwrights made minor modifications in this formula.

19. J. Doebler, "Beaumont's *The Knight of the Burning Pestle* and the Prodigal Son Plays," *SEL*, 5 (1965), 333–44.

20. Cf. Quicksilver's earlier speech of repentance, IV.i.120–39. Other critics have briefly suggested that *Eastward Ho!* is a parody or have discussed parodic elements other than those I emphasize: L. C. Knights, *Drama and Society in the Age of Jonson*, p. 252n; M. Bradbrook, *The Growth and Structure of Elizabethan Comedy* (London: Chatto and Windus, 1961), pp. 47 and 138–40; C. Leech, "Three Times *Ho* and a Brace of Widows," in *Elizabethan Theatre* III, ed.

D. Galloway (Hamden: Archon Books, 1973), pp. 20–24; R. Horwich, "Hamlet and Eastward Ho," SEL, 11 (1971), 223–32; A. Leggatt, Citizen Comedy, pp. 47–53, and Sylvia Feldman, The Morality-Patterned Comedy of the Renaissance (Mouton: The Hague, 1970), pp. 99–101.
   21. S. Henning, ed., A Mad World, My Masters (Lincoln: University of Nebraska Press, 1965), p. xv, notices that these "moralizing set pieces" are "burdened with rhymed sententiae, and . . . hindered by ellipses and other distortions of syntax," but concludes that "it is as if Middleton's esthetic sense were instinctively balking at the forced, contrived morality which has no organic place in his world of rogues." A. Leggatt, Citizen Comedy, p. 138, agrees that the subplot is an artistic failure: "When the three figures of the triangle are posed in a final tableau of forgiveness, love, and friendship . . . , we are still rubbing our eyes in disbelief; and the rest of the play moves on to its amusing, amoral conclusion. . . ." For a moralistic defense of the subplot, see C. A. Hallett, "Penitent Brothel, the Succubus and Parson's Resolution," SP, 69 (1972), 72–86. Cf. W. E. Slights, "The Trickster-Hero in Middleton's A Mad World, My Masters," CompD, 3 (1969), 95, 97.
   22. Foakes, PQ, 41 (1962), 29–39; T. S. Eliot, Essays on Elizabethan Drama (New York: Harcourt Brace, 1932), p. 166; R. Ornstein, The Moral Vision of Jacobean Tragedy (Madison: University of Wisconsin Press, 1960), p. 155; S. Schoenbaum, "The Precarious Balance of John Marston," PMLA, 67 (1952), 1069–78; G. K. Hunter, ed., Antonio and Mellida (Lincoln: University of Nebraska Press, 1965), pp. xii–xxi; Hunter, ed., Antonio's Revenge (Lincoln: University of Nebraska Press, 1965), pp. ix–xxi; and Hunter, "English Folly and Italian Vice," in Jacobean Theatre, pp. 84–111.
   23. A. Bergson, "Dramatic Style as Parody in Marston's Antonio and Mellida," SEL, 11 (1971), 307–25.
   24. P. Finkelpearl, John Marston of the Middle Temple, pp. 140–61; P. Ayres, "Marston's Antonio's Revenge: The Morality of the Revenging Hero," SEL, 12 (1972), 359–74; and E. Berland, "The Function of Irony in Marston's Antonio and Mellida," SP, 66 (1969), 739–55.

Chapter Five: The Plays (1)
1. Edward Hall, Chronicle (London: J. Johnson et al., 1809), p. 723.
2. Revels Accounts as quoted in CA, p. 132. I follow the specula-

tive reconstructions of lost plays acted by the children's troupes made by J. P. Brawner, ed., *The Wars of Cyrus, Illinois Studies in Language and Literature*, 28, nos. 3–4 (Urbana: University of Illinois Press, 1942), 51–57; and "Early Classical Narrative Plays by Sebastian Westcott and Richard Mulcaster," *MLQ*, 4 (1943), 455–64. Arthur Brown, "A Note on Sebastian Westcott and the Plays Presented by the Children of Paul's," *MLQ*, 12 (1951), 134–36, challenges the assumption that the choirmasters themselves wrote the plays.

3. Hall, *Chronicle*, pp. 517–18.

4. For criticism of the work as a masque, see H. Lesnick, *SP*, 65 (1968), 163–70; and A. von Hendy, "The Triumph of Chastity: Form and Meaning in *The Arraignment of Paris*," *RD*, n.s., 1 (1968), 87–101. For criticsm of the work as a play, see G. K. Hunter, *John Lyly*, pp. 154–55.

5. Revels Accounts, as quoted by Brawner, ed., *The Wars of Cyrus*, p. 60n.

6. Lesnick, *SP*, 65 (1968), 164; and von Hendy, *RD*, n.s., 1 (1968), 92. The painting of "Elizabeth I and the Three Goddesses" by the monogrammist "HE" or "HM" is reproduced in R. Strong, *Portraits of Queen Elizabeth* (Oxford: Clarendon Press, 1963), Plate VI, and discussed on p. 79. See also J. D. Reeves, "The Judgment of Paris as a Device of Tudor Flattery," *N & Q*, 199 (1954), 7–11, and Inga-Stina Ekeblad, "On the Background of Peele's 'Araygnement of Paris,' " *N & Q*, 201 (1956), 246–49.

7. *ES*, III, 416–17; *CA*, pp. 142, 288; and G. K. Hunter, *John Lyly*, pp. 81–83.

8. G. K. Hunter, *John Lyly*, p. 217. M. R. Best, "Lyly's Static Drama," *RD*, n.s., 1 (1968), 77–78, writes: "Lyly's plays present a series of tableaux exploring paradoxical states of mind, particularly those of love. . . ."

9. M. R. Best, *PQ*, 48 (1969), 1–11, contends that the play is Nashe's expansion of an earlier entertainment by Lyly, but he overlooks the simpler possibility that Nashe is merely satirizing an old-fashioned theatrical form. See above, chapter 3.

10. *ES*, I, 232n7, *CA*, p. 87, and Brawner, ed., *The Wars of Cyrus*, p. 60n.

11. Prodigal-son plays are discussed by Herrick, *Tragicomedy*, pp. 37–46; R. W. Bond, ed., *Early Plays from the Italian*, pp. xciv ff.; M. Doran, *Endeavors of Art* (Madison: University of Wisconsin Press,

1954), pp. 161–62; S. Feldman, *The Morality-Patterned Comedy of the Renaissance* (The Hague: Mouton, 1970), pp. 138–50; and E. Beck, "Terence Improved: The Paradigm of the Prodigal Son in English Renaissance Comedy," *RD*, n.s., 6 (1973), 107–22.

12. D. M. Bevington, *From "Mankind" to Marlowe*, p. 65. The scholarly controversy over the date of *Ralph Roister Doister* is summarized by W. L. Edgerton, *Nicholas Udall* (New York: Twayne Publishers, Inc., 1965), pp. 89–94. The conventionality of final prayers is discussed in *ES*, II, 550, and III, 179–80.

13. *ES*, IV, 30, and Craik, *The Tudor Interlude*, pp. 15–16, identify *The Marriage of Wit and Science* with the *Wit and Will* mentioned in the Revels Accounts for 1567–68. *CA*, 128–31, identifies *The Contention between Liberality and Prodigality* with the *Prodigality* mentioned in the same document. Lennam, *Sebastian Westcott*, pp. 61, 64–65, and 90 ff., argues that both plays were performed at court by the Children of Paul's in 1567–68 and elaborates Hillebrand's argument that the troupe revived *The Contention* for court production in 1574–75. See my forthcoming review. The latter play was not published until 1602, when it was advertised on the title page as having been printed "As it was played before her Majesty" but without mention of any company. The text (l. 1261) mentions a crime alleged to have occurred on Feb. 4, 1601, from which Chambers, *ES*, IV, 26, deduces that it was revived by the Chapel Children, who gave the next recorded court performance after that date.

14. *The Case Is Altered* first appeared in print in 1609 under three different title pages, all of them assigning the play to "the Children of the Blackfriars," the name used by Chapel Children or Queen's Revels troupe between 1606 and 1609. Most scholars think the play was written earlier, perhaps as early as 1598 for an adult troupe, and was revised after 1605, presumably for a boy company. See *ES*, III, 357–58; *CA*, p. 154; and Herford and Simpson, eds., *Ben Jonson*, I, 305–7, and IX, 166–67.

15. Herrick, *Tragicomedy*, pp. 46–51. For similar trends in university plays, see F. S. Boas, *University Drama in the Tudor Age* (Oxford: Clarendon Press, 1914), 41, 49–61, 94, and 183–91.

16. Chambers, *ES*, II, 13–14, and III, 465–66, argues that Phillip was the "Master Phelypes" who appeared with Westcote, Heywood, and the Children of Paul's before Elizabeth at Nonsuch on Aug. 7, 1559, and Hillebrand, *CA*, 117n identifies him as an organist at Paul's. On

the basis of these arguments, one can hesitantly assign the play to the Children of Paul's. However, T. S. Graves, "The Heywood Circle and the Reformation," *MP*, 10 (1912–13), 566*n*, thinks that the "Master Phelypes" of the Nonsuch performance was a singer from the Chapel Royal.

17. As quoted in *CA*, p. 324.

18. G. E. P. Arkwright, "Elizabethan Choirboy Plays and their Music," *PRMA*, 40 (1913–14), 118–19 and 129–30, and "The Death Songs of Pyramus and Thisbe," *N & Q*, 84 (1906), 341, noted his discovery of the lament, "Alas, you salt sea Gods," found in the Dawe part-books at Christ Church, Oxford, where it is set for treble voice and strings, and attributed to "Farrant." Noting Ferrant's connection with Children of the Chapel Royal and the names in the song, W. J. Lawrence, "The Earliest Private-Theatre Play," *TLS*, Aug. 11, 1921, p. 514, linked the piece with *The Wars of Cyrus*, which was apparently performed by the Chapel Children. Both Lawrence and Brawner, ed., *The Wars of Cyrus*, p. 19, believe that the Chapel Children performed the play in the late 1570s, although Chambers, *ES*, IV, 52, dates it 1587–94, on the grounds that it imitates *Tamburlaine*. However, G. K. Hunter, "*The Wars of Cyrus* and *Tamburlaine*," *N & Q*, 206 (1961), 395–96, suggests that Marlovian phrases may have been added during revision, after *Tamburlaine*. For evidence of revision, see Brawner, ed., *The Wars of Cyrus*, pp. 12–13, 28–34. Cf. Anne Lancashire and Jill Levinson, "Anonymous Plays," in *The Predecessors of Shakespeare*, ed. T. P. Logan and D. S. Smith (Lincoln: University of Nebraska Press, 1973), pp. 189–92, where the scholarship dealing with the date and authorship of this play is summarized.

19. Jackson Cope, "Marlowe's *Dido* and the Titillating Children," *ELR*, 4 (1974), 315–24. Cf. B. Morris, " 'Unstable Proteus': *The Tragedy of Dido Queen of Carthage*," in *Christopher Marlowe*, ed. B. Morris (London: Ernest Benn Ltd., 1968), pp. 27–46; and D. Cole, *Suffering and Evil in the Plays of Christopher Marlowe* (Princeton: Princeton University Press, 1962), pp. 75–86.

20. H. J. Oliver, ed., *Dido Queen of Carthage and The Massacre of Paris* (Cambridge, Mass.: Harvard University Press, 1968), p. xxxiii.

21. M. Doran, *Endeavors of Art*, p. 149.

22. N. Frye, *Anatomy of Criticism* (Princeton: Princeton University Press, 1957), pp. 182–83.

23. W. Habicht, "The *Wit*-Interludes and the Form of Pre-Shakespearean 'Romantic Comedy,' " *RD*, 8 (1965), 73–88.

24. For information about Edwardes' reputation as an author of comedies, see *ES*, III, 309, and *CA*, 82–84.

25. Harbage, *Shakespeare and the Rival Traditions*, p. 67.

26. The influence of Lyly on the early Shakespeare is discussed by G. K. Hunter, *John Lyly*, pp. 298–349. Cf. M. Mincoff, "Shakespeare and Lyly," *ShS*, 14 (1961), 15–24.

Chapter Six: The Plays (2)

1. A. Harbage, *Shakespeare and the Rival Traditions*, p. 71.

2. R. W. Bond, ed., *The Complete Works of John Lyly*, III, 295–98, suggests that Lyly wrote *Love's Metamorphosis* between 1586 and 1588, and revised it in 1599, and Chambers, *ES*, III, 416, suggests 1589–90, although there is no solid evidence for either dating. Bond thinks that *Love's Metamorphosis* is alluded to in *The Woman in the Moon* (written sometime before it was entered in the *Stationers' Register* on September 22, 1595) and so must precede it, but the line in question—Learchus' swearing "by *Ceres* and her sacred Nymphs" (III.i.50)—may not be an allusion to the play. Bond's chief argument for his dating is that the play's euphuistic style and Ovidian pastoral subject matter connect it in time to Lyly's earlier plays, but his reluctance to place it in the early or mid-1580s undermines this view. Lyly could still write euphuistically in the late 1590s, as he does in the letter to Cecil and the petitions to Elizabeth, where he wants to reassert his identity as a courtier-entertainer. (Bond himself suggests that Lyly was correcting *Euphues* for the new edition of 1595–97.) Similarly, euphuistic prose and Ovidian pastoral material could also be the result of a deliberate attempt on Lyly's part to imitate the mode of his earlier plays. If Lyly had written *Love's Metamorphosis* in 1589–90, the play would probably have been released for publication when the playhouse in Paul's closed in 1591, as were *Gallathea*, *Endimion*, and *Midas*. On this point Hunter speculates that the troupe had not yet produced *Love's Metamorphosis* at the time of its suspension and therefore held the text for some future time when it would again be performing. Perhaps, but why then did the company release so many of its plays? On the whole, there is as much evidence for 1596–97 as

there is for 1589–90 as the date of composition. Dating the revision, if any, is also tricky. Bond argues for 1599 or 1600 on the basis of highly questionable allegorical parallels to Essex, and Hunter refutes Bond's notion that the absence of a satiric subplot points to revision. There is really no clear evidence that *Love's Metamorphosis* was revised, let alone when such revision took place, but for purposes of my argument, it hardly matters whether Lyly wrote or revised the play around 1596 or whether the production that followed the reopening of Paul's was the first one or a revival.

3. R. W. Bond, *The Complete Works of John Lyly*, I, 68–69. G. K. Hunter, *John Lyly*, pp. 83–87, discusses this phase of Lyly's life and quotes the same passage.

4. Quoted in *ES*, III, 416. At least two other plays passed from one boy company to another. According to title page statements, the Children of the Queen's Revels acquired *A Trick to Catch the Old One* from the Children of Paul's, perhaps after the latter troupe disbanded, while *The Fawn* traveled in the opposite direction. Nothing is known about the circumstances of these transfers.

5. G. K. Hunter, *John Lyly*, pp. 280–84.

6. R. W. Bond, ed., *The Complete Works of John Lyly*, I, 73, and III, 334–39, attributes the bulk of the play to Day but finds some evidence of Lyly's hand; W. W. Greg, "The Authorship of the Songs in Lyly's Plays," *MLR*, 1 (1905), 44–46, denies Lyly's authorship, while S. R. Golding, "The Authorship of *The Maid's Metamorphosis*," *RES*, 2 (1926), 270–79, argues for Peele's. Because Peele died in November 1596, many scholars have been unwilling to consider the possibility of his having written plays for the revived children's troupes. Hans-Joachim Hermes, *Die Lieder im Anonymen Englischen Renaissance-Drama 1580–1603, Elizabethan and Renaissance Studies*, 40 (Salzburg: Salzburg University, 1974), pp. 96–148, argues persuasively for two stages of composition. He thinks the original version was written before 1590, perhaps by Peele, and that the work was revised in the late 1590s, after Paul's reopened. Hermes' theory offers a plausible explanation (though not the only one) for the play's ambivalence toward its Lylyesque models.

7. G. K. Hunter, *John Lyly*, pp. 291–97.

8. W. W. Greg, *Pastoral Poetry and Pastoral Drama* (London: A. H. Bullen, 1906), p. 266.

9. *ES*, IV, 54; and M. N. Matson, ed., *The Wisdom of Doctor Dody-*

poll, MSR (1965), pp. v–vi; Peele's authorship of this play is argued by John P. Cutts, "Peele's *Hunting of Cupid,*" *SRen,* 5 (1955), 121–32. For a discussion of the shift from Lylyesque comedy to New Romantic Comedy, and of the differences between them, see E. J. Jensen, "The Changing Faces of Love in English Renaissance Comedy," *CompD,* 6 (1972–73), 294–309.

10. M. C. Andrews, *Sidney's "Arcadia" on the English Stage,* unpublished doctoral dissertation (Duke, 1966), pp. 82–96. Cf. W. W. Greg, *Pastoral Poetry and Pastoral Drama,* pp. 322–26. Andrews also discusses other children's plays derived in part from the *Arcadia*— *Jack Drum's Entertainment* and *The Gentleman Usher,* as well as Beaumont's and Fletcher's *Cupid's Revenge* (Queen's Revels, 1607–8), which is based entirely on material borrowed from Sidney, but sensationalized rather than vulgarized. See also J. E. Savage, "The Date of Beaumont and Fletcher's *Cupid's Revenge,*" *ELH,* 15 (1948), 286–94.

11. Northrop Frye, "The Argument of Comedy," in *English Institute Essays, 1948* (New York: Columbia University Press, 1949), p. 70.

12. The main action of *What You Will* is summarized above, pp. 78–79, as well as in M. T. Herrick, *Italian Comedy in the Renaissance* (Urbana: University of Illinois Press, 1960), pp. 188 ff.; A. Caputi, *John Marston, Satirist,* pp. 160 ff.; and H. H. Wood, ed., *The Plays of John Marston* (Edinburgh: Oliver and Boyd, 1934–39), II, xx. Chapman too made *All Fool's* and *May Day* more satiric than his sources; see D. C. McPherson, "Chapman's Adaptations of New Comedy," *EM* 19 (1968), 51–64.

13. O. J. Campbell, *Comicall Satyre and Shakespeare's Troilus and Cressida,* pp. 48–49. See also, A. Kernan, *The Cankered Muse: Satire of the English Renaissance,* passim. Scholars have challenged Campbell's theory that the prohibition in 1599 of the printing of formal satire caused the writing of dramatic satire. Jonson never published verse satire and Marston probably began writing satiric drama before the edict; see D. G. O'Neill, "The Commencement of Marston's Career as a Dramatist," *RES,* n.s., 22 (1971), 442–45.

14. O. J. Campbell, *Comicall Satyre,* p. 79.

15. Jonson's *Every Man Out of his Humor,* which Campbell calls the earliest "comical satire," was performed by a troupe of adult actors, but may have been written for performance at court or at one of the inns of court; see Herford and Simpson, I, 22–23. Similarly,

some scholars argue that *Troilus and Cressida*, which Campbell calls a "comical satire," was also written primarily for performance at one of the inns of court; see R. Kimbrough, *Shakespeare's Troilus and Cressida and Its Setting* (Cambridge, Mass.: Harvard University Press, 1964), pp. 10–24. P. Finkelpearl, *John Marston of the Middle Temple*, pp. 119–24, argues convincingly that *Histriomastix* was also an inns-of-court play. In *The Case Is Altered* (III, 107) Jonson makes Antonio Balladino disparage the preference of "gentlemen" for "humors" satire.

16. John Wilcox, "Informal Publication of Late Sixteenth-Century Verse Satire," *HLQ*, 13 (1949–50), 191–200.

17. Hallett Smith, *Elizabethan Poetry* (Cambridge, Mass.: Harvard University Press, 1952), p. 205.

18. W. David Kay, *Ben Jonson, Horace, and the Poetomachia*, unpublished dissertation (Princeton, 1968), pp. 168–72, refutes the arguments identifying Brabant Senior with Jonson. The anonymous play, *Wily Beguiled*, whose Prologue may have come from the anti-Jonson side of the *poetomachia*, was probably acted by university students rather than a children's troupe. *ES*, IV, 53–54, thinks the "circled round" of the Epilogue points to production at Paul's, but the phrase need have no such precise significance. There is no other evidence of performance by a boy company. Cf. H.-J. Hermes, *Die Lieder* . . . , pp. 180–214.

19. R. A. Small, *The Stage-Quarrel between Ben Jonson and the So-called Poetasters* (Breslau: M. and H. Marcus, 1899), p. 106, points out that in *What You Will* Quadratus parodies one of Crites' speeches from *Cynthia's Revels*.

20. A. Nicoll, "The Dramatic Portrait of George Chapman," *PQ*, 41 (1962), 215–28; cf. R. Ornstein, "The Dates of Chapman's Tragedies, Once More," *MP*, 59 (1961–62), 61–64, who does not believe Bellamont to be a caricature of Chapman. For more evidence of the satirizing of the conventional satirist, see John Peter, *Complaint and Satire in Early English Literature* (Oxford: Clarendon Press, 1956), pp. 154 and 203–5; and A. Kernan, *The Cankered Muse*, pp. 150–64.

21. M. Doran, *Endeavors of Art*, p. 149. See also E. M. Waith, "The Comic Mirror and the World of Glass," *RORD*, 9 (1966), 16–23. The artistry of Middleton's comedies, as opposed to their photographic realism, is the theme of A. Covatta, *Thomas Middleton's City Comedies* (Lewisburg: Bucknell University Press, 1973), from whom I bor-

row the phrase "patina of realism." Cf. J. Jacquot, "Le Répertoire des Compagnies d'Enfants à Londres (1600–1610)," in *D & S*, II, 766. Covatta has profited from the wealth of scholarship on Middleton's use of literary sources, summarized in David George, "Thomas Middleton's Sources: A Survey," *N & Q*, 216 (1971), 17–24. Public-theater dramatists sometimes used London settings as early as the 1590s, but distanced these plays in a variety of ways; see B. Beckerman, *Shakespeare at the Globe*, p. 147.

22. The chronology of Middleton's city comedies is a vexing problem. For a convenient summary of the results of modern scholarship, see Covatta, *Thomas Middleton's City Comedies*, pp. 170–72.

23. B. Maxwell, *Studies in Beaumont, Fletcher, and Massinger* (Chapel Hill: University of North Carolina Press, 1939), pp. 17–28, argues for 1610 as the date of performance of *The Scornful Lady*. Cf. *ES*, III, 230, and *CA*, p. 319.

24. D. J. Lake, *The Canon of Thomas Middleton's Plays*, pp. 109–35, argues convincingly for Middleton's authorship of *The Puritan*.

25. S. Schoenbaum, "Middleton's Share in 'The Honest Whore,' " *N & Q*, 197 (1952), 3–4, argues that Middleton's contribution was relatively minor, but D. J. Lake, *The Canon of Thomas Middleton's Plays*, pp. 44–64, marshals impressive statistical evidence for the opposite view. H. Keyishian, "Dekker's *Whore* and Marston's *Courtesan*," *ELN*, 4 (1967), 261–66, contrasts public- and private-theater treatments of the same material. Cf. A. Leggatt, *Citizen Comedy*, pp. 99–124.

26. On the relative shares of the two authors, see *ES*, III, 295–96; and P. B. Murray, "The Collaboration of Dekker and Webster in *Northward Ho* and *Westward Ho*," *PBSA*, 56 (1962), 482–86; E. E. Stoll, *John Webster* (Boston: H. Mudge and Son, 1905), pp. 62–79, and F. E. Pierce, *The Collaboration of Webster and Dekker* (New Haven: Yale University Press, 1909).

27. R. Levin, ed., *Michaelmas Term* (Lincoln: University of Nebraska Press, 1966), p. xi.

28. R. B. Parker, ed., *A Chaste Maid in Cheapside* (London: Methuen, 1969), pp. xxix–xxxv.

29. B. Beckerman, *Shakespeare at the Globe*, p. 13.

30. W. J. Lawrence, *The Elizabethan Playhouse and Other Studies*, II (Stratford-upon-Avon: Shakespeare Head Press, 1913), pp. 71–73;

and G. E. Bentley, *The Profession of Dramatist in Shakespeare's Time, 1590–1642* (Princeton: Princeton University Press, 1971), pp. 60–61.

31. A. Kirsch, *Jacobean Dramatic Perspectives,* and J. Reibetanz, "Theatrical Emblems in *King Lear,*" in *Some Facets of "King Lear": Essays in Prismatic Criticism,* ed. R. L. Colie and F. T. Flahiff (Toronto: University of Toronto Press, 1974), pp. 39–57.

Appendix A

1. G. K. Hunter, *John Lyly,* includes an appendix on "The Authorship of the Songs in Lyly's Plays," pp. 367–72. The best available guide to settings for dramatic songs is Vincent Duckles, "Music for the Lyrics in Early Seventeenth-Century English Drama: A Bibliography of the Primary Sources," in *Music in English Renaissance Drama,* ed. John H. Long (Lexington: University of Kentucky Press, 1968), pp. 117–60.

2. A version of this song occurs in *2 Henry IV.* See F. W. Sternfeld, "Lasso's Music for Shakespeare's 'Samingo,' " *SQ,* 9 (1958), 111.

3. A. J. Sabol, "Two Songs with Accompaniment for an Elizabethan Choirboy Play," *SRen,* 5 (1958), 153n; and Mary [Joiner] Chan, "*Cynthia's Revels* and Music for a Choir School: Christ Church Manuscript Mus 439," *SRen,* 18 (1971), 141. Cf. E. S. Lindsey, "The Music in Ben Jonson's Plays," *MLN,* 44 (1929), 87–88; and W. M. Evans, *Ben Jonson and Elizabethan Music* (Lancaster: Lancaster Press, 1929), pp. 48–49.

4. See chapter 1, note 43.

5. F. W. Sternfeld, *Music in Shakespearean Tragedy* (London: Routledge and Kegan Paul, 1963), p. 15.

6. W. R. Bowden, *The English Dramatic Lyric, 1603–1641* (New Haven: Yale University Press, 1951), pp. 126–28; and my unpublished dissertation, *The Plays Acted by the Children of Paul's, 1599–1607* (Columbia, 1967), p. 346. J. S. Colley, "Music in the Elizabethan Private Theatres," *YES,* 4 (1974), 62–69, agrees with Bowden's general conclusions but argues that the amount of music and song in children's plays varies, depending on the intentions of the playwright and the nature of the particular play. K. Eggar, "The Blackfriars Plays and their Music, 1576–1610," *PRMA,* 87 (1960–61), 57–68, despite the

title, discusses the history of the Blackfriars operation and not the plays or their music.

7. Mary [Joiner] Chan, *SRen*, 18 (1971), 145.

8. Ibid.

9. R. W. Ingram, "The Use of Music in the Plays of Marston," *M & L*, 37 (1956), 154–64; C. Kiefer, "Music and Marston's *The Malcontent*," *SP*, 51 (1954), 163–71; and F. W. Sternfeld, *Music in Shakespearean Tragedy*, pp. 15–16.

10. W. R. Bowden, *The English Dramatic Lyric*, pp. 23–26; see also A. J. Sabol, "Two Unpublished Stage Songs for the 'Aery of Children,' " *RN*, 13 (1960), 224–25.

11. Philip Brett, "The English Consort Song, 1570–1625," *PRMA*, 88 (1961–62), 74; see also p. 79. Cf. G. Reese, *Music in the Renaissance*, rev. ed. (New York: W. W. Norton, 1959), p. 817.

12. J. H. Long, "Music for a Song in 'Damon and Pythias,' " *M & L*, 48 (1967), 247–50. See the response by Mary Joiner [Chan], *M & L*, 49 (1968), 98–100.

13. G. E. P. Arkwright, "The Death Songs of Pyramus and Thisbe," *N & Q*, 84 (1906), 341–43 and 401–3; "Early Elizabethan Stage Music," *The Musical Antiquary*, I (1909), 30–40 and IV (1913), 112–17; and "Elizabethan Choirboy Plays and their Music," *PRMA*, 40 (1913–14), 117–38.

14. See chapter 5 above. The setting is printed in Philip Brett, ed., *Consort Songs*, in *Musica Britannica* (London: Royal Musical Association, 1967), XXII, 15, along with other dramatic laments.

15. Sabol, *SRen*, 5 (1958), 147–48.

16. Sabol, "Ravenscroft's 'Melismata' and the Children of Paul's," *RN*, 12 (1959), 8.

17. Bowden, *The Dramatic Lyric*, p. 129, argues that polyphonic settings were rarely used in children's plays.

18. Sabol, *SRen*, 5 (1958), 149. The setting is printed at the end of Sabol's article, pp. 155–57, and in P. Brett, ed., *Consort Songs*, pp. 92–93.

19. Settings for two fairy songs in *The Maid's Metamorphosis* appear in Ravenscroft's *A Brief Discourse*; see Sabol, *SRen*, 5 (1958), 153n; and W. J. Lawrence, *MLR*, 19 (1924), 420–22. The text of this play does not print the lyrics to the shepherds' song, but Sabol, *RN*, 12 (1959), 7–8, suggests "The Crowning of Belphebe" from Ravenscroft's *Melismata*.

20. Richmond Noble, *Shakespeare's Use of Song* (Oxford: Clarendon Press, 1923), p. 127–28; Sternfeld, *Music in Shakespearean Tragedy*, pp. 86–87; and P. J. Seng, *The Vocal Songs in the Plays of Shakespeare* (Cambridge: Harvard University Press, 1967), pp. 211–13.

21. D. G. O'Neill, *M & L*, 53 (1972), 122–33, 293–308, 400–10; see also Sabol, *SRen*, 5 (1958), 150; and Bowden, *The Dramatic Lyric*, pp. 26–34.

22. Sabol, *RN*, 13 (1960), 231–32. The setting is printed on p. 230 and in P. Brett, ed., *Consort Songs*, p. 95. See also A. J. Sabol, "Recent Studies in Music and English Renaissance Drama," *SRO*, 4 (1968/69), 12–13.

23. Sabol, *SRen*, V (1958), 158–59, transcribes Imperia's song from Ravenscroft's *A Brief Discourse*, where it is attributed to "Edward Pearce," probably the choirmaster of St. Paul's. Sabol also suggests, *RN*, 12 (1959), 8, that Birdlime might have sung "The Painters' Song of London" from Ravenscroft's *Melismata*.

24. Sabol, *RN*, 13 (1960), 228. The setting is printed on p. 229. See also M. [J.] Chan, *SRen*, 18 (1971), 137.

25. Sabol, *RN*, 12 (1959), 6.

26. Sternfeld, *Music in Shakespearean Tragedy*, pp. 14–15; W. J. Lawrence, "Music in the Elizabethan Theatre," *MQ*, 6 (1920), 194; J. R. Moore, "The Songs of the Public Theaters in the Time of Shakespeare," *JEGP*, 28 (1929), 194–95; and G. K. Hunter, ed., *The Malcontent*, pp. lii–liii. Printed texts of private-theater plays are generally divided into acts, unlike texts of public-theater plays, perhaps because of the custom of entr'acte music. See W. W. Greg, "Act-Divisions in Shakespeare," *RES*, 4 (1928), 152–58; A. Harbage, *Theatre for Shakespeare* (Toronto: University of Toronto Press, 1955), pp. 46–47; H. L. Snuggs, *Shakespeare and Five Acts* (New York: Vantage Press, 1960), pp. 37–45; and W. T. Jewkes, *Act Division in Elizabethan and Jacobean Plays, 1583–1616* (Hamden, Connecticut: The Shoe String Press, 1958), pp. 61–79.

27. R. von Liliencron, "Die Choresänge des lateinisch-deutschen Schuldramas im XVI. Jahrhundert," *Vierteljahrsschrift für Musikwissenschaft*, 6 (1890), 309–53.

28. Francis Bacon, *Sylva Sylvarum*, in *The Works of Francis Bacon*, ed. James Spedding et al. (Boston: Brown and Taggard, 1862), IV, 255. We have no idea of where musicians were placed in the private theaters. A stage direction in a Paul's play (*Antonio's Revenge*

V.iii.49) indicates the existence of two "music-houses," but not their precise location.

29. G. H. Cowling, *Music on the Shakespearian Stage* (Cambridge: Cambridge University Press, 1913), pp. 53–64; and John H. Long, *Shakespeare's Use of Music* (Gainesville: University of Florida Press, 1955–72), I, 33.

30. G. C. Moore Smith, *College Plays Performed in the University of Cambridge* (Cambridge: Cambridge University Press, 1923), p. 32; W. W. Greg, ed., *The Academic Drama of Cambridge*, in *MSC*, II, part 2 (1923), 207–8; J. H. Long, *Shakespeare's Use of Music*, I, 32–34; W. L. Woodfill, *Musicians in English Society from Elizabeth to Charles I*, pp. 40–41; and J. P. Cutts, *La Musique de scène de la troupe de Shakespeare* (Paris: Centre National de la Recherche Scientifique, 1959), p. xlii and Appendix B.

Appendix B

1. This list is based on the Court Calendar in *ES*, IV, 75–130. I have also consulted *CA*; Mary Susan Steele, *Plays & Masques at Court* (New Haven: Yale University Press, 1926); Alfred Harbage, ed., *Annals of English Drama*, rev. S. Schoenbaum (London: Methuen, 1964); and A. Feuillerat, ed. *Documents Relating to the Office of the Revels in the Time of Queen Elizabeth* (Louvain: A. Uystpruyst, 1908).

2. G. R. Price, "The Early Editions of *A Trick to catch the old one*," *Library*, 5th series, 22 (1967), 222–23, argues that this play was performed at court on Jan. 1, 1607–8, in an unrecorded appearance by the Children of the Queen's Revels. This supposition is in accord with the statement on the second title-page (see Appendix C) of the 1608 quarto, presumably accurate, "Presented before his Majesty on New Year's Night last."

Appendix C

1. These lists are based on *ES*, *CA*, and A. Harbage, *Annals of English Drama, 975–1700*. I have also consulted J. Jacquot, "Le Repertoire des Compagnies d'Enfants à Londres (1600–1610)," in *D & S*, II, 795–81; and the following unpublished dissertations: R. T. Thornberry, *Shakespeare and the Blackfriars Tradition* (Ohio State, 1964),

pp. 302–7 and 311–19; and R. M. Wren, *The Blackfriars Theatre and Its Repertory, 1600–1608* (Princeton, 1965), pp. 79–123. I have cited relevant scholarship on the auspices, authorship, and dates of individual plays at appropriate points above.

2. Of this play, and the one following, only fragments survive. They were found in the manuscript containing *Wit and Science* and have been published with the text of that play in the *MSR* series.

3. *The Fawn* was entered in the *Stationers' Register* by William Cotton on March 12, 1616. In that year, Thomas Purfoot printed the play for Cotton in two quarto versions, under different title pages, indicating different auspices of production:

Q ^{1} __, as it hath been diverse times presented at the Blackfriars, by the Children of the Queen's Majesty's Revels. . . .

Q ^{2} __, as it hath been diverse times presented at the Blackfriars, by the Children of the Queen's Majesty's Revels and since at Paul's. . . .

If accurate, the second title page suggests a Paul's production sometime after the printing of Q ^{1}. Chambers, *ES*, II, 21–22, thinks Edward Kirkham brought the play to the Children of Paul's when he joined the directorate of that troupe around 1605. If the copy for Q ^{1} came from Blackfriars, as its title page suggests, then both quartos furnish the version of the play performed by the Children of the Queen's Revels: half of Q ^{2} was printed from standing type used for Q ^{1}, and the "faults," which the title page and a note in Q ^{2} claim to have corrected, are chiefly compositorial errors. See R. E. Brettle, "Bibliographical Notes on Some Marston Quartos and Early Collected Editions," *Library*, 4th series, 8 (1927–28), 337–48; F. T. Bowers, "Notes on Standing Type in Elizabethan Printing," *PBSA*, 40 (1946), 218–24; and W. L. Halstead, "An Explanation for the Two Editions of Marston's *Fawne*," *SP*, 40 (1943), 25–32.

4. Entered in the *Stationers' Register* on Oct. 7, 1607, by George Eld, *A Trick to Catch the Old One* was first published in 1608 under two different title pages, indicating different auspices of production:

A. __, as it hath been lately acted, by the Children of Paul's. . . .

B. __, as it hath been often in action, both at Paul's and the Blackfriars. Presented before his Majesty on New Year's Night last. . . .

The first title page was printed on sig. A2^r; the second on sig. A1^r after which the first was cancelled. G. R. Price, *Library*, 5th series, 22 (1967), 219, informs us that "the second title page was printed by passing sheet A through the press a second time after an interval. . . ." Scholars disagree about the length of this interval. Chambers, *ES*, III, 439 believes the 1608 date on the second title page to be an error for 1608–9, when the Children of the Queen's Revels gave a New Year's performance. Hillebrand, *CA*, p. 310, thinks the second title page refers to a performance on Jan. 1, 1606, which is surely too early. Price, quite plausibly, hypothesizes an unrecorded court performance on Jan. 1, 1607–8, a few months after Eld had registered his copy of the play. Instead of trying to link the play with a recorded court performance, Price bases his theory of a short interval on Eld's use of an existing blank space on sheet A for the second title page; a Jacobean printer, he maintains, would have found it unprofitable to store unbound printed sheets for very long.

Eld's copy probably came from Paul's. Between May 9 and Aug. 6, 1607, six plays attributed on their title pages only to the Children of Paul's were entered in the *Stationers' Register: The Phoenix* (May 9), *Michaelmas Term* (May 15), *The Woman Hater* (May 20), *Bussy D'Ambois* (June 3), *Northward Ho!* (Aug. 6), and *The Puritan* (Aug. 6). A seventh play, *What You Will*, almost certainly a Paul's play though its title page mentions no troupe, was also entered on Aug. 6. The managers of the recently dissolved Children of Paul's apparently released some of their texts for publication during the spring and summer of 1607. Significantly, not a single Blackfriars play was entered in the *Stationers' Register* in that year. Moreover, Eld himself entered *Northward Ho!* and *The Puritan,* and printed *What You Will* for Thomas Thorpe, a collaborator. It is not unreasonable to suppose that Eld also acquired the text of *A Trick to Catch the Old One* from the Children of Paul's in the later part of 1607. Shortly after New Year's Day, 1607–8, with the play on its way through his press(es), he discovered that the title page he had already printed did not advertise the play as effectively as it might, given the recent court performance by the Children of the Queen's Revels. He therefore printed a new title page on a blank portion of sheet A (sig. A1^r) and cut out sig. A2, which had the old title page on its recto side and nothing on the verso. The text itself, unaltered, was still the same one performed by the Children of Paul's.

5. Mentioned in the diary of the Duke of Stettin-Pomerania. See chapter 1, note 43.

6. See *ES*, II, 65.

7. This play and the one following are dialogues presented at Mercers' Hall on the occasion of the St. Paul's Grammar School dinner. The texts are reprinted in *MSC*, II (1954), 142–64.

8. The Westminster Choirboys may have acted in conjunction with the pupils of the Westminster Grammar School, as there were unusually close relations between the two institutions. See *ES*, II, 69–73.

Index

Foakes, R. A., 131, 132
Frye, Northrop, 39, 171, 196
Fulwell, Ulpian, *Like Will to Like,* 150

Game of Cards, A, 47, 259, 264
Garter, Thomas, 4; *The Virtuous and Godly Susanna,* 155, 215, 235, 268
Gascoigne, George: *The Glass of Government,* 150, 268
Gay, John, *The Beggar's Opera,* 41-42
Genus Humanum, 263
Gesta Greyorum, 53-54
Giles, Nathaniel, 24-25, 27
Gnapheus, 3, 149
Godly Queen Hester, 47, 155, 177, 215, 244, 268
Gombrich, E., 113
Greene, Robert, 176, 183, 189, 195, 196, 223, 228
Greene, T. M., 84
Greville, Fulke, 96
Gyles, Thomas, 17-18, 20-21

Harbage, Alfred, 15, 68, 107, 172-73, 179, 227
Harington, John, 47, 205
Hall, Edward, 140, 142-43
Harrison, John: *Philomathes' Dream,* 267; *Philomathes' Second Dream,* 267
Harrowing of Hell, The, 11
Harvey, Gabriel, 17
Henry VII, 11
Henry VIII, 4
Henslowe, Philip, 19, 196
Heywood, John, 11, 12, 17; *The Play of the Weather,* 141, 261
Heywood, Thomas, 51, 122, 215
Hillebrand, H. N., 2, 18, 23
History of Error, The, 153, 258, 262
Hollybrand, C., 105
Horace, 47

How a Man May Choose a Good Wife from a Bad, 120-21, 212
Huizinga, J., 38
Hunnis, William, 14-15, 16, 24
Hunter, G. K., 42, 83, 105, 131, 143, 146, 186

Impressment, 20-21, 24-25, 27
Inductions, 105, 111-12, 128-29, 131
Ingelond, Thomas, *The Disobediant Child,* 3-4, 150-52, 268
Inns of court, 7, 18-19, 51, 53, 55, 68, 69, 155, 205, 227
Iphigenia, 158, 258, 262

Jack Juggler, 148, 268
Jacob and Esau, 149-52, 268
James I, 27, 28, 29, 33, 42, 46, 54, 56, 95, 96, 117, 195, 231, 232
Jeffere, John, *The Bugbears,* 148, 149, 239-40, 268
Johnson, Samuel, 103
Jonson, Ben, 24, 26, 29, 50, 56, 70, 72-74, 132, 144, 154, 204, 210, 216, 223, 232; *Cynthia's Revels,* 43-44, 46, 48-50, 73-74, 83-84, 87, 94, 106, 111, 116-18, 183-84, 186-87, 204, 206, 229, 234, 248-49, 259, 264; *Poetaster,* 48-50, 83, 128, 204, 206, 215, 264; *Epicoene,* 53, 56-57, 74, 82-90, 91, 101, 115-16, 213, 265; "To Penshurst," 84; *Everyman Out of His Humor,* 87, 204, 205; elegy on Salomon Pavy, 104, 113; *Eastward Ho!,* 121-23, 213, 214, 216, 265; *The Case Is Altered,* 154, 197, 264; *The Alchemist,* 217; *Volpone,* 223
Juvenal, 83, 205

Kernan, Alvin, 58, 204
Keysar, Robert, 28
King of Scots, 257, 264

Kirkham, Edward, 23, 25
Kirsch, Arthur, 232
Kyd, Thomas, *The Spanish Tragedy*, 120, 128, 131, 136

Lasso, Orlando di, 6
Leicester, Earl of, 12, 15
Leto, Pomponio, 4
Levin, Richard, 192-93
Libanius, 83-84
Lily, William, 4
Livy, 141
London Prodigal, The, 120-21
Long, John H., 239
Love and Riches, 7, 263
Loyalty and Beauty, 141, 258, 264
Lyly, John, 16, 17, 48, 49, 56, 72, 73, 77, 105-6, 116, 132, 139, 143, 144-45, 146, 147, 149, 172-89, 192, 194, 195, 202, 206, 228, 229, 230, 239-41, 243, 253; *Sapho and Phao*, 16, 35-36, 43, 174-75, 180-82, 188, 239, 259, 262, 264; *Campaspe*, 16, 35-36, 46, 117, 156-57, 158, 173, 174, 176, 180, 182, 190, 240, 259, 262, 264; *Endimion*, 18, 46, 116, 175, 182, 185, 186, 192, 243, 259, 262; *Gallathea*, 43, 174, 182, 243, 259, 262; *Midas*, 47, 72, 145, 173, 177, 259, 262; *The Woman in the Moon*, 145-46, 173, 180, 182, 262; *Mother Bombie*, 149, 174, 180, 182, 188, 262; *Love's Metamorphosis*, 174, 180-83, 187, 262, 264; euphuism, 183-84, 187

Machiavelli, Niccolo, 69
Machin, Lewis: *The Dumb Knight*, 216-17, 266; *Everywoman in Her Humor*, 266
Macropedius, Georgius, 149
Maid's Metamorphosis, The, 43, 116-17, 184-86, 191, 230, 239, 243, 244, 253, 262

Markham, Gervase: *The Dumb Knight*, see Machin
Marlowe, Christopher, 130; *Dido, Queen of Carthage*, 116, 147, 148, 166-71, 264; *Tamburlaine*, 158
Marprelate controversy, 18, 114, 177-78
Marriage of Mind and Measure, The, 153, 258, 262
Marriage of Wit and Science, The, 12, 153, 172, 261; see also *Wit and Will*
Marston, John, 25-26, 50, 72, 73, 74, 105, 113-14, 128, 198, 204-11, 216, 219, 230, 232, 237; *Antonio's Revenge*, 34, 127-37, 189, 199-200, 207, 244, 250, 262; *The Fawn*, 44-45, 50, 57, 72, 106-7, 118, 206, 207, 263, 264; *Jack Drum's Entertainment*, 44, 109-10, 112, 183-84, 198-201, 207-8, 213, 227, 245-46, 247, 253, 262; *What You Will*, 48, 73, 78-79, 86-87, 110, 112, 154, 201-4, 207-8, 241, 246, 262; *Antonio and Mellida*, 73, 111-12, 127-37, 183-84, 197, 199-200, 202, 203, 207, 241, 251, 253, 262; *Sophonisba*, 118, 170-71, 228, 237, 244, 252, 253, 265; *The Dutch Courtesan*, 204, 246-47, 253, 254, 264; *Histriomastix*, 205; *The Malcontent*, 207, 250, 252, 264; *The Scourge of Villainy*, 208; *The Insatiate Countess*, see Barkstead; *Eastward Ho!*, see Jonson; *Satiromastix*, see Dekker
Mary I, 5
Mason, John, *The Turk*, 24, 266
Masques, 5, 29, 39-40, 43-46, 148, 177, 186
Master of the Revels, 5, 16, 26, 32, 35
Medwall, Henry, 140
Middleton, Thomas, 56-57, 60-63, 86, 91, 105, 113-14, 132, 154, 198, 213-15, 217-18, 221-27; *Michaelmas Term*,

Walpole, Robert, 41-42

Walsingham, Francis, 47

Wars of Cyrus, The, 46, *158-66*, 170, 239, 264

Webster, John, 113-14, 216, 219; *Northward Ho!*, see Dekker; *Westward Ho!*, see Dekker

Westcote, Sebastian, 11-19, 32-33, 105, 153-54

Whitgift, John, 18, 75

Wilcox, John, 205

Wisdom of Doctor Dodypoll, The, 57, 116-17, 189-91, 243, 262

Wise Woman of Hogsden, The, 212

Wit and Will, 257

Wolsey, Thomas, 4, 5, 47, 148, 155

Woodford, Thomas, 21-24

Xenophon: *Cyropaedia*, 159, 163, 165

Xerxes, 258, 267

Youll, Henry, 234, 248